CW01668956

Weihaiwei

Let me guard China's most ancient sea[1], once more,
Our great philosopher's tomb lies back of this shoreline[2].
Mother, don't forget that I am the brave guardian of the sea,
I have the island of Liugong[3] for my shield.
Make haste to rescue me; the time is ripe![4]
Behind me are buried the remains of our great forebears![5]
Mother! I want to return to you, Mother!
– by Wen Yiduo, "Song of Seven Sons"[6]

米字旗下的威海卫

Weihaiwei Under British Rule

Writers：张建国　张军勇
Translators：Alec Hill　马向红

Shandong Pictorial Publishing House

图书在版编目（CIP）数据

米字旗下的威海卫：英文／张建国、张军勇编著．
—济南：山东画报出版社，2006.10
ISBN 7-80713-409-7

Ⅰ.米… Ⅱ.张… Ⅲ.威海市－史料－1898～
1930－图集 Ⅳ.K295.23-64

中国版本图书馆CIP数据核字（2006）第118746号

Executive Editor：Feng Keli
Designer：Song Xiaoming
Publication：Shangdong Pictorial Publishing House
Add：39 Shengli Street，Jingjiu Road，Jinan City，P.O.：250001
Tel：Editor-in-Chief，(0531) 82098470
Market Dept.，(0531) 82098042 (Fax)，82098047
Printing：Shandong People's Printing House
Number of Publication：First published October，2006
Number of Printing：First printed October，2006
Specification：200 mm × 265 mm
21.5 printed sheet，258 images，and 150,000words
Impression：1-2000
Price：150.00RMB

Foreword

When the members of the Cheltenham branch of SACU (Society for Anglo-Chinese Understanding), and of the Cheltenham Weihai Link organisation (concerned with the twinning relationship between our two towns), saw for the first time the original Chinese edition of the book "Weihai under British Rule" they realised that an English language version would be of particular interest to many families, both locally and nationally, who would have relatives, including many sailors, marines and soldiers, businessmen, diplomats, hoteliers, traders, educationalists, or missionaries, who had spent time in Weihaiwei, and on Liugong Island, for many years the summer station of the British China Fleet, and former base of the first modern navy during the Qing Dynasty. It would also be of great interest to any other English speakers who wished to learn more about China, and in particular the history of its relations with Britain.

When Ian Johnson, the present chairman of the Weihai Link, discovered a mysterious box in the attic of his house, abandoned by a previous owner, containing the original photographic plates recording the take-over ceremonies of 1898, pictures of leaders, troops, warships and street scenes in the territory of Weihaiwei, this reinforced the determination of the branch to form a town-twinning friendship link.

In 1985 SACU was invited by the Chinese Friendship Association to send five of its national members to study urban changes taking place in China. When they arrived in that country, having already decided to confine their investigations to Shandong Province to avoid long distance travelling, the Chinese officials proposed to them a location which might suit Cheltenham as a twin – the city of Weihai at the easternmost tip of the Shandong Peninsula. When the group arrived in Weihai they were overwhelmed by the hospitality, the fresh sea air, the coastal scenery, not to mention the incredible large contour model of the proposed ten year development plan for the town and surrounding district Councillor Pennington, the group leader, decided they should spend four days undertaking urban research at Weihai since it was located in Shandong Province.

The population of Weihai at that time was similar to Cheltenham's, just over 70,000. The fact that the mayor of Weihai had administrative responsibility for an additional 220,000 people in surrounding villages and towns was overlooked. The differences between the powers of our respective mayors were not fully understood until several years later, after the initial friendship link was signed in 1985. The initial astonishment and reservations of the

British visitors regarding the scale and speed of the development were dispelled when they visited a construction site and saw a section of the new ring road already completed, with trees and shrubs along the sides of the roads and in the central reservation, and huge holes already excavated for the foundations of the overhead flyovers. The group discovered there were sixteen construction teams working together, sent by the Chinese Government as part of its plan to open up fourteen ports for direct trade with foreign companies. Cheltenham's own ring road had by then been forty years in planning, and even today, twenty years later, is still incomplete!

During the twenty years since the link was set up, Weihai City has expanded to become six times the size of Cheltenham, and there are 2.5 million people under the jurisdiction of its Mayor and Municipality. After thirteen years of campaigning by SACU, Cheltenham Council finally accepted Weihai as its twin-town in 1998 rather than merely a "friendship link", thus joining Annecy in France, G?ttingen in Germany and Sochi on the Black Sea in Russia, also another Cheltenham - a suburb of Philadelphia in the USA.

In the meantime, many exchanges of visiting mayors and other officials took place. Cheltenham people had to pay their own fares and expenses, as the only people who could be paid out of public funds were six officials or councillors involved in organising joint activities. Under our own local governmental system the budgets for such exchanges are strictly limited. The entertainment and hospitality offered us by other countries is usually far more lavish, which causes us some embarrassment.

With the guidance of Cheltenham Borough's Chief Executive, SACU sought assistance from companies who were trading with China, and several of these gave donations to the Weihai Link where needed. A Twinning Forum of elected members oversees the projects, but volunteers do most of the work. There is one part-time Twinning Officer who handles relations with five twin towns, also half-a-dozen friendship links with other towns.

SACU members and friends rallied to help translate the Chinese text into English. Dr Alec Hill, who had taken over as Secretary of the Cheltenham Branch of SACU and of the Weihai Link, spent many weeks bringing the various chapters together. Many Chinese friends within the UK, namely: Zhang Yaying, Sun Meiling, Zhou Hui, Marina Poon, and within Cheltenham itself, Frank Wing Yow Soo and Helen Bishop, together with David Tan, have all worked on various chapters as volunteers. The task proved too much for our own limited resources, so Weihai offered the services of their own people to help. Lu Dan of the Foreign Cooperation Bureau of Hi-Tech Zone, Weihai, translated chapter 7 and epilogue, and made the initial check through chapters already translated by British friends. In 2006, the Weihai Municipal Archives Bureau decided to publish its English version in October, so the original authors, according to academic custom, began to revise the whole book, add notes, and rewrite some chapters and sections which were then translated by Ma Xianghong of the Archives Bureau, and checked by Alec Hill. At the end of April 2006, Alec spent six weeks in Weihai, as a guest of the Bureau, working closely with Xianghong, an activity which continued online after his return to the UK. In the UK Lieutenant Commander Ronald Childs proposed some amendments to certain sections, and Dr Frances Wood, a vice-president of SACU, checked through the final version at short notice. All those involved in the production of this edition appreciate that the book presents the facts concerning the British presence in Weihai from a Chinese viewpoint, which is sometimes very critical of British actions. However the authors have done much excellent research and have given an objective description of the understanding, scholarship and skills of the two leading British Commissioners: Stewart Lockhart and Reginald Johnston. During their administrations they were regarded as "good magistrates" by the Chinese and were able to influence village headmen and regional chiefs to accept British laws and regulations but adapted to traditional Chinese customs and practices. The authors' scholarship conveys vivid impressions, especially in their accounts of the extremely valuable contribution, but sad mistreatment, of those Chinese labourers recruited during the First World War, plus the performance of the soldiers of the Chinese Regiment, trained by British officers, who helped control the borders of Weihaiwei, and who won praise for their abilities and loyalty during the struggles against the Boxers and during the capture of Beijing alongside the armies of other Imperial powers. Most British readers will appreciate the efforts of the authors to present the facts from reliable sources. Some sections may be regarded as controversial. It is undeniable that British presence in Weihaiwei was forced upon its people, and some of the actions described may make us ashamed of what was done in the name of our country. On the other hand many of those actions displayed understanding and sympathy towards the Chinese people and we can be proud of that fact. I believe the authors are to be commended on having gone a long way towards achieving a balance in this record of turbulent times.

Jim Pennington

Preface

At the end of 19th century, Britain, taking advantage of a period in which China had become partitioned by powerful invaders, forced the Qing government to lease Hong Kong, then subsequently Weihaiwei. From that moment on, the demeaning history of the "British Lease of Weihaiwei" commenced, and lasted for as long as 32 years, adding another heavy link to China's continued chain of misfortune. People should never forget that history. When the British finally withdrew from Weihaiwei, they took all the records of that period with them, thus creating a gap in the history of China, which has made it very difficult for the people of today to know about and to comment on those times.

Since the implementation of the open and reform policies in China, with China's importance in the world increasing everyday, and with the improvement in the relations between China and Britain, it has now become possible to have those historical records restored to their home and for the true history to become known. The Weihai Archive Bureau started the work of collecting those records in 1996, and now presents that information in this book <<Weihaiwei Under British Rule>>. In the book, the information contained in thousands of records has been compiled. By combining pictures and words together, it shows the true and first hand story of a painful period of time over 100 years ago. It is worth mentioning that by showing the first hand history in this book, that period of time may be analysed and understood. For instance, it exposes the nature of the colonial invasion of China's politics, economy, and culture; it also analyses how, if a nation is backward, its people can be defeated. It further analyses the reason for China's being backwards, and the reasons that are limiting its development even today. This writing combines both historical and current thinking. To understand history is to understand the present day, which gives that history a practical significance. It helps us to remember the historical disgrace of our nation, and encourages every Chinese to understand his/her responsibilities to make our great nation strong again.

In addition to describing how the colonialists controlled Weihai, this book tells the truth of both their positive and negative influences on the development of Weihai's society. In my opinion, this book displays the editors' spirit of respecting history and reality. It also reflects the openness and confidence of today's Weihai people. The past must not be forgotten, it is the teacher of the future. Weihai was not the only place in Chinese history which was once forced to be leased. The Weihai people's particular experience is also a memory for the whole Chinese nation. Therefore, the publishing of this book is not merely the concern of the Weihai people, it is obviously the concern of the whole nation.

Cui Yuechen,
General Secretary of the Weihai Municipal Committee of the CPC, and Chairman of the Standing Committee of the Weihai Municipal People's Congress.

October 2002

The British leasing of Weihaiwai – An attempt to maintain the balance of power

1

Britain did not lag behind the other powers in the scramble to carve up China

The First Sino-Japanese War (1894-5) not only destroyed the myth of the Qing Dynasty as a 'Heavenly Dynasty and Great Court', but also upset the balance between the western powers in the Far East,changing the traditional pattern of international affairs, and sharpening their scramble for China. Not until after the war had ended did the western powers, one by one, commence the scramble to carve up China. During the next several years, the Chinese government rapidly gave up many of its rights to build railways, explore mines and collect revenue; coastal areas became dotted with foreign military stations, and inland regions became divided into spheres of influence, which not only caused China to face a disastrous national calamity, but was also of very great concern to Britain.

As an experienced imperial power, Britain had the greatest influence on China's politics and economy prior to the Sino-Japanese War. She had come to possess the largest vested interests, not only acquiring a lot of privileges in the rich Yangtze River area, but also stretching out greedy hands into the north, south and southwest of China. Moreover, she had an important political influence on the Qing government through the control of China's military and civil enterprises. In order to maintain and enlarge its monopoly, and to resist the enlargement of other foreign powers in China, Britain took advantage of its established strong position to carry out an 'Open Door' policy towards that country. Its basic foreign policy in dealing with China had been to preserve the territorial integrity and full sovereignty of China in its existing form, and it had been strongly against the carving up of the country.

However, after the Sino-Japanese War, Britain encountered a challenge to its monopoly status and vested interests in China. Japan had suddenly become powerful as a result of the Meiji Restoration and the Sino-Japanese War, and was now the major Asian military power competing in the scramble for China against the other powers. Germany and other rising nations also lost little time in invading China. Russia, Britain's old enemy, actively allied

Japanese troops constructing fortifications at Beizhudao Village after they arrived in Weihaiwei. (February 1895)

itself with France in attempting to attack British interests in the north and south of China. This situation showed that Britain's monopoly days in China had passed, and all other powers were now trying to share it. Meanwhile, Britain had really declined, as its total industrial output was successively surpassed by America and Germany in the late 19th century and early 20th century, and its proportion of foreign trade in the world trade also gradually fell[1]. The glory of its position as the "World's factory" had become a thing of the past. Faced with the offensive in China by the other powers, especially by Russia, it became impossible for Britain to continue to enjoy its unique privileges in China. "To defend in an age of competition that which Great Britain had obtained in an age of monopoly"[2], became an urgent problem confronting the British government.

In the period shortly after the end of the Sino-Japanese War, British public opinion repeatedly demanded that the government should take part in the carving up of China, but the Prime Minister and Foreign Secretary, Lord

A coastal battery on Sun Island, Weihaiwei. The site of fierce fighting for several days between Chinese sailors, led by Sa Zhenbing, Captain of S.S. Kangji, and Japanese sailors, during the Siege of Weihaiwei in 1895. The battery was largely destroyed and finally given up by the Chinese who were hopelessly outnumbered. (1898)

Salisbury, insisted on maintaining Britain's traditional foreign policy towards China. However the emergence of this new political situation undermined his hopes of maintaining that policy.

The murder of two German missionaries in the west Shandong Province in November 1897 provided the opportunity for which the German Kaiser had been seeking and he immediately ordered his Far Eastern naval squadron to Jiaozhou. Then on 6th March the following year, the Qing government was forced to sign The Convention for the Lease of Tsingtao by which a 99 year lease of Jiaozhou Bay was bestowed upon Germany. Germany was also given special privileges: to build the Jiaoji Railway, to exploit mineral resources along the railway, and to make other investments. Shandong Province thus came under Germany's sphere of influence. While Germany and China were negotiating over Jiaozhou Bay, Germany informed Britain that the Qing government had proposed ceding a port to Germany within south China, which was within the British sphere of influence, in order to warn Britain that she would only harm herself by obstructing the German occupation of Jiaozhou Bay[3]. Meanwhile, Britain also had a mind to seek support from Germany in resisting Russia, and so decided not to offend Germany publicly in the matter of Jiaozhou. However, Germany's behaviour set a precedent for the direct seizure by foreign powers of territory from China's coastal regions in order to extend their spheres of influence in China, and gave an indication of the future carving up of China. Almost at the same time, Tsarist Russia, on the pretext of protecting China from a German invasion, commenced stationing its fleets in Port Arthur.

Russia's intention to control northern China, and furthermore to become the leading power in China, produced an immediate reaction from Britain. On 29th December 1897, the British Under-Secretary for Foreign Affairs, Lord Curzon, wrote to Lord Salisbury, proposing that a British presence in Weihaiwei would at least counter Russian and German influences in the north and would be in alliance with Japan[4]. The Secretary of the Colonial Office, Joseph Chamberlain, also actively urged the government to establish a naval base which would counter the Russian action[5]. However, Lord Salisbury was afraid that the occupation of Weihaiwei would lead to similar actions by the other powers which might endanger Britain itself, thus he rejected all the above proposals. At the same time, he still hoped to use military and diplomatic channels to compel Russia to give way. On 25th December 1897, two British cruisers sailed into Port Arthur, signaling the hope of meeting and talking, while the main force of the British China Fleet assembled in Inchon, to display its strength to Russia[6]. The British Minister in Beijing – Sir Claude MacDonald warned Zongli Yamen (the Qing Government's Dept of Foreign Affairs) that: "if all your ports are occupied by a foreign country,

November 1897, German forces invading Jiaozhou Bay (near Qingdao). (1897)

Russian Squadron stationed in Port Arthur. (1904)

that means disintegration"[7]. Meanwhile, Britain carried out a fierce confrontation with Russia over the matter of Port Arthur and the payment of China's remaining indemnities to Japan after the recent Sino-Japanese War.

At the beginning of the negotiations between Britain and Russia, Lord Salisbury first proposed the plan that the Yellow River valley and the area to its north should fall within the Russian sphere of influence, and that the Yangtze River valley should fall within the British sphere of influence, in order to reach a compromise with Russia on the basis of sharing the spoils. However, the basis of disagreement between them lay in the question of the balance of power in China, and although Russia was prepared to compromise over the question of a loan to pay off the indemnities, Britain would never yield in the matter of Port Arthur[8]. In February 1898, the Qing government had to promise Britain not to mortgage, lease or cede any territory from the Yangtze valley to any other power, and to continue to reserve the position of Inspector General of the Maritime Customs Service for a British official as long as the volume of trade between Britain and China still ranked as the highest[9]. Therefore, Britain regarded "the loan and the agreement with Russia as unimportant"[10], so took a more uncompromising stand in the matter of Port Arthur

This picture of the situation in the Far East was the work of a Chinese revolutionary named Xie Zuantai, based in Hong Kong in June of 1898. It depicts the situation in which China was divided up between the World Powers in the late 19th century and shows the Chinese people's clear awareness of that situation.

On 25th February 1898, MacDonald cabled Salisbury that the Chinese government was eager to counterbalance Russian pressures in the north. Thus it would be prepared to grant Britain the lease of Weihaiwei if it appeared that such an offer would be acceptable[11]. But Salisbury declined again, taking the view that "no substantial change in the current situation had occurred, though other powers had leased some Chinese territories", and fearing that any such action would immediately lead to the Russian seizure of Port Arthur[12]. On 1st March, the British Parliament passed another resolution concerning its foreign policy towards China: "the maintenance of Chinese territorial integrity had a great influence on Britain and its trade"[13]. However, only two days later, Russia made a formal approach to the Qing government, demanding to lease Port Arthur, and later, on 27th March and 7th May forced the Qing Court to sign The Convention for the Lease of Port Arthur and The Renewed Convention for the Lease of Port Arthur successively by which 25 year leases for both Port Arthur and Dalian were bestowed on Russia, and Manchuria also came under its sphere of influence.

In the face of Russia and Germany's rapid expansion, Salisbury's hesitation to move forward aroused wide opposition from the British public and government who all demanded a searching reappraisal of British foreign policy. The British Cabinet also began a fierce debate on the territorial carving up of the Chinese cake and sought more commercial privileges. On 7th March 1898, it was reported in The Times that Russia was threatening to send troops to Manchuria in order to enforce her demands for the lease of Port

The British barracks on Liugong Island. circa. 1910

Arthur and Dalian. Lord Balfour, at that time in temporary charge of the government in the absence of Salisbury, ordered Curzon to draw up a detailed statement of the position regarding Weihaiwei for submission to the Cabinet[14]. On 15th March 1898, the British Cabinet formally debated the leasing of Weihaiwei. For Britain, acquiring Weihaiwei as a 'make–weight' would signify a complete abandonment of the policy which had called for the maintenance of Chinese territorial integrity, but this could avoid going to war with Russia, and possibly France and Germany, and furthermore, a counter–poise to their influence in the north would be acquired[15]. Therefore, on 25th March 1898, after a long Cabinet debate, MacDonald was told to obtain the first refusal for the leasing of Weihaiwei[16].

The decision to lease and occupy Weihaiwei was an indication that Britain had significantly modified its policy towards China. As Lord Balfour stated in the Commons in late April of 1898: 'As long as China is unable to maintain its current position, we should change our policy towards her, and that is to make sure that we take a fair share in carving up of the Chinese cake, and that portion should not be less than that of the other powers'. Britain thus began its first step on the road to carve up China, Weihaiwei being the first prize.

As the Sun Flag fell, the Union Jack was hoisted aloft

McDonald submitted the demand to lease Weihaiwei as a formal request on behalf of the British Government on 28th March 1898. It alleged that: "Russia could pose a threat to China because Port Arthur could used as a military harbour to station her fleets, thus only by leasing Weihaiwei to Britain would the domination of Russia be alleviated"[17].

To use one foreign devil to contend with another was a common trick employed by the Qing Court in the modern diplomatic process. After its strategy of allying itself with Russia to stop the other powers had failed, the Qing government endeavoured to gain an alliance with Britain in order to oppose Russia. This strategy received support from several local Governors including Wang Wenshao (Governor of Zhili), Liu Kunyi (Governor of Liangjiang) and Zhang Zhidong (Governor of Huguang)[18]. The Railway Minister, Sheng Xuanhuai claimed publicly that: "the best way to gain control over Russia and Germany is by leasing Weihaiwei to Britain"[19]. Constitutional reform figures such as Kang Youwei also recognized that they could make use of the confrontational situation between Britain and Russia, and so they submitted a written statement to the Guangxu Emperor strongly proposing an alliance with Britain against Russia[20]. The extant historical records also showed that as early as in January 1898, Mr. Luo Fenglu, Chinese Minister in London, had taken up the matter of Weihaiwei with the British government[21], then in February, the Chinese intention to grant Britain the lease of Weihaiwei was passed on to the British government by the Inspector General of the Maritime Customs Service, Sir Robert Hart[22]. However, when the Qing Court was faced with the critical question of China being carved up, it predicted that Britain might not be content with leasing just Weihaiwei, thus they neither pursued the lease nor repudiated it resolutely, but rather attempted delaying tactics in the hope of gaining a better bargain.

During the two negotiations with Britain on the 28th and 31st March, the Qing Court argued that since Weihaiwei was still occupied by the Japanese, they would suggest that negotiations should commence subsequent to the departure of the Japanese fleet, and recommended that Britain might occupy another coastal location in order to contend with Russia, or by way of a compromise, China would open up Weihaiwei as a commercial port and give special benefits to British ships. MacDonald refused all of these suggestions and declared that if no reply was received before the deadline, the matter would be taken over by a British Naval Admiral[23].

On the 2nd April, MacDonald arrived as scheduled. Britain's assertion that they might take military action caused anxieties within the Qing Court, alerting them to the urgency of the matter. Prince Yi Kuang participated in these discussions, and proposed three demands: firstly, the terms and conditions leasing to Britain should be the same as those to Russia; secondly, it should be possible for China to use Weihaiwei after leasing; thirdly, Britain should refrain from demanding any further territory. MacDonald replied that Britain had acquired many privileges in the north and south of China, and that it was unacceptable that Britain should give up its interests in southern China in order to protect its interests in northern China. After further

The Royal Marine detachment onboard HMS Alacrity prior to taking part in the Lease Ceremony (24 May 1898)

Chinese sailors from the Chinese men of war "Fuchi" forming a guard of honour while taking part in the Occupation Ceremony.

consideration, the Qing government yielded and in principle concurred with Britain's request to lease [24].

While negotiating with China, Britain also speeded up its negotiations with Japan, Germany and other interested countries. According to the articles of the Treaty of Shimonoseki, Weihaiwei would be occupied by Japan until the Chinese government had paid off its indemnity. Therefore, it was still uncertain just when and how the Japanese troop would leave Weihaiwei. At the same time, it was inevitable that Britain would be in dispute with Germany as Weihaiwei lay in Shandong province which was under the German sphere of influence.

In order to obtain Germany's support, the British government firstly promised that "Britain shall not use Weihaiwei as a base to interfere with Germany's political and commercial interests in Shandong Province"[25]. Then, over the construction of any railway about which Germany was the most concerned, officially announced on the 20th of April: "After Britain has obtained Weihaiwei, she will not jeopardize Germany's interests in Shandong Province, and will not cause any trouble for Germany in that Province. In particular, Britain shall not build any railway in Weihaiwei to link up with Shandong Province's inland railway system."[26]

In comparison with the negotiations between Britain and Germany, it was much easier for Britain and Japan to reach an agreement. The controversy between the Japanese and Russia was very serious. In particular Tsarist Russia's pressure on Japan to return the Liaodong peninsula to China, had led to intense hostility between Japan and Russia. Although Japan had suggested an alliance with the Qing Court to oppose Russia, the reaction had been a chilly one. The decision taken by Britain to oppose Russia was certainly going to benefit Japan's interests. When the British Minister inquired about Japan's reaction on 15th March, the Japanese government definitely expressed no objection. Thus, on 31st March, Lord Salisbury telegrammed Sir Ernest Satow, the British Minister in Japan, to officially inform the Japanese Government of the intention to lease Weihaiwei, and to request Japan's agreement and support[27]. The Japanese government agreed spontaneously, but requested as a condition of that support that the British Government must "agree with and support" Japan "if at any point in the future, due to the need to defend or encourage its interests, it should decide on the necessity of adopting similar measures"[28].

Captain King-Hall reading the Declaration of Occupation. (24th May 1898)

Britain's concerns were directed towards Russia's fleets that were stationed in Port Arthur and Dalian. Tsarist Russia would definitely make some reaction. Firstly Russia suggested to Germany, before turning to Japan, that, after the departure of the Japanese, Weihaiwei should be returned to China, and that China must promise never to relinquish sovereignty over it to any other country. However, this suggestion was repudiated by both Germany and Japan[29]. Russia considered that a single log was not strong enough to support a tottering building, and so began to accept reality in silence.

While the diplomatic discussions were progressing, the British Government took further actions for the occupation of Weihaiwei. The British China Squadron was ordered to move to northern China. As the departure date of the Japanese troops approached, on 29th April, MacDonald suggested that London should take over the area occupied by the Japanese troops ahead of time and regard it as the basis for future negotiation[30]. On the 9th and 13th May, the Royal Navy sent a telegram to its Commander-in-chief in China, Vice-Admiral Seymour requesting him to take over Weihaiwei and to carry out the relevant investigations[31]. On the 16th of May, MacDonald, before confirming the leasing of the area and the size of the Territory, presented Britain's wish to take over Weihaiwei to the Qing Foreign Affairs Department. However, the Qing Court was adamantly opposed to this request, and

British sailors giving three cheers for the Queen to celebrate the flying of the British flag over Weihaiwei, the easternmost point of the Chinese Mainland. Weihaiwei had become a part of the "British Empire upon which the sun never set". (24th May 1898)

The British flag being raised during the occupation ceremony (24th May 1898)

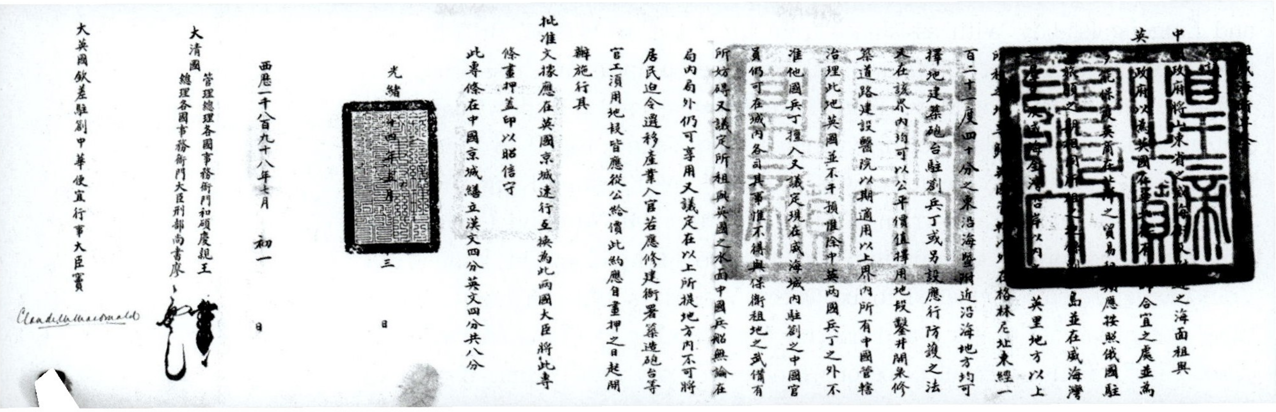
中[illegible]之海面租與
英[illegible]合宜之處並為
[illegible]之貿易[illegible]應按照俄國駐
[illegible]島並在威海灣
[illegible]英里地方以上
[illegible]格林尼址東經一
百二十一度四十分之東沿海暨附近沿海地方均可
擇地建築砲台駐劄兵丁或另設應行防護之法
又在該界內均可以公平價值擇用地段鑿井開泉修
築道路建設醫院以期適用以上界內所有中國管轄
治理此地英國並不干預惟除中英兩國兵丁之外不
准他國兵丁擅入又議定現在威海城內駐劄之中國官
員仍可在城內各司其事惟不得與保衛租地之武備有
所妨礙又議定所租與英國之水面中國兵船無論在
局內局外仍可享用又議定在以上所提地方內不可將
居民迫令遷移產業入官若應修建衙署築造砲台等
官工須用地段皆應從公給價此約應自畫押之日起開
辦施行其
批准文據應在英國京城速行互換為此兩國大臣將此專
條畫押蓋印以昭信守
此專條在中國京城繕立漢文四分英文四分共八分
光緒[illegible]三 日
西歷一千八百九十八年七月 初一 日
大清國 管理總理各國事務衙門和碩慶親王
總理各國事務衙門大臣刑部尚書廖
大英國欽差駐劄中華便宜行事大臣竇

Soldiers of the Qing Court (the last imperial dynasty of China) taking part in the Lease Ceremony (24th May 1898).

preferred to wait until the official agreements were approved and signed. MacDonald objected to this. Meanwhile, Japan once again demonstrated its enthusiasm and began to propose to the Qing Court that all the buildings Japan had constructed in Weihaiwei during its occupation should be transferred to the Qing Court, with the condition that once the British troops arrived, they should be given the privilege of using them. After that, Japan also suggested to Britain on several occasions that their officers should take over Weihaiwei in advance. The Japanese Government also sent a telegram to General Myoshi, who was stationed in Weihaiwei, that he must assist the British wherever necessary. Under these circumstances, the Chinese Foreign Affairs Department ordered Wang Wenshao, Governor of Zhili, on the 17th May, to meet the British officers to hand over Weihaiwei after withdrawal of the Japanese[32].

On the 7th May 1898, the Qing Court paid the final installment of its indemnity obligation to Japan for the war of 1894–5 in London. The Japanese troops started their withdrawal, commencing from the 9th of May. On the 19th of May, Vice–Admiral Seymour assigned the Commissioner, Captain King–Hall of HMS Narcissus to station his ship in Weihaiwei, where he was to meet the Chinese Commissioners Mr Yan Daohong (the expectant Daotai) and Captain Lin Yingqi of the Chinese man–of–war Fuchi who were in charge of the takeover matter. At 4pm., King–Hall accompanied by the diplomatic military attach é Brown, visited General Myoshi at the Japanese Headquarters in Weihaiwei and both sides agreed that British troops should, together with the Chinese government, take over the territory once the Japanese troops had left, in order to prevent the local people's resistance. At mid–day, 22nd of May, Mr. Lionel Charles Hopkins, British Consul in Chefoo arrived on HMS Alacrity at Weihaiwei. By the afternoon of the 23rd of May, the handover of Weihaiwei between the Qing Court and Japan was concluded, and Japanese troop were evacuated from the Weihaiwei mainland and Liugong Island. With assistance from the Japanese troops, British troops took over the barracks, forts, and stations once occupied by those troops. At 1.30pm, on the 24th of May, British troops were landed under Commander Napier and held the Flag hoisting ceremony on Yellow Island to the west of Liugong Island. The ceremony was attended by Captain King-Hall, Mr Hopkins, Captain Smith Dorrion of HMS Alacrity, Mr Yan and Captain Lin. The Proclamation of Occupation was then read by Captain King-Hall. Coincidentally, this happened to be Queen Victoria's 79th birthday. Finally three cheers for her Majesty and one for the Emperor of China concluded the ceremonial[33]. Thus, a small piece of Chinese territory had become part of the British Empire.

On the 1st of July 1898, a delegation from the Qing Court, consisting of Prince Yi Kuang, plus Liao Shouheng, an official from the Department of Foreign Affairs and the Minister of the Board of Punishment, met the representative of Britain, Sir Claude MacDonald, in Beijing where they

Soldiers of the Qing Court [the last imperial dynasty of China] stationed in the walled city of Weihaiwei (1898)

A map of the territory of Weihaiwei.

officially signed the Sino-British agreement Convention for the Lease of Weihaiwei. It was stipulated in the Convention that Weihaiwei was to be leased from the Chinese to Britain for as long as the Russians should occupy Port Arthur; the leased territory would include Weihaiwei and all adjacent waters; and in addition to the leasehold, the British also had permission to erect fortifications and station troops or take any other measures necessary for defensive purposes at any point on or near the region east of the meridian 121° 40' east of Greenwich. However, China still retained the right to allow its troop to enter and leave Weihaiwei without restrictions; the walled city was still under Chinese administrative jurisdiction, where officials would continue their business as before; Chinese warships would retain the right to use the harbour at any time. Subsequently, both officials from China and Britain demarcated the territorial boundary between 25th April and 17th May 1900: the territorial boundary line was drawn from a point (Caomiaozi) toward the south of the bay and continued in a semicircle to the east (Dalantou) and the west (Mashanzui). In total area, apart from the walled city of Weihaiwei, the territory consisted of 288 square miles (738.15 square km) with 120,000 inhabitants. Thus, Britain had obtained a strategic port in northern China, and its influence in China had reached its highest point.

The people of Weihaiwei rise up against the invaders

After the signing of Sino–British Convention for the Lease of Weihaiwei, both parties agreed that Britain could only exercise its power when the demarcation of territorial boundaries was completed by the Boundary Mission. In the early stages, Britain was not eager to administer the Territory formally because of insufficient preparation. However during that period, Britain speeded up all its surveys, preparing for the boundary demarcation and overall administration; at the same time urging the local authorities to assist with their surveys and to notify their people of the matter of the Lease. However, due to the Sino–Japanese War and the continued invasion of China by Germany and Britain, this not only intensified the anti–foreign feeling among the local people, but also displeased quite a number of local officials. The successive governors of Shandong, Zhang Rumei, Yu Xian and other high officials, adopted an attitude of hostility towards western rule[34]. They were therefore uncooperative, and conducted undercover resistance towards Britain's colonial authority in Weihaiwei. The neighbouring authorities such as the Wendeng and Rongcheng Yamens exercised their power by collecting taxes, and called the courts to order as usual. This caused uneasiness among the British Colonial authorities. They realized that if this continued, it would bring problems for their takeover as well as for financial control in the future. Thus, China was ignored. On the 12th of March 1899, the British authorities announced to the public, without consultation, that the citizens within their borders were prohibited from paying taxes to the Chinese authorities. They also prevented Chinese officials from exercising their administrative and judicial activities in Weihaiwei[35]. Their actions met with resistance from local officials and from the people.

The people of Weihaiwei had been renowned for their reputation for resisting invasion and defending their homeland. "The two districts of Wendeng and Rongcheng were concerned and all the villagers in Weihaiwei Territory were 'as sad as orphans'"[36]. The delimitation of borders became a hot topic discussed everywhere. Meetings of both villagers and elders were organized continuously. There was hostility and feelings of unrest among the people which were becoming difficult to control. Under the leadership of the village elders, the people began to participate wholeheartedly in the fight against the foreign invasion.

In May 1899, Colonel Lewis, of the Royal Engineers was sent by the British Army, to lead a military survey party to work at Ludaokou in the west of Weihaiwei. Upon learning of this information, the villagers used weapons such as hoes, sticks and stones, and surrounded the survey party, which was forced to stop its investigations and retreat to Weihaiwei. The British army stationed in Weihaiwei realized the gravity of this uprising, and they immediately contacted the Qing Foreign Affairs Department, via the British Minister in Beijing, demanding that they curb the villagers' rebellion against the British rule. However, the Foreign Affairs Department suggested that the British should consult with the local officials[37]. According to historical records, the local government in Shandong did not accede to the request made by the British.

After more than a year's surveying, Britain then drew up a boundary demarcation scheme at the end of 1899. Dorward, the British military commissioner of Weihaiwei, surmised that matters were in order, and began to press the Chinese authorities to send their officials to demarcate the border. However, the Qing Court insisted they should delay their survey until March the next year. In response Dorward ignored the Chinese authorities, and issued two public notices in January 1900, for the first time announcing that the British government would take over Weihaiwei, and appointed British

The fields outside Ludaokou Village, where Weihaiwei villagers blocked the way of a British military survey party in the spring of 1899. (1904)

officials to govern Weihaiwei, except within the walled city to which Chinese authority was limited. Additionally, Dorward also demanded that people living in the leased area must pay their taxes in the form of money or crops to the British officials, according to the original tax rate[38]. On the 18th of March, the British officials attempted to arrest some Chinese tax collectors from the Wenden Yamen. All these actions caused further resentment and animosity among local officials towards the colonial authority. After March 1900, anti-British gatherings had reached their peak within the Territory, "on average more than 2000 people participated", and "their main and public purpose was to drive the Britons away." [39]

A local teacher, Mr Cui Shoushan, who was nearly in his seventies, held an anti-British assembly in Jiangnanzhuang village on the 14th of March 1900 to discuss strategies for fighting against the British. Mr Cui, a local famous gentleman, had passed the imperial examination at the county level and was nicknamed "Guanzi", commonly known as Mr Cui Guan. He contacted Gu Huiting from the same village, and Dong Shaohui from Laihai village, to enroll and train militiamen, and to collect money for procuring weapons. They claimed publicly, applauded by the people, that their aim was to move against the British. That day, more than 700 people, armed with long spears, big knives, pistols and carrying mortars participated in this assembly. The meeting proposed that each village should set up militia units, training a certain number of armed militiamen. All the militia units should have three training sessions each month in order to improve their competence in martial arts as well as shooting practice. After the meeting, militia units expanded rapidly within southwestern Weihaiwei. Led by heads of the village militia units, local people went on training exercises and became better organized.

Cisheng temple at Zhangcun Village, built in the Tang Dynasty (618–707 AD), the site of a gathering of villagers led by Cui Shoushan, protesting against British occupation. (26th March 1900)

This spirited anti-British movement alerted the British colonial authorities that something alarming was going on. The gathering in Jiangnanzhuang village had been spied upon by members of the Chinese Regiment. After the meeting, the Chinese Regiment selected suitable soldiers to disguise themselves as villagers in order to collect more information[40]. The result of this was that the British authorities decided that they should destroy this anti-British movement while it was still in its embryonic stage.

Mr Cui Shoushan held another anti-Brit-

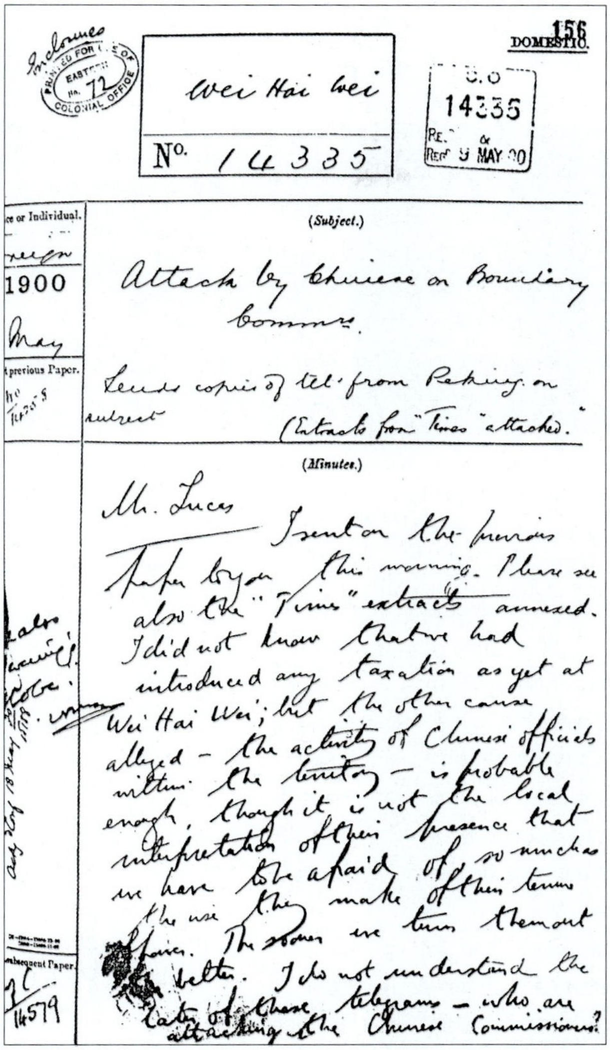

A note sent in May 1900 from the British Minister in Beijing to Prime Minister Salisbury concerning the Weihaiwei tragedy. [Note: Between March and May 1900, a number of local Chinese people were killed by troops under British control.]

ish meeting at Cisheng temple in Zhang village on the 26th of March. The main intention was to review the progress of military training and to discuss specific procedures for the insurrection. On the 25th of March, Dorward who was already aware of this uprising, commanded the Chinese Regiment to suppress it the next day. On the morning of the 26th, the head of the Chinese Regiment, Colonel Bower, led 420 fully–armed soldiers to the place where the meeting was being held. More than 700 people were surrounded. However, the people just ignored the troops and continued to hold their meeting. Just as Colonel Bower was about to command the public to put down their weapons, Mr Cui Shoushan demanded that first he should dismount from his horse to answer their questions. The people in the meeting unanimously voiced their support for this. In spite of Bower's stern command for them to abandon their weapons, he was ignored. The people refused to budge, and so Colonel Bower ordered the soldiers to use bayonets to force the people to surrender their weapons. Subsequently, the three leaders, Mr Cui Shoushan, Mr Gu Huitin and Mr Dong Shaohui were arrested and imprisoned on Liugong Island[41].

In order to placate the people's growing hostility, Dorward, held a meeting of the village headmen of the Territory on 2nd April. He claimed that the leasing of Weihaiwei had been agreed by the Qing government. In order to secure the release of the prisoners, almost all the village headmen attended this meeting. During the meeting, village headmen suggested that the British and Chinese government must reach a unanimous agreement before it could be accepted. They also appealed for the immediate release of the three prisoners. Dorward tactfully declined the requests made by the headmen, but he was satisfied with their attitude. He definitely reckoned that hostilities were due to villagers' ignorance, and their readiness to believe in rumours[42]. Of course, Dorward was not so na?ve as to sit back and relax. After the suppression of these village meetings, the British colonial authority installed cavalry units in the Chinese Regiment to effectively deter any further anti–British incidents.

On the 13th of April 1900, Mr Li Xijie, Daotai of Denglaiqing and the

Inspector of the Eastern Customs, Mr. Cheng Peiqing, expectant District-Magistrate, and other boundary officials of the Chinese authority arrived at Weihaiwei to meet Dorward and the other British officers, to debate the delimitation of the border. There followed numerous inconclusive meetings, and continuous argument. On the 25th of April, before they could conclude a unanimous agreement, Li Xijie, Colonel Bower, Major Penrose and other British boundary officers began to set up tablets marking their borders. The escort was formed from No.7 Company, under Captain Pereira, with Lieutenant Brooke and Colour-Sergeant Brook, and numbered some sixty men[43]. But since the delimitation, Mr Li Xijie refused to accept protection by the Chinese Regiment and with his party camped outside the territory during the night in order to keep a distance from the British side.

A dispatch by Chinese imperial Inspector General Gaoxi to the Qing Court reporting the deaths of Chinese people at the hands of the British.

It was nearly dark when the Boundary Commission had set up the 25th boundary stone on the 28th of April. Li Xijie stayed in the Cong family's temple in Dongdaotou village outside the leased border for the night, which was 3 miles distant from the British camp site at the foot of Duoding Mountain. In the night, around 600 people gathered at Dongdaotou village, beseeching Li and the team to stop delimitating the border. At the same time, thousands of people from neighbouring villages gathered outside the British camps, and shouted loudly that they were never going to sell their land. Unwillingly, Bower stepped out of his tent, trying to explain to the villagers that they were only setting up the boundary tablet, without the intention to purchase their land. However, the people did not believe him, and continued with their protests. Realising that the situation was getting out of hand and increasing in ferocity, Bower ordered the arrest of 6 of the leaders. This inflamed the anger of the people and they refused to leave. At the end of his wits, Bower reprimanded them and released all the leaders[44]. The following day, around 2000 people gathered outside the British campsite. The British were outnumbered, so the officers could only stay in the camp, and were unable to exit via the border. On the 30th of April Dorward, after receiving a message for help, sent reinforcement, led by Lieutenant Toke. At 1am on 1st May, further reinforcements of 170 soldiers, commanded by Major Bruce, were sent, and another battalion was stationed at Yangjiatan Village in the south of Weihaiwei, preparing to suppress the anti–British villagers by force.

That day, more than 5000 villagers had gathered around Dongdaotou village, and even more climbed up surrounding hills to watch the British army. In their communications Li Xijie and Bower blamed each other. Bower blamed the disturbance on the Chinese authorities because the lease issue had not been explained clearly to the people, who thus would not accept the British explanation. Following this, he demanded that Li announce that the delimiting of the border was carried out according to an agreement, and that there should not be any interference from anyone. The next day Li wrote to Dorward, suggesting that the border delimitation should be delayed until the people's hostilities had subsided. Bower insisted that border delimitation should be carried out regardless of the participation of the Chinese, otherwise they would be regarded as cowards[45]. On the 3rd of May, Bower led his soldiers eastwards to demarcate the border without participation of the Chinese. At the same time, 60 soldiers from the Chinese Regiment led by Captain Watson were stationed at Duoding Mountain in case of resistance by the local people.

On the 5th of May, the British boundary party arrived at Baoxin Village. That day at 2.30pm, the first attack took place in the dry Linquan River–bed, along which Major Penrose and his team of 15 soldiers were making their way back to camp after they had finished setting up their 32nd boundary stone. They suddenly found about 1,500 villagers, armed with

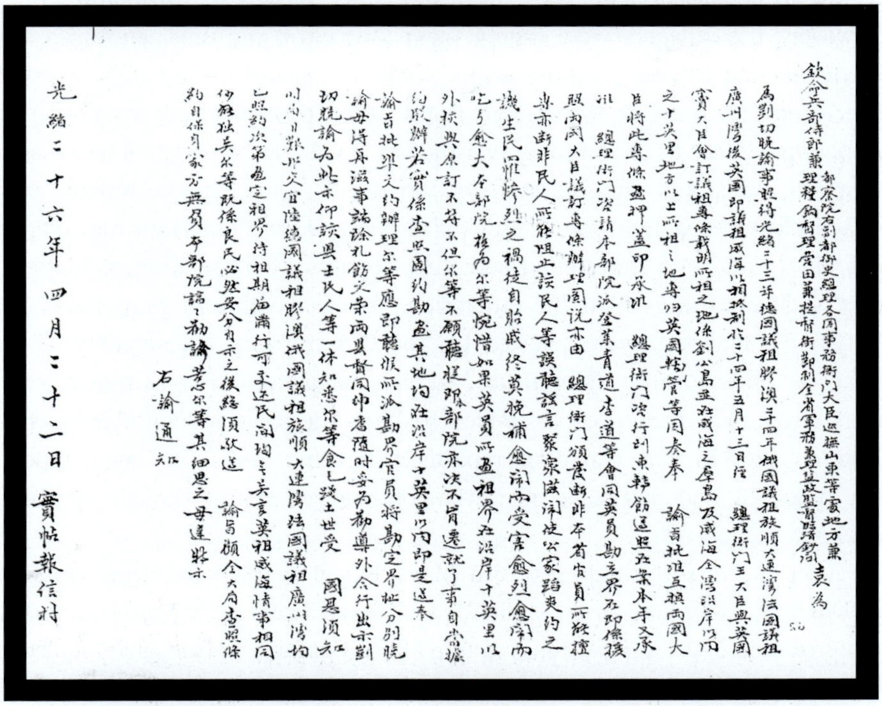
欽命兵部侍郎兼都察院右副都御史總理各國事務衙門大臣巡撫山東等處地方兼理糧餉督理營田兼提督銜節制全省軍務兼理鹽政監督臨清鈔關 袁 為
剴切曉諭事照得光緒二十三年德國議租膠澳二十四年俄國議租旅順大連灣法國議租
廣州灣後英國即議租威海以相抵制於二十四年五月十三日經 總理衙門王大臣與英國
竇大臣會訂議租專條載明所租之地係劉公島並在威海之群島及威海全灣沿岸以內
之十英里地方以上所租之地專歸英國轄管等因奏奉 諭旨批准互換兩國大
臣將此專條畫押蓋印承准 總理衙門咨行到東轉飭遵照在案本年又承
准 總理衙門咨請本部院派登萊青道李道等會同英員勘立界石即係按
照兩國大臣議訂專條辦理圖說亦由 總理衙門頒發斷非本省官員所能擅
專亦斷非民人所能阻止該民人等誤聽謠言聚眾滋鬧徒使公家蹈爽約之
譏生民罹慘烈之禍徒自貽戚終莫挽補愈鬧而受害愈烈愈鬧而
吃虧愈大本部院推為爾等惋惜如果英員所畫租界在沿岸十英里以
外核與原訂不符不但爾等不願聽從即本部院亦決不肯遷就了事自當據
約駁辯若實係查照圖約勘畫其地均在沿岸十英里以內即是遵奉
諭旨批准之約辦理爾等應即聽候所派勘界官員將勘定界址分別曉
諭毋得再滋事端除札飭文登榮成兩縣督同紳耆隨時妥為勸導外合行出示剴
切曉諭為此示仰該縣士民人等一體知悉爾等食毛踐土世受 國恩須知
[illegible]德國議租膠澳俄國議租旅順大連灣法國議租廣州灣均
已照約次第畫定租界待租期屆滿仍可交還民間詢之英官英租威海情事相同
仍維爾等既係良民必然安分自示之後務須欽遵 諭旨顧全大局查照條
約自保身家無負本部院諄諄勸諭苦心爾等其細思之毋違特示
右諭通知
光緒二十六年四月二十二日 實帖報信村

An order issued by Yuan Shikai, Governor of Shandong. [Yuan Shikai become the second president of the Republic of China for a short period after the 1911 revolution, then later tried to have himself declared emperor].

spades, hoes, sticks and stones approaching them quickly. When they were several metres off, the villagers began to throw stones at them and then attack with farm tools. Penrose was hit on the head by a stone. The British team then fired back and 3 villagers were killed. After this the British retreated back to their camp to the south of the river and at the foot of Taibo Hill, and were constantly firing during their retreat. The people pursued them relentlessly, and the battle resumed. At this moment Penrose was wounded by a brave anti–British warrior who attacked him in the head and legs, causing him to fall to the ground. The Chinese Regiment, realising the gravity of this attack, then began to open fire fiercely and managed to rescue Penrose, and then retreated once again. The British party's ammunition was spent by the time they had reached their camp. When they were very close to the camp, British soldiers who were on duty were alerted by the sound of shooting. They immediately sounded the alarm in the camp. Two companies led by Bower, Pereira and Toke, came out to the rescue. It was difficult to draw a clear distinction between the parties who were fighting, thus making it difficult to help. However, the villagers were totally inexperienced in fighting, and once they discovered the British reinforcements, they rushed out of the hills to try to deter them by throwing stones, but instead they became sitting targets on the open river bank. Several people were killed by Bower's party. The villagers began to retreat but were pursued by the British army. In the retreat, some villagers continued fighting as they withdrew. During this fighting, Pereira was pitch–forked to the ground and three soldiers from the Chinese Regiment were seriously injured; on the other side, nineteen villagers were dead. The British commanders were amazed by the bravery and the tenacity of the villagers. Subsequently Major Bruce, second commander of the Chinese Regiment wrote that many people seemed to have the same indomitable spirit as those of the Yihetuan (Boxers), repeatedly fighting even after being repeatedly repulsed, and that some men even continued to charge though they were seriously wounded[46].

One of the posts marking the boundary of the British leased territory. The characters on the post read: "Great Britain Leased Territories"

After the intense fighting of 5th May, Bower warned the army stationed on Duoding Mountain to be vigilant, and asked Dorward to provide further reinforcements. On the morning of 6th May, Captain Watson and Lieutenant Bray (stationed on the Duoding Mountain), while patrolling on horseback to the west of the camp, found groups of people shouldering guns surrounding the camp in all directions. It was estimated that around 3000 people took part in the attack. The two sides were only 600 metres apart. Once the villagers noticed Bray and Watson, they shouted furiously and vigorously charged towards them. Watson dashed back to the camp where he provided more ammunition for the soldiers. Later, Watson led half the company towards the southwest, while Bray led his party towards the highland in the north of the camp. The British Army started shooting at 11.30am. They killed three villagers. The villagers counter-attacked forcefully and attacked the British party again and again under the cover of poor mortars. Though they possessed heroic and tenacious spirits, unfortunately, their weapons were of low quality and were ineffective in the attack. Bullets, slugs, nails and odd bits of metal fell around in profusion over the positions of the British army, but caused no harm to any British soldiers. "A piece of ordinance, carried by several men, made a terrific noise and emitted an immense volume of smoke, but no projectile ever seemed to come out of it". The fighting lasted for more than one hour. The energy of the villagers was diminishing, and they had to retreat after rescuing their dead and injured from the battleground. This action resulted in the deaths of ten people, and there were numerous casualties[47].

After these two tragic incidents, angry villagers hastened to the Chinese boundary party's site in Dongdaotou village, demanding that the officials should dispatch their army for revenge. The Chinese authority recognised the gravity of the situation, and repeatedly restarted their negotiations with the British, beseeching them to temporarily stop demarcating the border. How-

The camp of the Chinese Regiment before the fierce battle at Taibo Hill on 6th May 1900.

The Chinese Regiment 1903— mercenary troops who served Britain, and were used to put down anti—British movements. (1903)

ever the Colonial British were determined in their course, there was no stopping them in their mission, and more soldiers were sent to strengthen the border. None of the Chinese authority's demands were heeded. On the 17th May, the demarcation of the border was accomplished by the British army. On the 12th June, Yuan Shikai, the provincial governor of Shandong, accepted the border line drawn up by the British army[48].

The Weihaiwei people's anti—British military struggle is an inspiring example in modern history. The members of the anti—British group were mainly peasants living in unfortunate circumstances. They were suppressed by society, and suffered from many hardships and misfortunes, and they were disregarded because of their humble origins. Without anyone to rely on, based on their determination to defend their homes against attack, and to prevent their relatives being killed and on other simple emotions, they spontaneously organized, using their flesh and blood to combat modern guns and cannons in relentless warfare. Like the rising wind and scattering clouds, all these historical events eventually quietened down, but as a pioneer movement in the 20th century, the Weihaiwei people's achievements and heroic spirits should be respected and commemorated forever by later generations.

onfucius and Mencius –
tactics of the colonizers

2

"Foreign Confucian scholars" and "Governing by Confucianism"

The British government established a temporary Weihaiwei Administrative Office in 1898. Initially the British Naval Commander in China controlled this office, which in 1899 was then transferred to the control of the War Office. On 17th May 1900, the Colonial Office sent Sir Frank Swettenham, Resident-General of the Federated Malay States, to Weihaiwei to make an investigation, after which, he wrote for the British government the Report on Weihaiwei and Its Future Administration in July of the same year. The report described the overall situation in Weihaiwei, including its politics, economy, society, natural conditions and so on. In addition, Swettenham gave the British government a number of important recommendations regarding the future administration of Weihaiwei, strongly recommending the advisability of ruling the Chinese by using Chinese ways, and insisting that all those traditional customs, which did not conflict with British rule, should be retained, never touching the traditional social and economical structures. The key-points of these recommendations were all adopted by the British government and became the basic political principles for the rule of Weihaiwei.[1] In 1901 the British Colonial Office formally took over Weihaiwei. On 24th July of the same year the British government produced a constitutional document entitled "The Weihaiwei Order-in-Council, 1901" (shortened to the Order-in-Council) which established the basic political system for Weihaiwei.

According to the Order-in-Council, the British government would send a civil commissioner to rule the territory, who would be appointed directly by the King and responsible to the Colonial Office. This Commissioner would have the power to make and enact the ordinances in Weihaiwei, in addition, he would hold jurisdiction over all affairs within the Colonial Office's functions and powers, and also have the power to appoint Weihaiwei government high officials, with the Colonial Office's approval, and to appoint and remove the middle and lower ranking officials, the clerks and temporary district officers by himself. Regarding his judicial functions, the Commissioner would have the power to sentence, grant special pardons and probation,

in addition to appointing the acting judge of the Weihaiwei High Court and to draw up the court regulations and legal procedures, etc. Therefore, though the Weihaiwei Commissioner was a little lower in rank than the governor of a British colony, his actual power was greater than that of a colonial governor as he himself commanded the three rights of legislation, administration and jurisdiction.

There were successive seven British commissioners in Weihaiwei during the period of the lease, namely Gaunt, Dorward, Cowan, Stewart Lockhart, Blunt, Russell Brown and Reginald Johnston.[2] The first three commissioners were all from the military, Blunt and Brown were from the Foreign Office. Those five commissioners contributed very little to the administration of Weihaiwei, but it was Lockhart and Johnston from the Colonial Office who were largely responsible for the style of administration which was established at Weihaiwei.

Sir James Haldane Stewart Lockhart (1858–1937) also went by the three

The House of the British Commissioner, Weihaiwei (1921)

The offices of the Senior District Officer.

Chinese names of Luo Bi, Luo Xi and Luo Renting. He was born in Scotland in 1858 and studied successively in King William's College in the Isle of Man, George Watson's College in Edinburgh, and finally graduated from Edinburgh University. In 1878 he was recruited by the British Colonial Service and then was sent to Hong Kong in 1879 and thus began his more than 40 years' political career in the colonial service within China. Lockhart gained speedy recognition from the Colonial Office thanks to his outstanding administrative abilities. Thus during the 13 short years from 1882 to 1895, he was rapidly promoted from the Clerk of Councils and Chief Clerk in the Colonial Secretary's office, then to Superintendent of Opium Revenue, first Assistant Colonial Secretary and Auditor-General, finally to Registrar-General to the Colonial Secretary. The post of Registrar-General was the second highest position in Hong Kong, second only to the Hong Kong Governor.[3]

In 1898 Britain forcefully leased the Hong Kong New Territories, also Weihaiwei. As a result of these actions they faced more complicated problems in setting up colonial rule. This special historical situation pushed Lockhart into being involved in some of the major events of modern China. He became the founder of British colonial rule in the Hong Kong New Territories and Weihaiwei.

In Hong Kong, Lockhart, as the British special commissioner, the chief negotiator and the first Special Commissioner of the New Territories, was responsible for a series of activities ranging from the New Territories survey, the boundary definition negotiations, the boundary demarcation for the takeover of the New Territories, and the design and establishment of the administrative system. In this, Lockhart was a faithful servant of Great Britain, and under his management, the New Territories were absorbed into the Hong Kong colonial system within a short time.

The territorial flag of British Weihaiwei.

Once they had settled the problems of the New Territories, the Colonial Office also took over responsibility for Weihaiwei from the military. Weihaiwei was the greatest headache because it faced not only the same problems concerning the establishment of administration as did the New Territories, but also presented a more complex economic problem. At that time, the plan to build a naval base was abandoned, so the colonial office hoped to develop businesses there, or at least to try to make it become self-sufficient, and so avoid becoming a financial burden on Britain. However, the commercial prospects for Weihaiwei seemed gloomy due to several major limiting factors such as the uncertainty of the lease period and the loss of railway construction rights. In view of these difficulties, it was essential for the Colonial Office to send a capable commissioner to Weihaiwei. The Colonial Office naturally selected Lockhart because his success in settling the New Territories had demonstrated his administrative abilities. More importantly, Lockhart had established a good rapport with the Chinese merchants in Hong Kong. They thus had strong reason to believe that under Lockhart's leadership Weihai would become another example of a British commercial success in Asia.[4] At this time Lockhart saw no chance of further advancement in Hong Kong, so he welcomed a transfer, accepted the appointment and arrived in Weihaiwei in May 1902.[5]

As soon as he started in his new job Lockhart moved the administrative office from Liugong Island to the mainland and changed its name to Port Edward, showing his ambition to rule and develop Weihaiwei. His ambition was a consequence of his confidence which resulted from his familiarity with Chinese culture.

Culture is rooted in every field of social life. It's not exceptional for an invader to achieve successful control over a territory if he has a deep understanding of that occupied territory's culture.

During his early stay in Hong Kong, Lockhart accepted formal and strict Chinese language training and began to spend lots of his energy in studying classical Chinese and Confucius. As time went on he became enchanted by traditional Chinese culture and studied not only classical Chinese history but also had an interest in Chinese music, chess and painting and all its customs. This interest remained with him all his life. He wrote and published several works on China such as A Manual of Chinese Quotations, The Currency of the Farther East, Index to the Tso Chuan, and Selected Chinese Verses. As a result, he had good relations, to varying degrees, with Gu Hongming, Zhang Yuanji, Xu Beihong and many other contemporary Chinese cultural figures. In the opinions of all of the above, he not only gained a reputation as an 'Overseas Confucian Scholar', but also became a famous collector of Chinese painting, calligraphy and old Chinese coins and Chinese crafts.

Compared to most contemporary colonialists, Lockhart was more fore-sighted and effective both in his understanding of China and also of its traditional form of administration, thanks to his profound sinological accomplishments. He understood very clearly that Confucianism not only had had a great influence on the scholar-officials of imperial times but that it was also deeply rooted in the mind of even the poorest peasant. He was also clear that it was the historical characteristic of Chinese rulers to rule the people through the strength of their culture and ethics, and he recognised the

The office of the Officer in Charge, Liugong Island. (1938)

Lockhart (left) and Johnston awaiting the visiting Governor of Shandong Province – Yang Shixiang. (11th July 1905)

importance of following local customs and taking advantage of Confucianism in order to rule an area of China. Therefore, he adopted Chinese traditional ruling ideas into his government in Weihaiwei, and established a unique Chinese–Western style of administration there.

In 1902, the Weihaiwei government staff consisted only of Lockhart and a Secretary to Government and Magistrate who was responsible for ordinance–drafting, judicial sentencing, policing, tax–collecting, registration and general affairs.[6] In 1906, the position of Senior Medical Officer was established, who was in charge of public health, the government hospital and the quarantining of ships. In the same year, the territory was divided into the north and south divisions, with two British magistrates, each of whom was responsible for his own division. One was Secretary to Government and Magistrate for the North Division, the other was District Officer and Magistrate for the South Division.[7] In 1916, the functions and positions of the North and South Magistrates were changed into those of the Senior and Junior District officers, who accordingly resided in Port Edward.[8] Senior District Officers would be from the Colonial Office or Foreign Office, and responsible for finance, civil affairs, official documents and correspondence, prisons and civil cases; Junior District Officers were selected mainly from among police officers in Hong Kong, Singapore and other colonies, or from army officers stationed in Weihaiwei, and were responsible for tax–collecting, the port, police and criminal cases, and also acted as court clerk. In addition, the Weihaiwei colonial government established two non–governmental advisory bodies for policy–

In 1920, when was a serious famine in Weihaiwei, the British distributed grain to the Chinese residents. The Chinese returned this grain to the British after the harvest of 1921. The photograph shows the (British) authorities erecting a tablet to mark the honesty of the Chinese population in Edward Port.

making; one consisting of foreign businessmen from Weihaiwei, the other of Chinese businessmen from the local Chamber of Commerce and also district headmen.

From the development of the structure of the colonial government, we can see that, no matter however that structure changed, the most important functional officer – the District Officer in charge of both administration and justice all the times – was similar to the traditional Chinese district–magistrate. Thus, Lockhart's idea of using Chinese ways to rule the Chinese permeated into every corner of his administration.

Concerning the judicial system, this meant combining both the strict western principle of legislation and the traditional Chinese one of moral enlightenment, combining the trying of a case with the concept of mediation by a 'peace talker' such as the village headman or other elder of the village.

Regarding the highly complex village system, this meant making the traditional family system successfully become an important part of the British administrative system in Weihaiwei, by means of the continued use of the village headman system and the popularization of the district headman system.

Regarding cultural education, Confucianism had reached its highest point in the social position, and during Lockhart's civil administration, Confucianism featured both in his manner and speech, and he took pains to perform as a "father–and–mother official", employing folk morality and customs. Until his retirement from Weihaiwei, he would still admonish the native people to follow the ancient simple, honest and natural style of life, and never to change their scholarly and refined bearing.[9]

The evidence shows that Lockhart was well able to cope with a complicated situation successfully and that his idea of using Chinese ways to rule the Chinese was exactly right, as was reflected in the peaceful state of Weihaiwei during troubled times elsewhere in China, when the nationalist trend of thought was increasingly running high and the fierce conflicts between China and the foreign powers were seen everywhere in other areas. However, Lockhart, though successful in civil administration, repeatedly came under attack for his failure to develop Weihaiwei business which had once been the primary aim of his administration. In fact, he was originally quite confident of that first aim as he had special experience in Hong Kong Chinese society.

Lockhart present at the foundation stone laying ceremony of a new wing of Donghua Hospital, the largest nongovernmental charitable organization, when he was Colonial Secretary and Registrar–General in Hong Kong in 1898.

Lockhart had been responsible for Chinese affairs for a long time during his service in Hong Kong. He could remain impartial and usually respected the Chinese people's rights when settling any conflicts between foreigners and Chinese. By the late 19th century, the Chinese had played an important role in Hong Kong society, to which Lockhart contributed much, thus he gained the respect and friendship of the Chinese in Hong Kong, which became the major source for his ambitious plan to develop business at Weihaiwei. However, the uncertain lease period, poor infrastructure and many other inconveniences not only limited foreign businessmen but also hindered the northward movement of Hong Kong merchants. In view of the above limitations, Lockhart proposed many times that the Colonial Office should take

measures to define the lease period, and he also repeatedly requested recruiting capable officials to assist his work and the enlargement of financial aid and public expenditure, but all were refused. While negotiating with the Colonial Office, Lockhart kept in frequent contact with the Shandong Governor and they visited each other often. He strengthened contacts with provincial industrial and commercial circles, urged the Shandong provincial authorities to construct a road to Weihaiwei, and actively proposed that Shandong businessmen should develop Weihaiwei, but the way had been blocked. He had no choice but to cast his eyes at Weihaiwei itself, and he strongly advocated the business developments at Weihaiwei and tried to squeeze funds from the meager revenue in order to develop transportation, public health and public works. However, limited by London's policy of running Weihaiwei at the lowest cost,[10] he finally not only failed to develop Weihaiwei into the second Hong Kong, but also lagged behind Qingdao and Dalian, which had developed from the same starting point as Weihaiwei. Thus, Weihaiwei became the 'Cinderella of the British Empire' in European eyes in China.[11] Instead, Lockhart's performance caused dissatisfaction in the Colonial Office, so he had to remain in Weihaiwei for 19 years until he retired in 1921 and returned to Britain.

Farewell to Lockhart, on his departure from Hong Kong in 1902.

We wonder what Lockhart thought about his successes and failures at Weihaiwei, but as a far-sighted 'foreign Confucian scholar', he seemed to value the future compared with the present. Early on during his involvement with the New Territories, Hong Kong, Lockhart had said: "Hong Kong may be returned to China some day in the future, when its history will be rewritten, and I just hope that I, James Stewart Lockhart would not be depicted as an ogre with a green face and long teeth in their writings"[12]. History has shown that he was not such an ogre, at least not within Weihaiwei and Shandong political circles. He was not only regarded as a friend by Shandong officials, but also even regarded as a Chinese by Weihai people. It was said that a Weihai person became angry with someone who referred to Lockhart as a 'foreigner'. When he retired, the Weihai people erected a stone tablet to commemorate his good performance and presented him a bowl of pure water, with compliments implying that he was an upright and honest 'father-and-mother official'.[13] Lockhart was acknowledged by Weihai people, but behind such recognition, the future was silent as stagnant water in the realm of traditional ideology and values at Weihaiwei. In fact, every national culture has its own limitations and it would have been impossible for Lockhart, well versed in both Chinese and Western, and ancient and modern learning, not to be aware of this. However, "if it ever came to a choice between a bad law or a physical disturbance, his preference would always lie with the unjust law", so he maintained the traditional system irrespective of good or bad, and so his actions really "were not due to altruistic humanitarianism as some might suppose"[14]: in the final analysis he would place benefits to the British colonial system above all other considerations.

After Lockhart returned home, he still took part in social affairs and academic research relating to China. He became a member of the China Association and joined the Governing Body of the School of Oriental Studies at the University of London, then became Secretary of the Royal Asiatic Society. On 26th February 1937, Lockhart died in his London house with the great reputation of having been "one of the foremost authorities in this country on Chinese affairs".[15]

Sir Reginald Fleming Johnston (1874 – 1938) was another high colonial official who stayed at Weihaiwei for a long period, second only to Lockhart. He was a famous figure not only in the colonial history of Weihaiwei but also in the history of foreign relations with China. Johnson was born in Edinburgh, Scotland, in 1874. After studying in Edinburgh University, he then went on to Magdalen College, Oxford where he graduated with a Master's degree in history. In 1898 Johnson was recruited by the British Colonial Service, became a Far East cadet and was sent to Hong Kong in the same year. In Hong Kong government, he successively worked as Clerk of Councils, Assistant Colonial Secretary and Private Secretary to the Governor. In 1904, thanks to Lockhart's strong commendation, he was sent to Weihaiwei by the Colonial Office and became Acting Secretary to Government and Magistrate, then District Officer and Magistrate for the South Division, later Senior District Officer.

Lockhart recommended Johnston not only because of their close personal friendship, but because they shared the same obsession with Chinese culture and had "the ability to win the trust of the Chinese".[16] This led Lockhart to

Commissioner Lockhart outside Government House. (1921)

believe that Johnston would be capable of carrying out his policy of using Chinese ways to rule the Chinese. In this, Lockhart had been Johnston's mentor from the time they worked together in Hong Kong. Lockhart taught him that if you wanted to understand China, you must understand her culture and society, not just her language.[17] Johnston lived up to Lockhart's expectations and he went even farther than Lockhart in his obsession with Chinese culture, especially Confucianism. Later he gained fame, not even matched by Lockhart, not only in Weihai but also throughout China. During his stay in China, Johnston read all the Confucian classics and many other texts. His travels extended all over famous mountains and rivers, scenic spots and relics in China. He was familiar with Confucianism, Taoism, Mohism and Buddhism, also Chinese astronomy, geography and prose, all of which he had studied and knew quite well. Thus, he could understand the Chinese culture more deeply than many ordinary Chinese people. He wrote many books and articles about China including From Peking to Mandalay, Lion and Dragon in Northern China, A Chinese Appeal Concerning Christian Missions, Buddhist China, Confucianism in Modern China, and Twilight in the Forbidden City, which are still valuable historical documents and also important for academic research today.

Unlike Lockhart, Johnston gave almost wholehearted support to Chinese culture. For example, he not only gave himself a Chinese name full of Confucian significance – 'Zhuang Shidun', but also acquired another name – 'Zhi Dao' from the phrase 'Shi Zhi Yu Dao', meaning 'a gentleman faithful to the Way', in the Confucian Analects, showing that he was determined to maintain their fundamental values. Witnessing the various criticisms of and attacks on the traditional Chinese culture, this westerner unexpectedly regarded the promotion of Confucianism as his duty, and was keen on advocating Chinese culture and Confucian classics. He sternly refuted the belief that Western culture and its social systems were superior to those of China and opposed the attempt to import western ideas into China. There was almost no hint of discrimination and prejudice in his works, unlike those of his contemporary westerners, although the Chinese were badly discriminated against at that time. When the Chinese were at a loss to know how to resist the pressures from a strong western civilization, he pointed out that the Chinese culture and social structures contained many things that were good for China and even for the world. When Confucianism was regarded as the root of all evil and became an object of public denunciation, he reminded the Chinese that the destruction of Confucianism would result in an irretrievable loss to China and predicted that China would lose more excellent and great qualities if China became totally westernized. When the Chinese cast their eyes upon a more material civilization, he warned them to pay more attention to their own spiritual values and cultural heritage and he especially pointed out that the right way for China to be lifted out of poverty and backwardness was to carry out a complete political reform and eradicate corruption, but "to retain the moral force of traditional religion and not to destroy all ancient ethical values"[18]. All the above ideas and actions made Johnston an unusual western figure in the modern history of cultural exchanges between China and the western nations, and also became the ideological basis for his

21st April 1921. Lockhart's farewell speech on the occasion of his retirement from Weihaiwei.

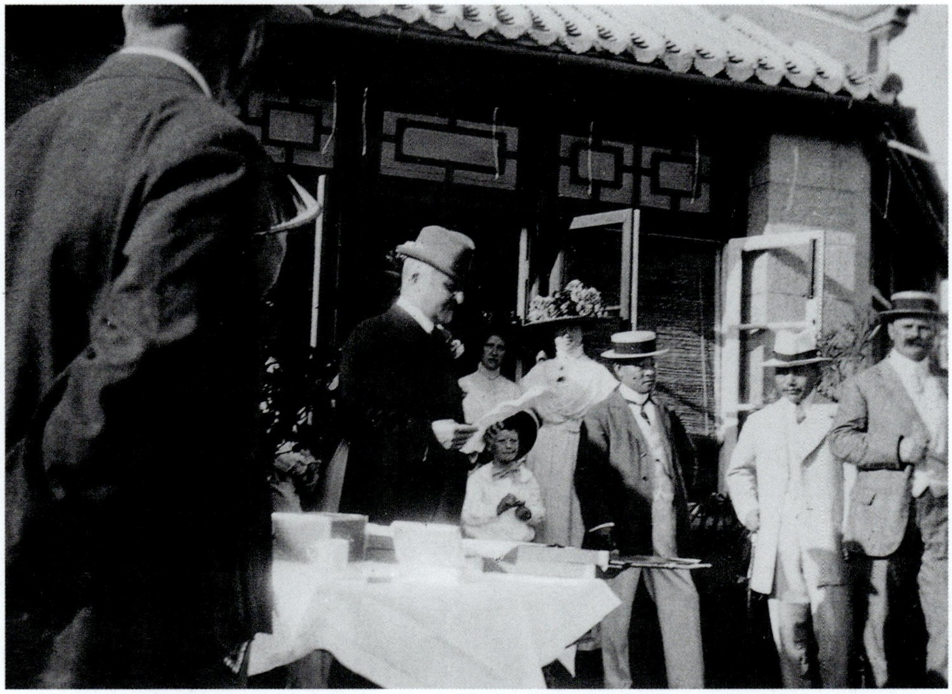

exceptional performance in the administration of Weihaiwei.

Johnston's political ambition was, in direct line with his cultural position, to become a traditional Chinese 'father–and–mother official' and 'scholar–official'. His behaviour was even louder than his words in this respect, and he earnestly practiced what he preached. During his service in Weihaiwei, he participated in the design and popularization of the district headman system, the reform of the judicial system, the division of the administrative districts and so on. He was also responsible for most administrative affairs. He stressed that government officials should not set themselves high above the masses, simply relying on their junior officials' reports, but should go down to the grass–roots level to gain an understanding of the true situation, and gained the confidence of the ordinary village people through direct contact and by treating worthy men with courtesy.[19] He also strongly deprecated ignorance of the people's true concerns and pointed out that although some small cases might seem unimportant to a foreigner, they were very important to the humble country folk.[20] Therefore, he spent most of time travelling throughout the territory, trying to understand what was going on at the most basic levels. He talked with the villagers using a pure local dialect and would settle their disputes at any time and in any place. In court, he always tried to hear each case according to the Chinese customs and moral values, so

The merchants of Liugong Island saying farewell to Lockhart (1921)

R.F Johnston spending Christmas Day at Beikou Temple in Weihaiwei, 1906.

there was almost no difference between him and the ordinary Chinese magistrates, except in his appearance, and maybe superior knowledge when quoting from some teaching from the Analects and the Sacred Edict to enlighten the litigants. Due to his western and Confucian accomplishments, Johnston quickly melted into the Weihaiwei social life, and the local people would even ask for Johnston's mediation in settling such trivial matters as quarrels between a husband and wife, a mother and daughter-in-law, or between neighbours. During the first year of his service in Weihai in 1904, the territory gentry presented him with a scroll and praised him as a 'father-and-mother official'.[21] In 1930 when he retired from the post of Commissioner, the local people presented him with a bowl of pure water, which was the highest honour for all officials when retiring from their posts.[22] Even today, some elderly people in Weihai can still remember the public praise for his love of the people.

Although Johnston, as a British colonial official, successfully followed the model of a 'father-and-mother official' which was valued by the traditional Chinese society in Weihaiwei, and also served an example to his colonial colleagues in how to realize Britain's colonial dream, he, in return, was regarded as a conservative and a Confucian by the Colonial Office and never achieved high office. The Colonial Office even regarded him as a sheer crank: "abnormal..., once almost became a monk..., fond of living in the wild".[23] Such accusations accompanied him all his life, and later even worse insults were used such as 'a British traitor who was wholeheartedly faithful to his foreign master' or even 'a homosexual'.[24] During his service in Weihaiwei, Johnston made several requests to be advanced or moved, but all were refused. It seemed to the Colonial Office that since he liked living in the wilds, then Weihaiwei was the best place for him to stay.[25] During this period, his only recognition from the Colonial Office was the reward of the CBE medal.[26] However, Johnston met his great life chance through a lucky meeting in 1918.

In the late October 1918, Johnston arrived in Shanghai. On 26th November, he came across Li Jingmai, a surviving adherent of the Qing Court, who was carrying out a secret mission.[27]

As a compromise result of the 1911 Revolution, the abdicated Emperor Puyi still kept the title of Emperor, but his rule was limited to the small Forbidden City in Beijing. In 1918, the Emperor's tutor Xu Shichang was offered the office of President of the Republic of China, so was forced to give up his position as tutor. He decided to choose a new tutor who could educate Puyi in the knowledge of European constitutional notions in order to meet the need if Puyi should ever be restored to power. The mission to look for such a qualified person was handed over to Li Jingmai, the second son of the late Viceroy and Grand Councillor Li Hongzhang.

Li Jingmai was once a high Qing official who, during the 1911 Revolution, had fled for refuge to Weihaiwei, where he was in frequent contact with Johnston. In his eyes, Johnston, as a foreigner with knowledge of both China and western countries, would be the best choice as the Emperor's tutor. Thus, when both of them met each other in Shanghai, Li immediately invited him to discuss this appointment which Johnston accepted without hesitation, because he was eager to leave Weihaiwei. Then, Xu Shichang negotiated with the British legation, which approved his plan, so Johnston left Weihaiwei for Beijing and began his career as tutor to the Emperor. This event promoted Johnston to a higher level and so he entered the mysterious Forbidden City, which was inaccessible for the common people, and he became a part of the Emperor's daily life. He was the only foreigner who ever lived in the Forbidden City in modern China, and also the only foreign tutor to the Emperor in several thousand years of Chinese of imperial history, as a result of which he became well known throughout the world.

After entering the Forbidden City, Johnston not only taught Puyi English, astronomy, geography, mathematics and European law, but also knowledge of British social customs and manners, also news about major social reforms in the world; he even brought Puyi some radical magazines such as New Youth, and introduced him to famous figures from China and other countries. Thus he became the bridge between Puyi and the new world outside. As a foreign tutor to the emperor, Johnston revealed to him a totally different world that greatly influenced Puyi, who began to be engrossed in the 'European style of life', which made both tutor and student become increasingly close as days went by. Puyi was eventually banished from the Forbidden City in 1924 when Johnston accompanied him in spending his darkest

Johnston in his sable coat and mandarin's hat at his home, Cherry Glen, in Beijing's Western Hills, after he was appointed Mandarin of the Second Rank with a Coral button, 1922.

days as a refugee, and finally after making great efforts on Puyi's behalf, arranged for him to take refuge in the Japanese legation. This was the end of Johnston's career as the Emperor's tutor.

In 1927, Johnston returned to Weihaiwei as the last commissioner. Just before his departure, the Colonial Office instructed him definitely that his present mission was to return Weihaiwei to China. Although he knew clearly that 'this appointment was not a smooth road covered with roses', Johnston found himself 'already in love with everything here' and 'had a feeling of returning home'.[28] He was not satisfied to idle away his time in Weihaiwei, instead, he managed to enlarge the public financial expenditure over education, transportation and municipal works, etc. He even considered delaying the rendition and proposed many extension plans. However, the rendition had been the trend of the times, so Johnston's hope was just an illusion. On 1st October 1930, Johnston, on behalf of the British government, attended the Rendition Ceremony and then retired to Britain, when the last words he left to the Weihaiwei people were that "I have no doubt you will in the future have Chinese Commissioners who, with greater abilities and wider opportunities than mine, will be able to do far more for your welfare than it had ever been possible for me to do; but I think I can assure you with confidence that you will never have an administrator who will have a deeper affection for Weihaiwei than I have."[29]

After returning to his homeland, Johnston was appointed to the Chair of Chinese at the University of London's School of Oriental Studies after recommendations from Lockhart and others. Although he now lived in Britain, China, especially Puyi, was still his biggest concern. He always sympathized with Puyi's miserable life. In 1934, Johnston wrote Twilight in the Forbidden City which was a best-seller at that time. This book described the end of the Qing Court – the period of decline from the foundation of the Republic of China to Puyi's banishment from the Forbidden City, after the Qing Court had existed almost 300 years. He wrote in his book: "To His Majesty Emperor Puyi, in the earnest hope that, after the passing of the twilight and the long night, the dawn of a new and happier day for himself, and also for

On 4th April 1927, local notables held a welcoming ceremony for Johnston when he returned to Weihaiwei as the Commissioner.

Johnston at the ceremony marking the return of Weihaiwei to China. 1st October 1930

his people on both sides of the Great Wall, is now breaking."[30] In 1935, Johnston travelled to China for the last time, and visited Puyi in Changchun, but politely refused Puyi's invitation to take up his post as tutor once again.[31]

In retirement Johnston bought an island in Edinburgh with his remuneration from Twilight in the Forbidden City. In his island home, he gave some of the rooms names such as: the Bamboo Room, the Weihaiwei Room, and the Emperor Room,[32] fondling his presents from Puyi every day, and ignoring the affairs of human life. On 6th March 1938, Johnston died at the age of 64 after endlessly recalling his past days in China.

In 1964, Puyi, by then just an ordinary citizen of the People's Republic of China, recalled Johnston in his autobiography From Emperor to Citizen as 'the important part of his soul'.[33] Many years later, Johnston was listed by Chinese contemporary historians as one of 100 foreigners who had influenced Chinese history.[34]

A Combination of Chinese and British practices in the administration of justice

The Weihaiwei Order–in–Council was the basis of the Weihaiwei judicial system during the period of the British lease. From the point of the governing principles and system defined by the Order–in–Council, in theory, this aimed to make British legal practices predominate in the Weihaiwei legal system through the introduction of British laws. All Chinese legal practices were rejected within the field of public law, but there were some limited concessions in private law; however, in practice, the Weihaiwei legal system showed considerable variation on the whole because of the deep–rooted local customs and traditional social system, the difference between the two cultures, the legal status of the territory, which was not actually a colony, and most importantly the appreciation of, and enthusiasm for, Chinese culture by the administrators such as Lockhart and Johnston.

Regarding legislation, the Order–in–Council ruled that ordinances in effect within Hong Kong should apply in Weihaiwei after some necessary modifications which took account of the local conditions. The Commissioner exercised the legislative power, but the produced ordinances could only be enacted as long the king/queen did not exercise any veto against them, based on the Colonial Secretary's advice.[35] In addition to the local authorities themselves drafting the ordinances, there was a legal advisor appointed by the Colonial Secretary who was responsible for offering legal advice and whenever necessary drafting the legal measures to be promulgated in the name of the Commissioner.[36] The Crown Advocate of the British Supreme Court at Shanghai was concurrently the legal advisor.

In fact, most legal disputes could be settled according to Chinese law and local custom, thus 'it has been found unnecessary to enact more than a very small number of ordinances for Weihaiwei',[37] in addition Britain was 'aware that Weihaiwei would one day revert to China, so laws were deliberately kept to a minimum and existing Chinese structures maintained',[38] thus 'it is only when the fact of British occupation introduces some new set of conditions for which local custom does not provide, that legislation becomes necessary'.[39]

Therefore, apart from local administrative regulations, the authorities only passed 114 ordinances from 1903 to 1930.[40] Such measures were generally copied from or closely modelled on laws already in force in England or in the Colony of Hong Kong,[41] so there were many obvious differences between these and Chinese laws.

Firstly, there was the principle of upgrading ethical considerations to a legal status. For example, it was regarded by the British as breaking the law if a man depended on a prostitute for his living,[42] failed to help to keep public order or to aid in the arrest of an offender at a police officer's request,[43] failed to turn in another person's lost property [44] or to return it to the owner,[45] and so on. Such acts were not considered by the Chinese as legal offences, but rather as moral offences. In addition, a system of rewards was also established for good moral behaviour. For example, if a bus driver turned in a passenger's lost property or returned it to the owner, he would get a maximum reward of not more than one fifth of the value of the lost property,[46] which took into consideration the natural human expectation of some material benefit.

Secondly, there was the principle of protecting the weak. The British authorities not only brought the vulnerable classes such as women, children, and employees under legislative protection, but the protection laws were also very strict. For example, it shall be no defence to a charge or indictment for an indecent assault upon a girl or a boy under the age of 13 years to prove

The Office of the Secretary to Government in 1902. All the civil and criminal cases in the North Division were handled by the Secretary to Government before 1916.

Rongcheng District magistrate's court (Rongcheng, in the east of the present Weihai City). During the period of the British lease, Weihaiwei court cases between Chinese residents might be referred to Wendeng (in the middle-south part of the present Weihai City), Rongcheng or other neighbouring magistrate's courts, or might resort to a joint hearing between those courts when necessary. (1905)

that she or he consented to the act of indecency.[47] An employer could be declared guilty if his behaviour might lead to the suffering of an apprentice or servant, which did not completely depend on actual injury to the sufferer, and the same principle was applied in the case of abandoned children;[48] someone could be convicted of a crime based on the fact that he beat a woman or a child not more than 14 years old whether the victims themselves charged him or not.[49]

Thirdly, there was the principle of giving priority to the interests of the public in a situation involving a conflict between public and private interests. For example, the Bus Regulations enacted in 1928 were far stricter towards bus drivers than towards pedestrians because Johnston wanted 'those drivers always to keep it in mind that they are not the masters of the roads, which are public property, and which do not simply belong to a small number of drivers.'[50]

For situations in which it became necessary to slaughter infected livestock, the authorities set up a comparatively fair system to make up the owner's losses,[51] which showed respect for and protection of the individual's legal rights and interests during such misfortune. Besides the above ordinances and regulations, what surprised the local people most was the ordinance against cruelty to animals[52] and the requirement to provide a comfortable living environment for them.[53] Although it is difficult to be clear today about the practical effects of such an ordinance without any actual evidence, this ordinance certainly reflected comparatively advanced modern concepts embodied in the legal system.

When introducing English laws, the authorities always consulted district and village headmen before enacting an ordinance that might impact Chinese customs and native life, in order to maintain the policy of taking advantage of Chinese ways to rule the Chinese.[54] There were also a few articles recognizing Chinese traditional legal practices in a series of British legal documents. For example, Article 2 of the Government Waste Lands ordinance 1919 said: "Government Waste Lands include all unoccupied land which is deemed by Chinese law or custom to be public property and to be vested in the State.[55] According to the Chinese Marriage Preservation Ordinance of 1913, the definition of a Chinese married woman was based on the Chinese traditional definition.[56]

The establishment of the Weihaiwei judicial system was a progress of absorbing what was useful and discarding what was not from both Chinese and British judicial notions.[57] The High Court of Weihaiwei, which the Order-in-Council had provided for, was a recording court that consisted of the commissioner and a judge, or either of them sitting separately.[58] Both of them were appointed by the British monarch. However, in practice, there were simply not sufficient resources to support a resident judge at Weihaiwei, thus the Judge, Assistant Judge or Crown Advocate of the British Supreme Court in Shanghai was the person designated to serve at Weihaiwei when necessary. The High Court had the power not only to hear all the cases within the territory, but also to bring a case from a lower court – the District Court or Magistrate's Court.[59] The Court of Appeal from the High Court of Weihaiwei was the Supreme Court of Hong Kong. By 1910, however, not a single appeal had been made to that court because of the lack of any system of lawyers, the expensive cost of appealing, and the fact that very few Chinese in the territory were even aware that it was possible to make such an appeal.[60] As the system of appeal performed practically no function, the authorities passed the Rehearing Ordinance in 1913 to provide for the rehearing by the Commissioner or Judge of civil cases tried before a Magistrate.[61]

According to the Order-in-Council, the District Court simply consisted of a magistrate who was appointed by the Colonial Secretary, and who executed all or part of the judicial powers held by the High Court.[62] Although there were no legal requirements concerning his qualifications, or ethnic status, the Magistrate, if that role was undertaken by a non-Briton, would have no power to try any case with a non-Chinese defendant.[63] Magistrates were able to judge a criminal case which carried a limited penalty not exceeding 400 dollars or imprisonment for any term not exceeding 12 months. However there were no such restrictions on civil cases.[64] If any litigant was not satisfied with a Magistrate's penalty of not less than 100 dollars, or of imprisonment not less than three months, then he or she could appeal to the High Court.[65] In addition, the Magistrate had also no power to hear any cases involving high treason, murder, rape, forgery and perjury.[66]

As a part of civil government, the judicial bodies also reached a final settlement after a series of changes. Early in May 1898 before the issue of the Order–in–Council, the Convention was still not final, but King–Hall and Hopkins (See Chapter1) executed the judicial power to ban drunkenness on Liugong Island and on the mainland outside the walled city of Weihaiwei.[67] On 14 December 1899, S. Barton of the British Consular Service in China was appointed District Officer and Magistrate, responsible for various kinds of cases.[68] In 1902 when Lockhart came to Weihaiwei as the Commissioner, all cases were in the hands of the Secretary to Government and Magistrate.[69] In 1906, the South and North Division Magistrates were separately responsible for all cases within their division.[70] In 1916, the positions of Senior and Junior District Officers were created, and then the Senior District officer was responsible for all civil cases, accordingly, the Junior District Officer was responsible for all criminal cases.[71]

From the above process, one can see that the authorities never set up an independent and professional court, and thus the judicial function was just one

In addition to the permanent courts, the authorities also held travelling courts in large market villages. The photograph shows Johnston at Shuangsikuan, one of the overnight stops on his circuit as District Magistrate in 1904.

of the District Officer's duties. Therefore, on the whole, a Weihaiwei magistrate (or District Officer) might be regarded as combining the duties of Registrar-General (Protector of Chinese), Puisne Judge, Police Magistrate and Captain-Superintendent of Police,[72] which duties were quite as broad as were those of the district-magistrates — the "father-and-mother" officials — of China. Meanwhile, because there were very few major cases in the territory, the High Court seldom sat, so except for a few major difficult cases, the magistrates (two district officer), acting as judges, made most of the legal decisions. From the point of case categories, major criminal cases were very few. Commercial disputes were also not many as the businessmen of Weihaiwei regarded it as a waste of time to go to court. Most business disputes were settled privately or by the arbitration of the Chamber of the Commerce according to Chinese commercial customs.[73] Thus the magistrate spent most time on civil disputes between family members or neighbours. These family disputes mainly involved rights of adoption, the remarriage of widows, guardianship rights, family property rights, and heritage rights. Disputes between neighbours usually concerned land ownership, debts, tombstones, grazing rights, bankruptcy and the violation of a contract, etc.[74] According to the Order-in-Ordinance, the laws applied in Weihaiwei mainly included British law, adapted Hong Kong law, local law, and Chinese law and customs.[75] In addition, in any civil case, if one of the litigants was Chinese, Chinese assessors, who were very familiar with Chinese law and customs, would be invited by the court whenever necessary and be present during the hearing, but not be participants in the judgment.[76] With the enactment of the Jury Ordinance, 1905,[77] the jury system was introduced into Weihaiwei, but in practice, most cases were heard without the presence of assessors and jury.

It was very common for there to be a conflict while executing the law because of the cultural differences between Eastern and Western customs. The matter of female suicide was a typical example. The authorities ruled that such cases must be reported immediately once known, but female suicide was common at that time in China, and basically did not involve any legal or moral questions, instead, the woman would gain social respect if she killed herself because her husband or betrothed had died. It was even the case that, during the early period of the British lease, there were still some people who requested that the authorities praise the practice of female suicide.[78] Another example was the matter of giving evidence in a criminal case. It seemed to the traditional Chinese that it was not only dangerous because he would run the risk of revenge, but it was even disgraceful to give evidence to prove another's crime, thus it was very difficult for the authorities to get evidence in a criminal case.[79] This conflict was more conspicuous in a civil case as the judge might need to seek guidance from many Chinese laws and customs. Therefore, Johnston adopted the principle of settling a civil dispute according to Chinese custom.[80] This practice was not unique, as there was a lack of lawyers and British legal proceedings were something completely new for the native people. Johnston had to extensively modify the court regulations. He not only adopted the procedure of inquiry,but also abandoned all or part of the British rule of evidence in order to enable civil disputes to be settled justly and fairly.[81] In the meanwhile, as Johnston was deeply influenced by Chinese traditional legal ideas, he regarded the court as a place to teach and enlighten the people, and he said, "I have frequently, in delivering judgments in both Civil and Criminal cases, used appropriate texts taken either from the Confucian classics themselves or from the Sacred Edict, for the purpose of giving my hearers little moral discourse on points suggested by the cases before me".[82] As a result of a series of changes and adaptations, the judicial system of Weihaiwei was tending to become similar to the Chinese traditional system. As Johnston commented, "in all essentials, therefore, cases are heard and dealt with in Weihaiwei very much as they are heard and dealt with in China; thus a man from the Chinese side of the frontier who comes into court as plaintiff in Weihaiwei finds himself – especially if he is used to litigation in his own country – quite at home".[83]

The court–house, Wenquantang, in 1907. Before 1916, more than 70% of the cases were heard in this court.

Changes in legal proceedings were most frequent during the process of finalizing the judicial system, which mainly led to the improvement that made the traditional Chinese mediation system standardized and official. During the Qing Dynasty, the authorities regarded folk litigation as a sign that public morality was not what it used to be, so tried to restrict them by adding many legal procedures and limiting the days allowed for prosecutions such as 'No Prosecutions during the Harvest Days', thus the ordinary Chinese regarded litigation as a dangerous route to take. However, since Lockhart came into power, in order to implant the idea of equality under the British rule in the hearts of the people, he ordered the court to be open for the people every day. Whether rich or poor, literate or illiterate, any one could bring a free lawsuit into court and the only small expense was caused by purchasing a standardized petition form that was printed by the government.[84] Such a petition form cost only 8 copper cash and was sold by D. Clark & Co. and a few other firms.[85] After Johnston came to his position at Weihaiwei in 1904, in order to publicize the fact that no bribes would be acceptable in the British judicial system, he demanded that all petitions be handed directly by the plaintiff to the magistrate in his court or house, whether early or late, which prevented the government clerk from taking a bribe.[86] All the above measures encouraged the great growth of litigation as villagers brought a large quantity of trivial things to the court such as the neighbours stealing grass, or the shrewish wife out of her husband's control,[87] which placed a great burden on the British magistrate. Recognising the inadequacy of traditional mediation, in order to reduce the magistrate's workload and strengthen the control of villages, the authorities divided the whole territory into 26 subdistricts in 1906, where each subdistrict contained average 12 villages. The head of each subdistrict was the district headman who was required to take advantage of his influence to settle disputes as a 'peace-talker',[88] however there were no official requirements concerning this procedure. In the meantime, in 1907, nearly a year after the establishment of the district headmen system, Johnston decided to revoke all the petition-writing licences because many writers had extorted bribes from litigants and sometimes overstated the facts deliberately in order to sharpen the disputes. Instead, those litigants who were illiterate or couldn't afford a petition-writer for themselves were allowed to plead their cases orally.[89] In addition, in order to encourage those who were wronged "to openly bring a lawsuit or make accusations legally against some influential person or family in their own village", Johnston set up a locked letter-box (petition-box) on the roadside in the neighbourhood of the South Division court.[90] But this measure still failed to decrease the lawsuits. Some illiterate peasant-folk were garrulous and inconsequential, so it took an English magistrate a long time to record long rambling statements made in rustic Chinese, which not only affected judicial efficiency, but also undermined the authority of the village elders and weakened the entire traditional rural social structure. Thus, it was decided to have salaried government petition-writers and to charge a fee for each petition in 1910. The fee for each petition was $2.[91] Thereafter, it was ruled that any litigant involved in a civil case should obtain a government form from their district headman and ask the peace-talkers to devise a settlement. If it proved impossible to settle, the form should be filled in stating the reason for failure and stamped with the seal of the district or village headman, then the litigant could go to the court with this form (certificate) and pay for a petition, otherwise, the court would reject the lawsuit. Thereafter, in order to keep the system running smoothly, in 1913 it proved necessary to raise the fee to $3,[92] then in 1916 it was raised to $5, then to $10 within the same year.[93] In China, it was a time-honoured custom to settle disputes among the people by using 'peace-talkers', but this kind of semi-official mediation system as employed by the British authorities was unique in the history of China, which was also a major reflection on the strategy of using Chinese ways to rule the Chinese within the British judicial system.

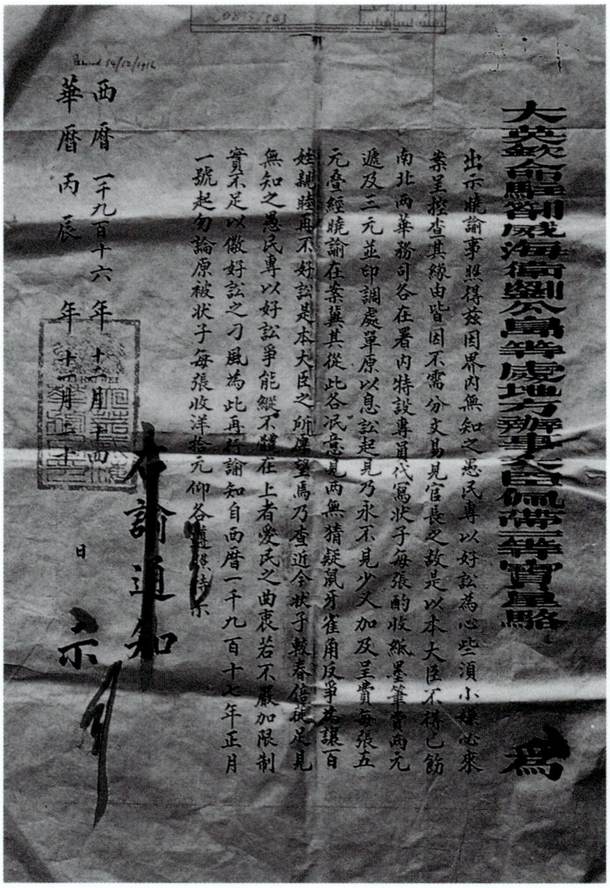
大英欽命駐劄威海衛管轄全島等處地方辦事大臣佩帶二等寶星駱　為

出示曉諭事照得茲因界內無知之愚民專以好訟為心些須小故必來
案呈控查其緣由皆因不需分文易見官長之故是以本大臣不得已飭
南北兩華務司各在署內特設專員代寫狀子每張酌收紙墨筆費兩元
遞及三元並印調處單原以息訟起見乃永不見少又加及呈貴每張五
元疊經曉諭在案冀其從此各泯意見兩無猜疑鼠牙雀角反爭為讓百
姓親睦再不好訟是本大臣之所厚望焉乃查近今狀子較春倍蓰足見
無知之愚民專以好訟爭能縱不體在上者愛民之由衷若不嚴加限制
實不足以儆好訟之刁風為此再行諭知自西曆一千九百十七年正月
一號起勿論原被狀子每張收洋拾元仰各遵照特示

右諭通知

西曆一千九百十六年十二月十四日
華曆丙辰年十一月二十日

示

An official notification of 1916, announcing an increase in court fees. The colonial authority increased court fees to discourage unnecessary court cases.

In other words, the judicial system at Weihaiwei during the period of the Lease was not a purely British one, neither was it a purely Chinese traditional one, but a complex of Chinese traditional laws and customs, British colonial practice and other complicated factors, which was both the result of the particular situation in Weihaiwei, and the reason why the native people were prepared to accept British rule to a certain extent.

Police and public order

The first modern style police force in Weihaiwei appeared on Liugong Island. A police force consisting of an inspector, a sergeant and about 12 constables had been established on the island prior to 1900. In that year, Sir Frank Swettenham, High Commissioner of the Malay States, submitted to the British government a proposal regarding the policing of Weihaiwei which recommended that the police force on Liugong Island should be reduced to just 3 persons, and instead, a 200—man force should be formed from the Chinese Regiment which would be responsible for social order throughout the whole territory.[94] This was welcomed by the Colonial Office, but opposed by the military authorities. Major C. D. Bruce, Commander of the Chinese Regiment at that time, stressed that any attempt to change the military status of

British police inspectors in Weihaiwei. Mr. Whittaker (middle) was in charge of the Weihaiwei police affairs for almost 30 years. (late1920s)

Chinese policemen made up the main body of the colonial police force in Weihaiwei. The photograph shows the highest rank (Police Sergeant) which could be attained by a Chinese policeman, locally known as 'three stripes'. (1918)

the Chinese Regiment would lead to serious and uncontrollable corruption within that Regiment, and what was more, that no officer would care to act as a police inspector. Therefore, he suggested that the Commissioner might request the military authorities to dispatch troops in order to put down a riot or to maintain public order whenever necessary, but that such actions should be purely military operations, not under the control of the administrative authorities.[95] This suggestion was supported by Dorward,[96] so no civil police force was established on the mainland until 1902.

After Lockhart took office, in order to minimise expenditure, he preferred to depend on the village headmen to maintain social order within the territory, so he took no action regarding any enlargement of the police force. Thus the mainland had only a single police inspector in 1902,[97] who was on loan from the Chinese Regiment. Although the colonial government issued a Police Force Ordinance in 1903 setting up a formal structure for a police force in Weihaiwei, the total force consisted of only 15 men at that time and all the police inspectors were concurrently officers of the Chinese Regiment.[98] The matter of the police force was considered again when the British government decided to disband the Chinese Regiment in 1906. However, Lockhart still insisted on maintaining his original position, and opposed the creation of any new police posts, and recommended that the Colonial Office should appoint a District Officer in the centre of the territory to strengthen the control over the countryside and to ensure the effective running of the village headman system.

Police duties were varied; one of the more important was security duty. The photograph shows Lockhart and his bodyguards at government house in 1921.

In the meantime, he proposed to station a small troop within Weihaiwei as a deterrent force.[99] However, when he learned that London government would refuse to send any military forces to Weihaiwei, he immediately realized that the current system would not be adequate for keeping public order and that it was imperative to form a effective police force.[100] In the same year, Weihaiwei was divided into three policing areas: Port Edward, Liugong Island and the Territory. Thirty-six soldiers who had retired from the Chinese Regiment were chosen for the new Territory Police.[101] Thereafter, the number and the distribution of the police were adjusted according to the changing public situation. Thus the authorities gradually established an ideal police system.

As regards the various police ranks in Weihaiwei, these consisted of police constable, senior police constable, police sergeant, senior police sergeant, police inspector and senior police inspector.[102] There were usually 3 police inspectors who were all Britons. Each inspector was in charge of one police district for a term of 5 years.[103] All police constables and sergeants were Chinese. Concerning the salary and fringe benefits, inspectors were paid in sterling. By 1930, their annual salary reached £300 (equivalent to ¥6000 or

7000), and in addition, they enjoyed free coal supplies and other allowances. Police constables and sergeants were paid in Chinese money and their salaries increased annually according to their number of working years, but there was a wide salary gap between them and an inspector.[104] Although all members of the police enjoyed free medical treatment, constables would be paid only half of their salary while on sick leave if the medical officer could prove that their illness was due to their own carelessness.[105] Because of the shortage of both police and instructors, all new constables would be placed on duty as soon as they were recruited, without any initial formal training. Instead the authorities established a strict training regime while they were working. Except for those constables actually on duty, all constables had to attend a daily training including physical fitness, exercise, shooting and horsemanship.[106] In 1925 the authorities ruled that all new constables must receive regular training for 6 weeks before they went on duty.[107] In order to ensure the police could carry out their tasks without hindrance, the Offences against the Person Ordinance, 1905, contained a special regulation that "every person who assaults, resists or willfully obstructs any constable or police officer in the due execution of his duty or any person acting in aid of such officer; or assaults any person with intent to resist or prevent the lawful apprehension or detention of himself or of any other person for any offence, shall be guilty of a misdemeanor and being convicted thereof, shall be liable at the discretion of the court, to imprisonment for any term not exceeding two years, with or without hard labour."[108]

When the Territory Police was established in 1906, all the constables were retired soldiers, who came together with their weaponry, from the Chinese Regiment. The military qualities of that regiment were high, but the policing skills were quite low, which led to an incident in which a number of village headmen were beaten by a mounted police patrol in that same year.[109] In 1907, a number of district and village headmen jointly submitted a written statement to the authorities reporting that police constables were abusing their power by threatening and arresting villagers.[110] Thereafter, the authorities strengthened their control and supervision over the police and enacted very strict and detailed regulations regarding rewards and punishments and policing standards. Meanwhile, a regular rotation system was established for the police. Constables were rotated every three months in 1906,[111] later once every half year.[112] The authorities set up a police supervision system in 1921. The Financial Assistant to the Senior District Officer was in charge of police supervision, and the Senior District Officer inspected each police station once a week while the Commissioner would do this once a month.[113] However, over the next few years, faced with the prospect of rendition, the British government demanded that the Weihaiwei authorities should reduce the staff numbers and try their best to cut down on expenditure, so all police inspec-

The prison in Dongcang Village, Port Edward. This was used for prisoners with sentences of two months or less. Those with heavier sentences were sent to Liugong Island or to Hong Kong. (1930s)

tors who had several functions were stationed at Port Edward and Liugong Island, which made it impossible to supervise constables who were stationed in the distant countryside.[114] Meantime, the incidence of taking bribes and exploiting the people was quite frequent because the Chinese police were not satisfied with their salary that did not keep pace with prices. Johnston put to an end to this dissatisfaction by increasing their salaries in 1928.[115]

For a long time after the establishment of the police force, the authorities concentrated most of its members within Port Edward, while there were just a few throughout the wider countryside. In 1903, only one police detective inspector and five detectives were responsible for public order in the countryside and for liaison between the government and the village headmen, and these would have in addition to conduct investigations into civil and criminal cases.[116] When the Territory Police was set up in 1906, the authorities stationed only 8 constables at Wenquantang,[117] the site of the Senior District Officer's office, which functioned both as an administrative office and court. These constables were mainly concerned with the daily duties of the Senior District Office, and never went on patrol duty.[118] The other Territory constables were stationed at Port Edward, carrying out their duties to patrol a limited village area. Although the police force was seriously deficient, major problems of public order seldom occurred because of the maintenance and strengthening of the traditional village headman system. After the Revolution of 1911 broke out, the districts neighbouring Weihaiwei suffered from successive years of conflict. Various groups of refugees and victims of natural calamities, also persons from different political factions, and armed personnel, came to Weihaiwei for refuge, which not only undermined public order in the territory, but also affected relations between the authorities of Weihaiwei and the surrounding districts. It was beyond the village and district headmen's control to deal with armed robbery, illegal crossing of the border and other problems disrupting public order within the territory. Because of the lack of any formal system of police patrols, villagers were unable to get any immediate help from the police constables. In addition, it took long time to report a case to the police due to the poor facilities for transport and communication, which meant that the offenders had usually fled before the police could take any action.[119] In view of this increasingly dangerous situation, the authorities had to enlarge the police force, especially in the countryside. In 1913, six police posts were set up within the larger villages and near to the border.[120] The number of these posts had increased to fifteen by 1930.[121] The size of the police force at each post would depend on the degree of that post's responsibility. The constables would patrol the area day and night, and also carry out irregular inspection of empty buildings, temples, sheds and empty sampans.[122] They concentrated much of their effort into striking blows at such crimes as illegal border crossing, armed illegal groups, highway robbery and smuggling.[123] The establishment of these posts and the formation of a regular system of patrols matched these new requirements and succeeded in maintaining public order within the whole territory.

A major duty for the police in Weihaiwei was the management of prisons and detention houses. At the beginning of the British lease period, the authorities set up one prison at Port Edward and another on Liugong Island.[124] In

Prisoners who had been sentenced to hard labour repairing roads on Liugong Island (late 1920s)

1902, the prison at Port Edward was changed into a detention house as it failed to reach the standards required of a prison.[125] Its staff consisted of several warders, headed by a single chief warder. Its main function was to lock up offenders awaiting trial[126] and those prisoners who had been sentenced to a term not exceeding two months.[127] Those who had been sentenced to a term exceeding two months were incarcerated within the island prison, which could accommodate more than 100 prisoners.[128] After 1902, any prisoners sentenced to long-term imprisonment were usually sent to Hong Kong Prison with the tacit permission of the British Hong Kong government.[129] On 29th July 1916, Lockhart, the Weihaiwei Commissioner, and the Hong Kong Governor Francis Henry May signed a formal agreement concerning the irregular transfer of prisoners from Weihaiwei to Hong Kong, which gained approval from the British parliament in the following year.[130] During the early stage of the British rule in Weihaiwei, the administration of the prison had its brutal side, but with the consolidation of British power, modern western ideas about prison administration began to play a major role. For example, not only were the male and female prisoners segregated, but prisoners convicted of minor or major crimes, adults and juveniles, first and frequent offenders, were all segregated while in custody.[131] Prisoners in Weihaiwei also enjoyed many legal rights. For instance, the commissioner would periodically send a supervisor to inspect each prison, and this supervisor would interview all the prisoners and listen to their complaints and advise on the running of that prison.[132] Representatives of the prisoners would be allowed to supervise the distribution of their food rations; and so on.[133] The teaching system in the prison became more progressive. The authorities ruled that all prisoners should receive education in Confucianism, basic knowledge about society, moral values and western democratic concepts from a full-time instructor. After 1910, there were teachers in the prisons both on Liugong Island and in Port Edward. They taught English, mathematics, reading and writing, etc, at a primary level for 24 hours each week.[134] This demonstrated that the aim of the British prisons in Weihaiwei was not simply to punish, but to help erring persons to reform themselves by persuasion and return them to a normal and useful social life.

If the Weihaiwei police force is compared with a more modern police force, it can be seen that its responsibilities were really quite broad. For instance, apart from his normal police business of crime prevention and detection, the Island police inspector was also responsible for tax-collection, forestry, public health, registration of births, deaths and marriage, fire prevention and control, the running of the lighthouse, etc., on the island. The Port Edward police inspector was responsible for public health, municipal administration, tax-collection, forestry, the lighthouse and investigations into criminal cases at Port Edward. The Territory inspector had responsibility

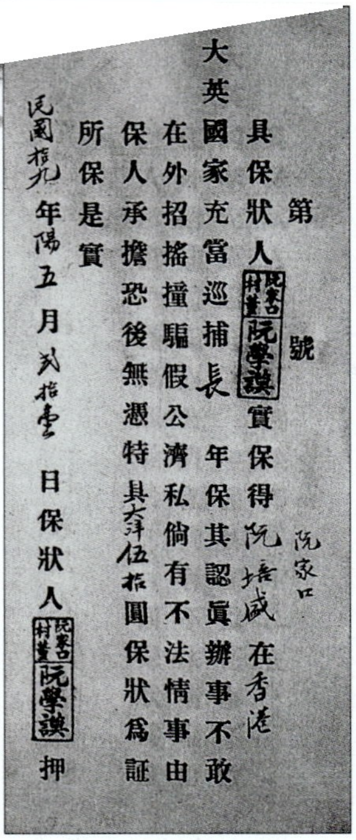

第　號
具保狀人阮學謨實保得阮墡成在香港　阮家口
大英國家充當巡捕長　年保其認眞辦事不敢
在外招搖撞騙假公濟私倘有不法情事由
保人承擔恐後無憑特具大洋伍拾圓保狀爲証
所保是實
民國拾九年陽五月貳拾壹日保狀人阮學謨押

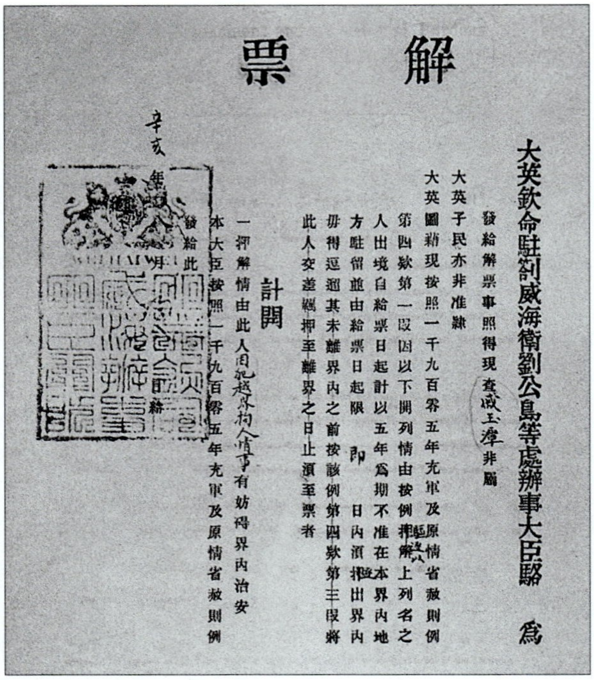

解票

大英欽命駐劄威海衛劉公島等處辦事大臣駱　爲
發給解票事照得現査戚玉潭非屬
大英子民亦非准隸
大英國籍現按照一千九百零五年充軍及原情省赦則例
第四款第一段因以下開列情由按例押解上列名之
人出境自給票日起計以五年爲期不准在本界內地
方駐留並由給票日起限即日內須押出界內
毋得逗遛其未離界內之前按該例第四款第三段將
此人交差羈押至離界之日止須至票者
計開
一押解情由此人因犯越界拘人情事有妨碍界內治安
本大臣按照一千九百零五年充軍及原情省赦則例
發給此
辛亥年

During the Lease period and in the following 1930's, the Hong Kong Authorities came to Weihaiwei to recruit for policemen. The photograph shows a certificate of good character issued by a village headman for a villager recruited as a Hong Kong policeman. (1930).

The photograph shows an order expelling Qi Yutan, Chairman of the walled city Chamber of Commerce, from the territory because he had contacted revolutionaries from Wendeng to help arrest the sub-district deputy magistrate of the walled city. (1911)

for fire-fighting in the countryside, public works, land registration, maintenance of roads and bridges, etc., throughout the whole territory.[135] All the above matters would actually be dealt with by his subordinate police constables and sergeants. In addition to similar duties to those of the Island and Port police, the constables in the countryside were also responsible for such activities as dissuading persons from suicide, controlling access to the government waste lands, investigation of civil cases and other miscellaneous tasks.[136] In 1921, out of the total of 124 policemen, only 21 had duties which were not strictly policing, such as acting as orderlies or armourers.[137] The remaining 103 provided an average of one policeman to every 1700 of the population, so they were very familiar with a number of social situations such as transport, business, buildings, residents' occupation and income,[138] which effectively strengthened social control and maintained public order. In addition, the municipal administrative power over Port Edward and Liugong Island was exercised by the police force, which further ensured uniform control over the whole territory and strict enforcement of the law.

The establishment of an auxiliary police force was another feature of the Weihaiwei police force. Early in 1902, a number of Chinese labourers were hired temporarily to assist the Port Edward Inspector of Police while he was carrying out his police duties and supervising public health. Such auxiliary assistants were empowered to act as constables at times if necessary.[139] The local inhabitants were able to request personal policing services, as was demonstrated in The Police Force Ordinance, 1903 which stated, "It shall be lawful for the Commissioner, if he shall think fit, upon the application of any householder, to appoint any member of the Police Force to do special police duty in and upon the premises of the applicant on payment of such sums as the Commissioner shall direct".[140] In 1905, when public order within Port Edward was in a bad state, local Chinese businessmen urged the British authorities to enlarge the police force and offered to fund half the costs.[141] After that, the British authorities set up three separate groups of auxiliary police.

The first force consisted of two voluntary fire brigades: one was formed at Port Edward in 1907,[142] the other on Liugong Island in 1909.[143] All members of these two fire brigades were clerks and sailors working for local Chinese firms and paid for by those firms. They would attend a monthly fire training organized by the official police force. The number of voluntary firemen reached 129 by 1921[144] and they carried out most of the fire fighting duties during the lease period.

New Commissioner Russell Brown inspecting the police force. (November 1923)

The second force was the countryside peace preservation teams formed in 1918. The district headman was responsible for the establishment and management of such a team within his own district. Usually there would be one

team member out of every ten families in each village and they would attend training for two hours each day under the guidance of a member of the regular police force. The village would buy guns that would be, however, handed in to the authorities for safekeeping when the situation became stable. During night patrols, at least four people would be on duty. If there were any unusual occurrences, these patrols would immediately alert the neighbouring village peace preservation team using gongs or whistles.[145]

The third force consisted of special constables. In order to control the difficult situation which arose after the Revolution of 1911, it became necessary to include some additional temporary constables within the police force, and village watchmen were appointed and paid by the villagers themselves in many of the villages of the Territory.[146] In 1913, the authorities took the advantage of these temporary constables and village watchmen to establish the village night patrol system.[147] In the early 1920's, affected by the anticipated rendition of Weihaiwei, the authorities were strictly limited in their ability to enlarge the police force, and what is more, part of the existing police force was transferred to Hong Kong, thus the shortfall in the size of the police force became an increasingly serious problem. To counter this, the authorities initiated the establishment of a formal system of special constables by issuing "The Peace Preservation Ordinance, 1921".

The consequence of this was that whenever it appeared, in the judgment of the Commissioner, that any tumult or riot had taken place or might be reasonably apprehended, and that the numbers of ordinary officers appointed were inadequate to deal with the situation, it became lawful for the Commissioner to authorize any Magistrate to summon in writing before him, any number of persons living within the Territory, to be appointed immediately to act as special constables.[148] Each special constable would have the same powers regarding the preservation of peace, the prevention of offences, the apprehension of offenders, and for many other purposes, and have the same privileges, protection, and immunities, as a full member of the police force, except with regard to pay and pensions or other financial reward.[149] The establishment of the auxiliary police force helped the authorities resolve the problem of the shortage of manpower without too great an expenditure.

How did the Territory manage to stay peaceful while the surrounding districts were often in a state of chaos during the lease period? The police force, including the auxiliary police, of course played a key part, but not the only one, in a way not even the major one. The traditional village system was the real guarantor of peace and was relied upon by the authorities in order to maintain their control. As we will see in the following section, this village and district headman system formed the basis of the British administrative system at Weihaiwei.

District headmen and self-running villages

The district headman system was an important part of the British administrative system in Weihaiwei, forming the foundation and pillars of the colonial administrative structure.

Before the British arrived in Weihaiwei, the native villages were basically under a closed patriarchal rule. The senior representative of the local squires and the senior branch of the patriarchal clan was responsible for ensuring village order and the good conduct of his fellow villagers. Most villages ran themselves according to family tradition and village regulations. Occasionally, several villages would jointly govern their own affairs. Generally, they enjoyed a high degree of autonomy. The local squires played a leading role in the village government. More than 90 percent of the Weihaiwei population lived in the countryside, thus the colonial government paid great attention to the control of the villages. In 1900, the British Colonial Office sent Sir Frank Swettenham, High Commissioner of the Federated Malay States, who had a rich experience in colonial rule, to Weihaiwei for an on-the-spot investigation. Following this investigation, he produced a draft plan for the British authorities concerning the way in which they should govern Weihaiwei. Swettenham proposed that the traditional system, to the extent that it was compatible with British rule, should be retained. Therefore, he strongly advocated trying to maintain the existing village government and to devise a judicial system to divide the village structure. He recommended that as far as possible all reconcilable conflicts and civil cases should be judged by the village institutions.[150] Swettenham's proposal was finally adopted by the British government and became the basic principle of colonial rule in Weihaiwei. Thus the colonial government took great pains to ensure effective control of the village areas on the basis of maintaining the traditional system.

During the early period of the British occupation, whilst they were preoccupied with the problem of the boundary demarcation, the colonial authorities had little time to concern themselves with village affairs within the territory. Once the civil administration had begun in 1900, the authorities

Lockhart receiving the village headmen at Weihaiwei for the first time. (8th May 1902)

began to pay greater attention to village government. In 1902, on the fifth day after he assumed office, Lockhart received all the village headmen within the Territory, then registered them and issued certificates of appointment, recognising their power and position within each village.[151] However the British did not interfere with the native customs. At first, the Secretary to Government and Magistrate took care of every single village matter personally, but the increasing burden of daily affairs prevented him from visiting villages often, so the contacts between the government and the people were not smooth, the government bodies could not run in a coordinated manner and the administrative system worked ineffectively. In addition there were also regional differences, which diminished colonial control over the villages. Another disadvantage was that the new judicial system in Weihaiwei had an unintended effect on the traditional ruling systems. For example, the court opened daily and charged no litigation fee, so any illiterate litigant who was unable to afford to pay for a written petition could simply go along to the court and make his statement by word of mouth. This resulted in large

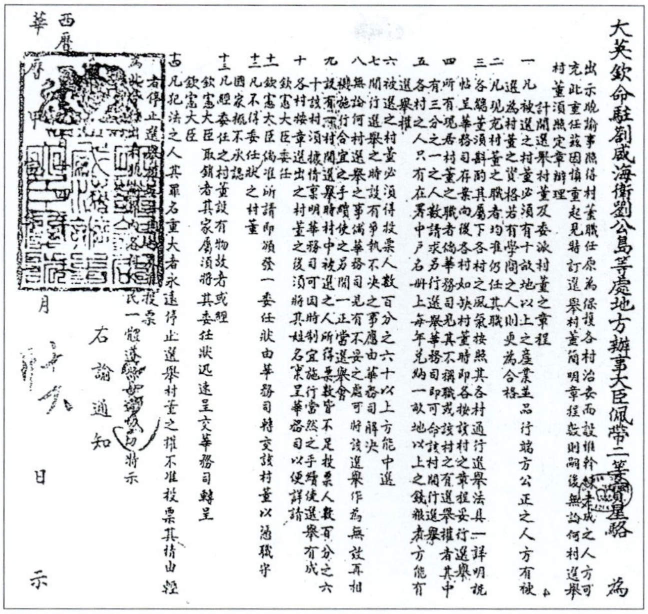
大英欽命駐劄威海衛劉公島等處地方辦事大臣佩帶二等寶星駱 為

Regulations for electing the village headmen issued by the authorities. (16th March 1914)

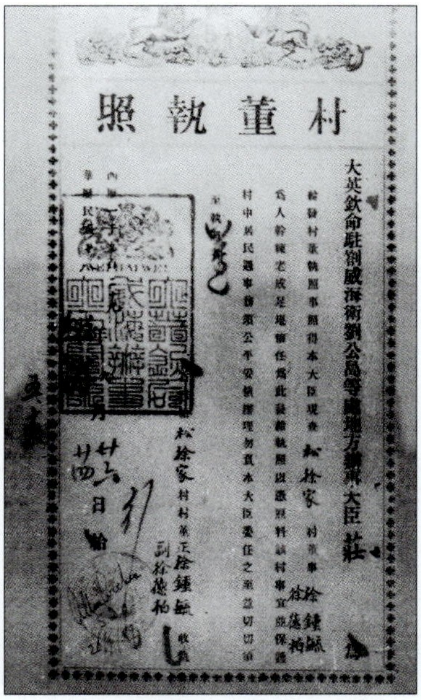
村董執照

大英欽命駐劄威海衛劉公島等處地方辦事大臣莊

Certificate of appointment of the village headmen issued by the authorities. (26th September, 1929)

numbers of disputes being brought to the court for settlement by villagers which in turn undermined the authority of the village elders, not only weakening the entire rural social structure, but also leading to resentment on the part of the village headmen and elders. In order to eliminate these problems, the colonial government began to seek new ways to place village affairs under the control of village headmen.

In 1905 Johnston proposed a district headman plan, which was implemented in 1906. Under this, the territory, comprising more than 300 villages, was divided into two main administrative districts known as the North and South Divisions, but within these twenty-six new subdistricts were created and each subdistrict had a district headman. The North Division contained nine of these districts, plus Liugong Island and Port Edward, and was placed under the jurisdiction of the North Division magistrate who was also Secretary to the Government. The South Division contained the remainder of the territory and was administered by the South Division District Officer and Magistrate whose headquarters lay in Wenquantang.[152] At first, this district headman was selected from among the village headmen within that subdistrict by the Senior District Officer and 'confirmed' by the Commissioner, receiving an official certificate of his appointment. Later on, the village headmen within the same subdistrict would vote for the district headman. This person was required to supervise the collection of land taxes within his subdistrict, distribute to village headmen copies of all notices and proclamations issued by the government, distribute deed forms to purchasers and sellers of property, and to use his influence generally in the interests of peace and good order, and in the discouragement of litigation, and the district headman also offered advice on village administration to the colonial authorities to help make a government decision.[153] The rule of village headmen was

Lockhart receiving local village headmen during his tour of inspection. (1905)

The group photograph of village headmen rewarded by the authorities. (1904)

Che Shuoxue, Head of Haixitou Village, awarded with a commemorative plaque and medal for his part in rescuing a merchant ship from peril. (1905)

also standardized and strengthened at the same time as the implementation of the system of district headmen. Each village would still retain a village headman, who would be chosen by those villagers within his village who had the right to vote, and he would be 'confirmed' by the Commissioner by receiving an official certificate of his appointment The chosen village headman had to possess property of more than 10 mou of land and gain 60 percent of the votes. The Senior District Officer had the right to dismiss any village headman and had the final jurisdiction regarding any problem occurring during his selection.[154] Each headman was held responsible for the maintenance of peace and good order within his subdistrict. He was also required to collect the land tax on behalf of the government, to communicate official notices to their fellow villagers, and to register deeds of sale and mortgages.

When the district headman system was first implemented, the rights and duties of the district headman had not been clearly specified, and as a result the Magistrate's administrative and judicial workload was still not reduced. Therefore, the colonial authorities decided to charge a litigation fee of $2 for each case in 1910 and later gradually increased this fee to deter frivolous litigation. At the same time, they clearly required that the litigant must present to the magistrate a certificate proving that the district headman had previously mediated in the dispute unsuccessfully; otherwise the court would not accept the case. This measure made mediation in the village become more efficient day by day, and to a certain extent encouraged the smooth running of the district headman system. The colonial government tried its best to improve the district headmen's prestige in the villages in order to attract local landowners to take part in social affairs. Thus, the district headman would receive a salary from the government of $5 per month as well as a small percentage from the sale of government deed forms, for which a fee was charged. In addition, he had the power of nominating persons for a scholarship offered by the government school.[155] From 1902, an annual meeting of village headman was held; from 1906, this became a quarterly meeting. From 1923, the government would hold two banquets annually to entertain district headmen, on New Year's Day and the King's Birthday. Meanwhile, in order to identify their interests more closely with those of the government, the custom of awarding tablets or medals for outstandingly meritorious behaviour was extended to include them. In 1904 during special Coronation Day ceremonies, all the village headmen assembled at Port Edward and those chosen as most diligent in their work were presented with medals. The entire group was then entertained at a banquet and taken to inspect the fleet anchored in the harbour. What's more, this event would be commemorated by a group photo.[156] As time went by, such events were held frequently. In 1914, medals or carved complimentary tablets (bian) were presented to head-men on many occasions such as risking one's life to save somebody else, making donations to build roads or schools, giving relief to the people in a disaster area and so on.

One district headman, Che Shuoxue, provides a typical example of the awards given by the colonial government. Che was a village headman of Haixitou Village in 1905 when a merchant junk from Fuzhou (the capital of Fujian Province), returning with cargo from the Korean Peninsula, encountered a storm in Weihaiwei. The junk ran onto rocks and became stranded to the north of his village. He and other people were personally instrumental in saving numbers of lives and in helping the crews of the wrecked junk to save their cargo and to repair the damage done to their vessel. Those who had shown themselves most energetic in this good action de-

*District headmen,
Lockhart and other
colonial officials in
front of the
Commissioner's office.
(the eve of Chinese
New Year, 1905)*

served special commendation. The junk owner, Wang Zuogang, wrote a letter of thanks to the Government of Weihaiwei once he had returned to Fuzhou. Lockhart paid great attention to this and ordered a special bian or carved complimentary tablet to be made from sandalwood in Hong Kong. He presented this to Che Shuoxue himself in Haixitou Village. The inscription read "Zheng Ren Yu Wei"—"Human lives rescued from peril".[157]

The implementation of the district headman system enabled the colonial authorities to involve the influential representatives from the villages within the colonial governmental system and to depend upon them to help maintain control, thus enabling overall control of the Weihaiwei villages.

Village headmen and local elders presenting a silk banner to Johnston. (1904)

Relations with Shandong local authorities

Weihaiwei became an independent administrative area of the British Government within Shandong Province from the start of its lease. During the period of colonial rule, contacts between the British authorities and the local Chinese authorities in Shandong increased greatly at all levels; after this, dealing with external affairs became an important task in the political life of the territory.

Regarding the initial mechanism for any communication between the British commissioner in Weihaiwei and the Shandong governor, the commissioner would first report any matter to the British minister in Beijing, then the minister would present it to the Zongli Yamen (the Chinese Foreign Office) who would then instruct the governor of Shandong, and vice versa. However in early 1900, in order to allow the demarcation of the territorial boundaries to proceed more smoothly, at the request of Dorward, the commissioner at that time,[158] the Zongli Yamen and the British minister in Beijing agreed that the Weihaiwei commissioner could directly contact the Shandong Government to settle any common disputes. If both sides failed to settle them, they should report them to the Zongli Yamen and the British Minister, who would then carry out negotiations.[159] Thereafter, all major official matters between Weihaiwei and the Shandong government were dealt with directly between the commissioner and the governor. The senior district officer and the junior district officer were responsible for any negotiations with the local authorities at all levels below the provincial government, following the commissioner's instructions, but they could settle certain external affairs which fell within their area of responsibility by themselves.[160]

The demarcation of the territorial boundaries was the first major negotiation between the British government and the Shandong government acting on the behalf of the Qing Court. After the Convention for the Lease of Weihaiwei was signed, the Chinese and British authorities agreed that Britain would not exercise its powers in Weihaiwei until both sides had formed a Boundary Commission to complete this demarcation. However, the colonial government

Lockhart with the visiting Governor of Shandong Province. (1902)

ignored this agreement, made a number of arbitrary decisions and persisted in going their own way. For example, in June of 1898, the British authorities sent 800 armed men, led by a military band, to march through the villages surrounding the town of Weihai as a means of 'overawing' the people with their superior military strength.[161] In the spring of 1899, notices were posted forbidding any further payment of taxes to the Chinese magistrates, which aroused the local people's indignation. The Wendeng and Rongcheng magistrates then issued instructions to ignore it. In October 1899, after more than one year's surveying, the British side worked out their plan for demarcation and obtained the approval of the Qing Court. Next the Shandong governor, Yuan Shikai, appointed Chinese boundary commissioners, headed by Li Xijie, Daotai (head) of the Denglaiqing circuit (or dao), within which the territory was located, to assist their British counterparts with the project and it was decided that the demarcation work would begin in late March 1900. However, prior to the arrival of the Chinese officials, in January 1900, Dorward became too impatient and issued two proclamations informing the local people including those in parts of the Wendeng and Rongcheng areas, that they should pay land taxes to the British authorities. This resulted in even greater annoyance to the Chinese people and officials. On 27th March of the same year, the Qing Court, in the face of the British threat to occupy

Wendeng and Rongcheng, instructed Yuan Shikai to 'look closely at it, argue strongly on just grounds, don't give way in case this should give other foreign authorities an excuse to follow this bad example.'[162] On 13th April, Li Xijie and other Chinese officials arrived in Weihaiwei. Dorward demanded the collection of taxes, which was refused by Li. On 18th April, Li held a meeting of local leaders and territorial headmen inside the walled town without the presence of Dorward, and stated during this meeting that the British had no right to collect taxes or exercise jurisdiction within the territory at all, and affirmed Cui Shoushan (a local leading elder and scholar who had passed the imperial examination at the county level during the Qing Dynasty) and other local people's anti–British stand to be in the public interests. Dorward inevitably delivered a severe rebuke to the Chinese commissioners for holding this meeting. On 21st April, both the Chinese and British sides held a joint demarcation meeting in which Li insisted on marking the boundaries in strict accordance with the convention, thus ignoring Dorward's various demands, and both sides argued endlessly.

On 25th April, the demarcation began. After a few days, a local crowd pinned down the boundary commissioners, and although Li at this point proposed suspending the demarcation, the British officer in charge flatly refused. In the meantime, Governor Yuan had wired Dorward that the

Lockhart with Chinese provincial officials during his visit to Jinan [capital of Shandong Province] (1903)

project should be halted, that he would not recognize any boundary already laid, and that he would accept no responsibility for any disturbance which might occur. Shortly thereafter, two actual violent incidents took place near the British camp and during the ensuing battle the British army killed some Chinese. Li protested strongly against this and stated that the Chinese side would not take part in the demarcation until the bloodshed was settled. The Zongli Yamen and the Shandong Provincial government also contacted the British repeatedly and urged them not to proceed with the demarcation and to deal with the aftermath of the bloodshed, but the British ignored all of them. Finally, the Qing Court had to give in to the more powerful Britain. The Shandong Governor Yuan and the Wendeng Magistrate Chen had to issue a notice, demanding that the local people should obey the Convention and play safe,[163] thus the matter of the bloodshed was left unsettled. Afterwards, Magistrate Chen Jingxing resigned in anger. His successor, Magistrate Zhu Xin, expressed his condolences to the families of the deceased.[164]

In 1900, soon after the boundary disturbances, the Eight-Power Allied Forces launched a war to suppress the anti-imperialist Boxer Movement in China. After this war, the Qing Court started modern reforms in order to save the nation from further insurgency. In Shandong, modern reforms were also carried forward steadily, but were suddenly accelerated once the new

Lockhart with the Commander of Yanzhou [a town in Shandong province] at the Commander's official residence. (1903)

The 76th descendent of Confucius receiving Lockhart at his Mansion. Lockhart was the first foreigner ever to be received at the Mansion of Confucius. (1903)

Governor, Zhou Fu, took office. Such modern reforms directly affected the attitude of the Shandong local authorities to the British authorities in Weihaiwei. At that time, Jiaozhou Bay and Weihaiwei were successively leased by Germany and Britain. Germany took advantage of the building of the Jiaoji Railway to advance their overall invasion in the political, economic, military and cultural spheres, which aroused public indignation and great concern within Shandong Province. Faced with this dangerous situation, all the Shandong people became unusually active and sought various measures to save the nation from doom. The officials, led by Zhou Fu, took some positive measures: for one thing, they speeded up modern reforms and developed business jointly with merchants; for another, they encouraged other nations except Germany to invest in Shandong. They placed great hopes in the British authorities at Weihaiwei – first of all because they wanted to offset the German influence by expanding the British one, and secondly because they wanted to build a bridge between British and Chinese politics and business.

On the other hand, the boundary disturbances made the British authorities realize that it would be very difficult to maintain public order in Weihaiwei without good relations with the Shandong local authorities. They said: "if diplomatic troubles were to arise between Great Britain and China, and a

During the 1903 visit to the Confucius Residence, the descendent asked for a picture of the British King. After obtaining permission from King Edward VII, a portrait of King Edward VII was delivered to the Mansion of Confucius by Johnston. (1904)

command, direct or indirect, were to go forth from the Governor that the British in Weihaiwei were no longer to be treated with respect, a few days or weeks would be sufficient to bring about a startling change in the direction of anti-foreign feeling among the inhabitants of the leased Territory".[165] In view of the British policy concerning Weihaiwei, which was that it held no attraction for merchants from Hong Kong and abroad, when Lockhart arrived in the Commissioner's post he cast his eyes towards Shandong Province. Lockhart wanted to encourage Shandong businessmen to develop Weihaiwei and also hoped that the Shandong local governments might invest in constructing provincial roads to Weihaiwei, in order to develop the territory's economy.

Driven by their mutual interests, both sides began to strengthen their contacts. In December 1902, Zhou Fu, who had served as Shandong Governor for only 4 months, paid a visit to Weihaiwei in spite of the snow. The following April, Lockhart began his first journey through Shandong in response to Zhou Fu's invitation.

On 20th April, Lockhart and his party – a total of 13 people – arrived at Chefoo where they transferred to a Chinese cruiser "Jing Hai", through Penglai, Yangjiaogou and travelled westward along the Xiaoqing River. On his way to Jinan, Lockhart made an investigation of the general situation within Shandong. At that time, Chefoo had been a treaty port for many years, but now faced sharp competition from the Jiaoji Railway. In order to build an independent inland waterway trade line, Shandong local authorities were actively dredging the Xiaoqing River. Lockhart thought that this measure would be helpful for the development of Weihaiwei, so he suggested in his confidential report to the Colonial Office that Great Britain should support this effort. This trip helped Lockhart gain direct experience of the

Lockhart with the Commander of Weixian [a town in Shandong province], showing Lockhart his gold watch rewarded by the British Government. (1903)

ordinary people in Shandong: "Throughout our journey up the canal we were treated most kindly by everyone. Large crowds assembled to have a look at our party when we anchored, but beyond evincing a natural curiosity at the unusual spectacle of Europeans travelling under the auspices of the Governor of the province, they behaved with great decorum and never uttered a rude word – a striking contrast to the crowds that flock to stare at Europeans in other parts of China and hail them with uncomplimentary epithets supported by brickbats".

On the afternoon of 27th April, after 5 days sailing on the Xiaoqing River, Lockhart and his party arrived at Huangtianqiao Pier in Jinan where they stayed until 5th May.

Shandong authorities made careful and considerate arrangements for Lockhart's visit, which make Lockhart and his party feel "the great care and solicitude that a mother bestows on her child". When they switched to a Chinese cruiser at Yangjiaogou on 23rd April, the local military and political officials held a special welcoming ceremony for them, and in addition, Zhou Fu sent eight bodyguards and three officials to escort them. When they sailed further and arrived at Gaoyuan, Zhou Fu also sent cavalry to escort them while Lockhart and his party made their way up the canal to Jinan, either by horse, or when they were weary by ship. The final leg of the journey was by sedan chair, at the end of which Lockhart surprisingly received a thirteen-gun salute. 1500 soldiers lined up to welcome them when they entered the walled city of Jinan. Continuous visits, meetings and meals followed, and a banquet which must have been the most sumptuous feast the Chinese could produce.

During his stay in Jinan, Lockhart, accompanied by Zhou Fu and one of his senior officials, visited Daming Lake, Baotuquan, Thousand Buddha Hill and other famous spots, and then visited Shandong University, the Military College, the Government manufacturing factory and Arsenal, etc. They also conducted an investigation at Luokou and in other spots. During this time, Lockhart had three official interviews with Zhou Fu, who talked about the difficulties in the industrial and commercial fields in the province. Zhou also said that the purpose of entertaining Lockhart was to show the common people how to treat the Europeans, and he urged that British financial investors should complete the Jinzhen railway construction as rapidly as possible so as to offset the German diversion of trade to Jiaozhou. Zhou Fu pointed out that once China was broken up, all the other powers' vested

Lockhart with Yang Shixiang – the visiting Governor of Shandong in front of the Senior District Officer's office. (11th July 1905)

Yang Shixiang, Governor of Shandong, and his party arriving at Port Edward. (10th July 1905)

interests in China should be harmed, and he also inquired about Lockhart's views of China's modern reforms, Empress Dowager Cixi's political position and the future of reformer Kang Youwei. Regarding those questions that had no direct relevance to Weihaiwei, Lockhart gave only ambiguous answers. Instead, he used the opportunity of making contact with the Jinan Chamber of Commerce to advocate commercial investment in Weihaiwei and promised to give them any support.

On 5th May, Lockhart left Jinan for Confucius' birthplace, Qufu, a place that had a strong appeal for him. During his several days' presence in Jinan, he had made a deep impression on Shandong's provincial senior officials. At the same time, Shandong high officials and leading 'gentry' figures also regarded him as one of their own because of his good diplomacy skills and his scholar behaviour which was almost in a traditional Chinese manner. When he left Jinan, Zhou Fu and his staff gave a farewell dinner for his party outside of the South Gate of the walled city of Jinan and saluted with fire to see them off.

On 9th May, Lockhart and his party arrived at Qufu via Yanzhou where General Tian of Yanzhou Town received them warmly.

On 10th May, as a foreign Confucian scholar, Lockhart went in uniform to the Temple of Confucius to show his respect for China's great Sage. Then he proceeded to the main building of the Temple, where the Duke Kong

Lingyi, the 76th descendant of Confucius, who was 32 years old, was waiting to receive him. Duke Kong appreciated Lockhart's knowledge of Confucianism and proposed taking a group photo with him and his party. In the same evening, Duke Kong paid a return visit and presented Lockhart with books referring to the life and works of Confucius with his inscription and with some articles made of wood from a tree planted by one of the sage's favourite disciples. The next day, Lockhart visited the Confucian Temple and attended a special banquet in his honour. During the banquet, Duke Kong expressed his gratitude for Lockhart's respect for Confucius and asked if he might receive a portrait of King Edward VII as a souvenir. After the banquet, Lockhart, accompanied by Kong Xianglin, an uncle of the present Duke Kong and an ex-Literary Chancellor, visited the Confucian woods, the tomb of Confucius, Zhougong Temple, Yanhui Temple and other historical sites.

Lockhart was always proud of his visit to Qufu. He was not only the first European who had talked with Duke Kong, but also the first European to attend a banquet at the Temple of Confucius. It should be pointed out that

Yuan Shuxun, Governor of Shandong, arriving at Port Edward. (1908)

Lockhart landing at Huangtianqiao Pier, Jinan. (27th April 1903)

Duke Kong had refused to meet the German Governor of Jiaozhou when he visited in Qufu in the same year.

On 12th May, Lockhart and his party left Qufu for Jining. On the way, they were received by the 74th descendant of Mencius (the philosopher, B.C. 372—289) and visited the Temple of Mencius, the tomb and woods of Mencius, and passed an arch marking the site of the home finally occupied by the mother of Mencius who moved her residence to a respectable location where her son could be brought up well.

On 13th May, Daotai Zhang Lianfen treated him with warm hospitality at Jining. At that time, Germany's plunder of Shandong mines had troubled the provincial authorities a great deal. They not only controlled the Fangzi Coal Mine, but also tried their best to seize the mining rights at Boshan including control of the Yixing Coal Mine which was under the jurisdiction of Zhang Lianfen. Zhang showed great concern about this and hoped that Lockhart would urge the British financial group to complete the Shandong section of Jinzhen railway as soon as possible in order to counter German influence. Later, Shandong Judge Shang Qiheng expressed the same concern as Zhang. However, Lockhart had no authority to deal with such things, and could only listen to what they had to say. The next day, Lockhart said farewell to Zhang and left for Taian where he visited Taishan Mountain with Judge Shang Qiheng who had arrived there before him and who would accompany him from Taian to Zichuan.

On 24th May, Lockhart and his party arrived at Weixian via Qingzhou.

Shandong Governor Sun Baoqi (second left) visiting Weihaiwei. (1910)

General Mei Dongyi of Weixian welcomed Lockhart warmly and held a review of his troops in Lockhart's honour. The British and Chinese national flags were raised at the barracks. At that time, in order to prevent Germany from stationing troops along the Jiaoji railway on the pretext of protecting it, General Mei had stationed troops who were mainly responsible for patrolling the railway. 1500 soldiers were sent for this purpose and the military expenditure was paid by the local government. General Mei was a typical Chinese who was pro-English and anti-German. He related to Lockhart what Li Hongzhang, the late Viceroy and Grand Councillor, commented about foreigners: the British – straightforward and peaceful, the French – happy so long as they have a good bottle of wine, the Germans – brutes! In the meantime, he hoped to send officers to Weihaiwei to learn the British military art of war. General Mei's troops were the smartest that Lockhart had seen in Shandong, so Lockhart supported his request actively and ensured his wish was granted at early date.

On 25th May, Lockhart boarded the train to Qingdao after saying goodbye to General Mei and his officers. In Qingdao, Lockhart hastened to make a wide investigation thanks to the arrangements of the German Governor. Germany's well established ruling system and strong situation impressed Lockhart a lot. However, ever since his trip to Jinan, he had felt aware of the strong resentment against Germany by all classes in Shandong and of their efforts to resist Germany. Thus he thought, "The Germans will never succeed as administrators of a population which is mostly oriental. They are quite ignorant of the Chinese and do not know how to deal with them". As Shandong local authorities treated Britain and Germany in two quite different ways, Weihaiwei should have a bright future in spite of difficulties. However, this proved not to be the case. On 30th May, Lockhart left Qiangdao by boat and arrived back in Weihaiwei the next day.[166]

Lockhart's first journey in Shandong did not lead to substantial material progress due to the lack of any specific planning, but he established close personal contact with senior Chinese officials in Shandong. Thereafter, they visited each other frequently and their relations remained surprisingly good.[167] Apart from these visits, Lockhart corresponded regularly with senior Chinese officials, "indeed, he seems to have kept in contact more frequently with them than he did with his London masters".[168] "The result is that through the medium of informal or semi-official correspondence, and by personal visits, a great deal of business is satisfactorily carried through without 'fuss' or waste of time, and that frontier matters which might conceivably grow into difficult international questions requiring intervention, are quickly and easily settled on the spot".[169] However, because of the fundamental conflicts between British and Chinese basic interests, the Shandong authorities did not realize their original intention of taking advantage of the British presence at Weihaiwei to balance the German influence; on the other hand, the British authorities in Weihaiwei also failed to realize their dream of "a second Hong Kong".

After the Revolution of 1911 which overthrew the Qing government, there were some major changes in the contacts between the colonial government and the Shandong authorities. In 1911, immediately after the last Shandong governor, Sun Baoqi, had declared Shandong's independence from the central government, he wrote to Lockhart to inform him of this action and stated he would try his best to protect the foreigners' rights in Shandong.[170] However, the turbulent situation after the Revolution could not be controlled by the provincial government. Soon afterward the Colonial Office instructed Lockhart to communicate with the revolutionary officials in the surrounding area only so far as was strictly necessary,[171] so as to avoid implying formal recognition of their authority. Lockhart's superiors were most anxious that British neutrality be preserved in this instance, but as will be seen, the commissioner was to have great difficulty in doing so as a revolutionary government had been established at Chefoo. At the beginning of the revolution, the colonial government issued notices prohibiting the people of the territory from taking part in political activities of any party, or any group within the territory advocating revolution. Meanwhile, he stationed more than 100 guards at several points along the territory's borders to keep

Lockhart with Luo Zhongming, District-Magistrate of Rongcheng. (1905)

During the period of the Lease, many Korean people came to Weihaiwei for refuge or travelled to other places via Weihaiwei, as Japan was speeding up its seizure of Korea. This photograph shows a minister and his son from Korea. (1904)

undesirable persons entering the territory from outside and banished any revolutionaries who were discovered within the territory. Upon learning that the magistrate of the walled city of Weihai had been arrested in his own Yamen by a band of revolutionaries who had marched through the territory from Wendeng, Johnston ordered the rebels out of the Yamen and urged, through the British consul at Chefoo, that the Chefoo authorities should reinstate the magistrate of the walled town.[172] But these measures did little to resist the development of the turbulent situation in the neighbouring area. In 1912, there occurred massive counter-revolutionary violence in Wendeng and Rongcheng. Commissioner Lockhart was finding the situation increasingly alarming with large numbers of refugees streaming into the territory from the two neighbouring counties and a growing possibility of violence and banditry spreading over the borders, so he decided to propose Port Edward as a neutral meeting-ground where representatives from Chefoo, Wendeng, and Rongcheng could come to discuss means of restoring peace to the area, but the Weihaiwei Peace Conference was fruitless.[173] Before the conference was held, counter-revolutionaries killed the Wendeng revolutionary, Yu Chunxuan, and then the Chefoo revolutionaries dispatched troops to Wendeng and Rongcheng to suppress the counter-revolution. It was not until 1913 that order was eventually restored in the neighbouring area.

In the 1920's, Shandong suffered chaos from the conflicts between the warlords. Regarding external affairs, the Weihaiwei commissioner had to communicate with the Chefoo authorities directly on every matter except those concerning legal actions,[174] thus contact with the provincial government became gradually less up to the time of the rendition of Weihaiwei.

Military Control and Utilization

3

The summer resort of the China Fleet

Weihaiwei was located at a very important military position by the Yellow Sea and the Bohai Sea. Across the water, Korea and Japan lay to the east and Port Arthur (Dalian) on the Liaodong Peninsula to the north. After the Sino–Japanese War, the ulterior motive for the leasing of Weihaiwei by Britain was to construct a permanent naval base whereby Russia and Germany could be contained, also to allow easy access to Beijing and Tianjin in order to win dominance over Chinese affairs. In 1898, a team led by the British Naval commander Vice–Admiral Simon and Colonel Lewis from the Royal Engineers, came to Weihaiwei for the purpose of military surveying and later submitted an ambitious "Weihaiwei Naval Base Construction Plan" to the British Government. The key defensive buildings in this plan were to be constructed on Liugong Island. These would include excellent defensive facilities and sufficient ammunition depots, with a strong garrison which could maintain powerful firepower to safeguard against attacks from whichever direction. The island barracks were designed to be large enough to accommodate an infantry battalion, a battery, most of the mechanical division, and heavy machine gun units. In addition, a succession of pillboxes, artilleries and barracks would be constructed on the mainland and the region east of meridian 121° 40′ Eastern Hemisphere. At the same time, the British army started to carry out some maintenance work on the old military facilities which had been left behind by the Japanese and the Qing Court army. They also built new forts, barracks, docks, trenches, shelters, pillboxes, coal warehouses, and a hospital.

However, there were grave reservations when the British government discussed this construction plan, as large sums for construction costs would be incurred, at a time of Britain's involvement in the Boer War in South Africa. Thus, construction work in Weihaiwei continued spasmodically. During the Boer War, the British Navy and Army had suffered serious losses, and the state treasury was exhausted. Britain could not afford to carry on with the construction. Especially after the experiences of the Boer War, the British

Government considered that for a long distance war, "a mobile naval fleet would be more valuable than a fixed land base". For the time being, the rise of the German Navy and the alliance between Russia and France were the main threat to British sea power. The Government trusted in "Investment in the military fleet rather than in bricks and mortar", so the priority of the British Navy was swiftly shifted to constructing warships. The British gave

The aircraft carrier H.M.S. Hermes anchored off Weihaiwei (1930s)

The British China Fleet (circa 1910)

up their grand defensive construction plan in February 1902, and in the end their policy changed to using Weihaiwei as a training base and convalescent home for the British Navy. Subsequently, Britain's investment in Weihaiwei was concentrated mainly on the supply of materials and provisions, maintenance of facilities, health and the hospital, recreation and so on. In order to make Liugong Island an exclusive military controlled area, the British colonial authority took command of all lands, including all the buildings on the Island. The British Marine corps was stationed on the island all year round to guard the port, to offer servicing facilities to the fleet, equipment maintenance and so on, and they were also prepared for action whenever necessary. All the British Fleets stationed in China could take part in military manoeuvres or take breaks for relaxation in Weihaiwei from the end of April to the end of October as Liugong Island and the nearby shores were blessed with good military facilities and an excellent climate.

The navy base on Liugong Island also became a spring board for Britain's military operations in China. In 1900 when the Eight-Power Allied Forces invaded China, Liugong Island became a supply base for the British Army. An Expeditionary Force consisting of mainly Indian soldiers was sent from Hong Kong to Weihaiwei at that time. Priests and foreigners escaping from Shandong were accepted onto Liugong Island. In September of 1914, more than 1000 British marines boarded ships from Liugong Island to Laoshan Bay (near Qingdao) to assist the Japanese army in their occupation of Qingdao. In 1927, when the people of Wuhan took back the Hankou concession from Britain, the British No.2 Fleet at Weihaiwei sailed to Hankou on the 10th of January trying to recapture the concession by force. Due to its very special

The photograph shows an official inspection of the 4th Submarine Flotilla at Weihaiwei (circa 1909)

A naval firing range on Liugong Island. (1910)

Aircraft from the aircraft carrier H.M.S. Hermes at Weihaiwei. (1935)

A Royal Navy funeral ceremony in progress at Majingzi, Liugong Island. (circa 1909)

Royal Navy Ceremonial contingent "stood down" following the Lease Ceremony – 24 May 1898.

strategic position and the natural conditions in Weihaiwei, the British military authority wanted to retain it. For this reason when, in 1930, Weihaiwei was restored to China, the lease of Liugong Island to the British was extended for a further 10 years.

During the British occupation of Liugong Island (except for the duration of the first world war, when all British fleets were sent to assist the war in Europe) a large number of ships would also anchor at Liugong Island each summer, and following the appearance of technologically advanced vessels, and the expansion of the navy, more and more ships came here. Especially between 1930–1937, around 30 or more ships would be anchored on the Island at any one time. According to official records, between spring and summer of 1931, when the British China Fleet arrived at Weihaiwei, the number of Navy officers and sailors totalled nearly 10,000. Apart from the aircraft carriers "Hermes", there were up to six cruisers of the 5th Cruiser Squadron, the submarine depot ship Medway, together with up to eleven submarines of the 4th Submarine Flotilla and more than twelve miscellaneous destroyers and sloops, a despatch vessel, oil tanker and minor auxiliary craft. The whole port was buzzing with activity. [1]

Naval exercises at sea and ships' movements in harbour sometimes pre–

Summer house of the Commander in Chief of the China Fleet on Liugong Island (1931)

The Commander in Chief, China Fleet, inspecting Indian troops (1923)

sented a hazard to local fishing boats and commercial craft and from time to time collisions occurred whereby damage was caused, which sometimes led to a vessel sinking. One of the most serious accidents was the sinking of the British submarine, HMS Poseidon. Poseidon was launched in June 1929. It was 89 metres long and 8.8 metres wide. Its displacement was 1,760 tons, fully loaded 2,040 tons. It had a surface speed of 17.5 knots, and carried a crew of 51. Its armaments consisted of one 4–inch gun, two machine guns, and eight 21–inch torpedo tubes. In November 1930, it left England for the far east and arrived in Hong Kong on 27th February 1931 before proceeding to Weihaiwei. During that same year, on the 9th of June, while conducting an exercise to the north of Weihaiwei, it was rammed by a Chinese commercial vessel "Yuta", and sank to the bottom of the sea within only 2 minutes. 31 sailors out of the 51 onboard escaped, including 4 who escaped by using the Davis Escape Apparatus.

The Royal Navy established a cemetery in Majingzi on Luigong Island for military personnel who died in Weihaiwei during the Lease Period which after the departure of the Royal Navy in 1940 was maintained by the British Consulate.

To satisfy the requirements for convalescence of British naval personnel, the colonial and military authorities, and also European businessmen, invested large sums of money in recreational and entertainment facilities in Weihaiwei.

The Officer in Charge of Luigong Island Naval Base, Surgeon Commander A.A. Pomfret R.N. (centre), and his staff. (February 1940)

For instance on the mainland were constructed: the "Four-eyes Building", the "Seven Star" Buildings, the "King's Hotel", the "Eastcliff Hotel" and so on. On the island were the "Admiral's House", "Naval Hospital", plus several bars. There were also 3 soccer fields, more than 10 tennis courts, two golf courses and cricket fields, bowling greens, badminton courts, etc. In addition to facilities developed by the government authorities, businessmen from more than 10 different countries obtained special permission to start up businesses, such as hotels, bars and other facilities providing services for the British sailors. There were printing houses, bakeries, launderettes, tailors, savings banks, butcher's shops, and grocery shops run by westerners, The Chinese businesses included photographic shops, shoe shops, barbers etc. A few hundred Chinese labourers were engaged in providing services for British sailors. Some were employed to clean, to provide transportation and other kinds of odd services. Businesses boomed during the summer months.[2]

On the 7th of March 1938, the Japanese army occupied Weihaiwei. They also occupied some of the Chinese navy's facilities on Liugong Island. The British presence had decreased significantly and by now only a few British naval personnel were stationed on the Island. On the 4th of November 1940, the British navy abandoned Liugong Island and thus ended its 42 years of occupation.

Chinese soldiers of the Eight–Power Allied Force

After they had occupied Weihaiwei in 1898, the British government soon realized that the security of Weihaiwei would depend on a land–based defence capability. Thus, in addition to a naval force, it would also be necessary to station sufficient troops there.[3] However, the military authorities were unable to support such an action. At that time, Great Britain was occupying a huge amount of overseas colonial territory which was about a hundred times larger than the size of its homeland, so it was clearly impossible for troops from Britain to meet the whole of the empire's land–based defence requirements. At the same time, Anglo–Boer relations were rapidly worsening and a fierce large–size conflict was inevitable, which meant that the main British force would not be free to help in other areas. Therefore, in order to meet the land defence needs for Weihaiwei, the British government finally decided to form a mercenary army.

This mercenary army became known as "The Chinese Regiment of Infantry",[4] and its size was initially fixed at 1000 staff members.[5]

The Chinese Regiment headquarters, constructed in 1899 (1902)

British officers of the Chinese Regiment. (1904)

In November 1898, Major Hamilton Bower, of the Indian Staff Corps, was appointed Commandant and was given the local rank of Lieutenant Colonel by the War Office. Commandant Bower arrived in Weihaiwei at the end of that same year, with two Chinese and one German interpreter between English and Chinese, who were all newly recruited.[6] Before long, Major C. D. Bruce, who was the Second-in-Command, plus 4 Captains and 6 Sergeants transferred from the Royal Infantry, also arrived in Weihaiwei.[7] After this, the establishment of the Chinese Regiment (the short form of the title Chinese Regiment of Infantry, also referred to as the 1st Chinese Regiment) was soon carried out.

The British actions were soon reported to the Qing Court by Mr Yan Daohong,[8] the prospective Daotai (a rank under Governor but above Prefecture) of Shandong, who was then in charge of foreign affairs in Weihaiwei, and these aroused public indignation. Presented with a protest lodged by Mr. Luo Fenglu, the Chinese Minister in London, Prime Minister Salisbury explained that it was solely for the purpose of protecting the Territory's security that a regiment was to be established at Weihaiwei. At the same time, he promised that soldiers would be recruited only from within the Weihaiwei area, and moreover, that the regiment would serve only in Weihaiwei, and would not be transferred to other locations.[9]

Lord Salisbury was just stalling Mr Luo. In fact, the British War Office from the very beginning "intended the Chinese Regiment to be, not merely the garrison of Weihaiwei, but also the nucleus of the body of military police which would be needed if, and when, we took over the government of our 'sphere of influence'".[10] Concerning the choice of regimental officers, the War Office tried to transfer high-grade officers from the British regular army to Weihaiwei. The standard for senior non-commissioned officers (or N.C.O.'s) was also high and they were normally given a local rank higher than their substantive rank and a special allowance for service at Weihaiwei.[11]

The recruited Chinese men were usually from 19 to 24 years old and "must be strong and honest".[12] They were enlisted for a term of three years general service, which might be prolonged, if necessity, to four years.[13] Of course, an adequate material reward was necessary to ensure that Chinese soldiers would follow their orders willingly. According to the British military rules, a soldier's monthly salary was 8 silver dollars, and a squad leader's could reach 12 silver dollars; sufficient rice, flour, meat and firewood were offered free each day; the necessary seasonal uniforms were also free. A soldier would gain 30 more silver cents after a service of two years if he had no record of violation of discipline. Extra reward was also given to any outstanding soldiers who gained excellent results during training.[14]

However, at first, it was not easy for the British authorities to recruit Chinese men in spite of the excellent pay and conditions. This was because the people of Weihaiwei hated the British invasion at that time and so refused the enlistment. Mrs. Phyllis Watson, the widow of W. M. Watson, Captain of the 1st Company of the Chinese Regiment, recalled: "The orderly room received recruits at the rate of perhaps four a month at first... The local Chinese authorities went out of their way to make recruitment difficult, and in this they were aided by the parents of the young men who enlisted. Both fathers and mothers besieged the barracks in order to persuade their sons to return to the fields".[15] But China at that time was full of illiterate refugees who had suffered a great deal from natural and man-made calamities and had to leave their hometowns for a living. Thus when the British authorities finally decided to break their promise and to recruit from other places in Shandong, Zhili, and north eastern China,[16] many young refugees came to Weihaiwei in a steady stream.

The Chinese Regiment was finally formed in 1899 [17] at which time there were seven companies [18] that consisted of 534 officers and men.[19] All officers above the level of N.C.O. were selected from the British regular army. The British usually referred to it as the Weihaiwei Regiment. The regiment consisted of a military band, a medical team, the Infantry Company and Cavalry, etc. Each company was provided with Chinese interpreters who were recruited from modern schools (i.e. as compared with traditional ones that taught only Chinese literature classics) within Hong Kong, Shanghai, Hankou and other cities. After a regular British–style training, these troops were sent to various posts within Weihaiwei and were responsible for the land–based defence and public order in the leased Territory.

The impression of their British officers was that these Chinese recruits were of good appearance and averaged 5 feet 8 inches, which was a good height for those days.[20] More importantly, "they are very amenable to the discipline and control of those they know; they are robust and well able to stand fatigue and hard work; they are very good shots, taken all round; are no trouble to feed, as they have no prejudices on the subject, except it be in the matter of quantity".[21] Thus, "...the finest men, and the finest soldiers in every way, are the Shandong men...".[22] However, these men were from an old nation with several thousands years of civilization, that promoted the ideal of noble character which poverty and obscurity could not divert, and neither threats nor violence itself could bend. So it was of great concern for Britain to know whether they would be faithful to a foreign country, especially when they had to fight against their own countrymen. Before long, the Chinese Regiment's wonderful performance dispelled their misgivings.

On 26th March 1900, the Chinese Regiment carried out its first task which was to suppress an anti–British gathering of local people led by the elder Cui Shoushan at Weihaiwei. It was a bloodless military action, but

Guards of the Chinese Regiment. (1902)

Chinese Regiment band (1904)

gave the colonial authorities a very pleasant surprise. Captain A.A.S.Barnes, commander of the 2nd company, said: "Trivial and bloodless as this, the regiment's first real test, may seem, a little reflection will prove that it was really of vast importance, as being the first indication of what was afterwards so often and so abundantly shown – namely, the readiness of the men to stand by their officers, even against their own people",[23] so he was convinced that "they could be fully relied on for sterner work, should the occasion arise".[24]

Barnes's opinion soon became justified. On 25th April in the same year, while under the escort of 60 men from the 7th company of the Chinese Regiment, both the Chinese and British sides began the boundary demarcation of the leased Territory. When a boundary disturbance broke out, the colonial authorities sent for the Chinese Regiment to help them. The British officer who participated in this recalled: Roused from their sleep at the dead of night and ordered to march out, armed and equipped, against their own people, by alien officers, not a murmur was heard, and not a man was there but showed the greatest zeal".[25]

On 5th and 6th May, at both the dried river bed and Duoding Mountain, faced with a group of Weihaiwei people who rushed to attack the British side armed with farming tools, stones and guns, Chinese soldiers from the Regiment fired on their own people without hesitation and killed 29 of them.

On 5th May, the father of one of the soldiers was killed during the attack on Captain Watson's camp. Even in the opinion of a British officer, this son

Chinese Regiment interpreters. (1904)

had strong reason to leave the Regiment, but he remained firm.[26]

Another scene then occurred during the battle, "An old man, apparently carrying all his worldly goods on a stick over his shoulder, came running towards the camp. He was the father of one of the soldiers of the regiment, and he had come to warn his son that thousands were on their way to wipe out the camp and all in it, and that if his son had any regard for his own skin he would get out as soon as he could. The son replied that if there was going to be a fight he preferred to remain where he was. The old man continued his flight through the camp alone.[27]

The British officers involved in the battle recalled that here were a great number of similar instances of loyalty in every company.[28]

The British authorities successfully employed the Chinese Regiment in suppressing the anti–British armed struggle and finally completed their boundary demarcation. In view of this, the British Minister MacDonald in Beijing sent a special telegram to the Weihaiwei Military Commissioner Arthur Dorward stating: "Please congratulate Colonel Bower on the splendid behaviour of his regiment".[29] A Reuter's telegram also praised the fact that: "the Chinese Regiment behaved splendidly".[30]

Those British officers who had participated in the establishment of the Regiment were even more enthusiastic: "... it is certain that their behaviour against their own folk in Weihaiwei is something to be very proud of. It proved, beyond a doubt that they were thoroughly to be relied on",[31] "At all events, it was a grand thing for the regiment, as it showed the officers that their hard work had borne the best of fruit; and, what is possibly more important, it proved the value of the regiment to others, and enabled us to justify our existence".[32]

Almost at the same time as the armed struggle against Britain at Weihaiwei, the Eight-Power Allied Forces invaded China in order to suppress the Boxer movement which had originated from inland within Shandong Province. At that time, Weihaiwei was appointed as the supply base for the British army in China. The Indian Detachment from the China Expeditionary Force was dispatched to Weihaiwei from India via Hong Kong. However, this aid was too slow in coming to be of any help. So the British army, facing repeated defeats in northern China, immediately decided to transfer the Chinese Regiment to take part in the battle.

It's not known whether the British government considered their earlier promise "not to move the Regiment to other places" when they made the above decision. However a relevant report in the British Central News Telegram at that time stated: "The 1st Chinese Regiment at Weihaiwei at the commencement of the crisis eagerly begged to be sent to the front to fight under their adopted flag, and as time went on without the arrival of the desired orders, dissatisfaction was openly expressed by the men. Finally it was decided to give the new regiment a chance, and there was wild rejoicing at Weihaiwei when the orders came to hand".[33]

On 21st June, 1900, Colonel Bower led the first 200 men to be selected from the Regiment aboard H.M.S. Orlando, and left for Tianjin.[34] It was this successful expedition against the Boxers and the well-armed Chinese regular troops that enabled the Chinese Regiment to finally gain its reputation.

Captain Barnes who took part in this expedition wrote in 1901: "The Chinese Regiment was represented in more expeditions than any other corps. To say nothing of the original troubles around Weihaiwei, we had our part in Tianjin, the relief of Beijing, and the smaller expeditions, on the 19th August, 1900 that to Duliu and the abortive one to Beicang. No other regiment was represented in all these actions."[35]

In Tianjin, in addition to their rearguard service, the Chinese Regiment, together with forces from others of the eight powers, also took part in the Zizhulin Settlement Battle, and fought for possession of the Eastern and Western Arsenals. They encircled and suppressed the Boxers and the Qing troops, and attacked Laolongtou (Tianjin) Railway Station. Finally, they were the first to rush into the walled city of Tianjin, through the South Gate, being the only representatives of the British Army who took part in the final assault and capture of the city of Tianjin.[36]

During these battles, the Chinese Regiment soldiers justified the confidence of their officers by their brave and faithful performance.

On 27th June, the Russian Army made the first attack on the Tianjin Eastern Arsenal which was regarded by the allied forces as a major threat to the security of the Zizhulin Settlement. The Settlement was less than 10 kms away from the Eastern Arsenal where more than 1000 Qing men and a large troop of Boxers were stationed. The Eastern Arsenal was not only the station that supplied ammunition to Qing troops at the front, but was also in an important position to bomb the Settlement and to cut the connection between Dagu and the Settlement foreign forces. The Russian Army's attack was rebuffed with a vigorous counterblow by the Qing troops, so Colonel Bower received orders to lead his men to assist. It was the first time for the Chinese Regiment to attend a regular battle, but its troops "behaved like old soldiers... and the section volley-firing was very good, the objects being clearly pointed out".[37]

In the same day, the Allied Forces occupied the Eastern Arsenal, thus clearing the way for their subsequent attacks. After the battle, Weihaiwei Military Commissioner Dorward telegrammed the War Office to record the Chinese Regiment's meritorious deeds in view of the fact that "the Regiment repulsed a flank attack of Boxers, inflicting considerable losses on the enemy".[38] Captain Barnes took delight in describing a cannon carried to the front by No. 4 Company of the Regiment, which fired a deadly shell at the Eastern Arsenal: "The explosion that followed was one of the most lovely, and, at the same time, the most extraordinary, sights I have ever seen. A huge pillar of snowy whiteness rose slowly and majestically into the air, and when its summit was five or six hundred feet above the earth, it slowly opened out like a vast sunshade, and after hanging in the air for ten minutes or so, slowly dissolved. I have since seen summer clouds of similar appearance, but never anything to surpass this death-dealing cloud for the beauty of its pure whiteness".[39]

When the Chinese Regiment reinforced Tianjin Railway Station on 4th July, the soldiers behaved splendidly again. One British Officer in his reminiscences said: "One shell landed in some lime only a few feet from the left of the No. 4 Company, which was lying down behind the row of trucks. It covered the men about there with lime, which they appeared to look on as an immense joke, judging from the shouts of laughter which

A British instructor demonstrating to Chinese soldiers how to use the Maxim heavy machine gun. (1904)

arose from them".[40]

On 9th July, some new modern cannon from the British Army arrived in Tianjin, then the allied forces launched a counterattack on the Qing troops stationed at Balitai. One Qing commander Nie Shicheng was killed during this battle.[41] The Chinese Regiment was responsible for the transportation of British army's cannons and ammunitions. Dorward said in the battlefield report: "The most arduous work of the day was done by the Chinese Regiment, who, as escort to the guns, worked indefatigably in getting them over broken and swampy country".[42]

In the early morning of 13th July, the allied forces launched the final general offensive upon the walled city of Tianjin. The western allied forces, consisting of Japanese, British, American, Italian and Austrian armies, first attacked the Western Arsenal, and then attacked the South Gate of Tianjin city from three directions.[43] Nos. 4 and 5 companies of the Chinese Regiment led by Captain Watson were one part of the western allied forces attacking the Western Arsenal and occupied the houses between the Western Arsenal and the South Gate of Tianjin. Major Pereira led No.7 Company in carrying stretchers and ammunition for this attack.[44]

Another British officer who attended the battle recorded in his memoirs the true situation when the Chinese Regiment fought against their own people. During the battle, the 9th United States Infantry suffered heavy casualties, and needed stretchers and medical workers urgently, so Major Pereira led No. 1 and 7 companies in risking their lives to aid the American troops. When the American commander discovered these relief troops, he stood up immediately and agitatedly signalled with his hands to request them to withdraw because the fierce fighting was just at its peak and he didn't believe that they could charge through the heavy firing from the Qing troops. However, "the Chinamen paid no attention to him, but trotted on until they reached their goal".[45] Major Pereira found that the American army had almost run out of ammunition, and so Captain Ollivant led No. 6 Company to transport new ammunition. Sadly, Captain Ollivant and the mule carrying the ammunition were killed on the way, but the soldiers still risked their lives to charge on.[46] Thereafter, the Chinese Regiment received an order to stay at the front, "they detained a considerable body of the enemy in front of them, and prevented any attack being made on the right flank of the Japanese".[47]

These memoirs especially mentioned a Chinese sergeant named Qi Diankui. At that time, he was leading half a company in charging under fire towards the walled city of Tianjin under the command of Captain Watson. While passing by some temporary barracks, Watson found Qi, surrounded by bullets, kneeling down in the middle of the road, and then rebuked him in a stern voice. However, Qi 'stood up quite calmly and saluted and explained

that as he had been told to take up his half company in exactly the same manner that his officer had done, and since he did not know what that manner was, he had come out into the open to watch. Now that he had seen how they were to advance he could continue. It did not seem to have occurred to him that he was taking any unusual risk".[48] Qi was killed later at Tongzhou [49] and rewarded the Distinguished Conduct Medal by the British Army.[50]

In the early morning of 14th July, under the command of Japanese Major General Fukushima, Watson led his companies to charge into the walled city of Tianjin, being the only representatives of the British Army. On the afternoon of that same day, Tianjin fell into the hand of allied forces.

Since 1840, China had fought two Opium Wars and one Sino-Japanese War and been defeated in every one of them, which made many westerners believe that it was impossible for the Chinese to become high-class soldiers. In their view, the Chinese would flee helter-skelter if they faced the enemy on the battlefield. During the boundary disturbances at Weihaiwei, the Chinese Regiment was merely dealing with a group of ordinary villagers who were armed only with farming tools and had no battle experience, so that action proved merely that Chinese soldiers would respond well to commands, but the British authorities still had doubts about their true fighting capacity. However Tianjin offered a great opportunity for the Chinese Regiment to finally display its high combat effectiveness before the colonial authorities.

From then on, the British press was full of the praise for the Chinese Regiment. Said The Times correspondent: "Whatever the future may show as regards the active fighting qualities of the 1st Chinese Regiment, they certainly possess in a highly developed degree the quality of passive courage."[51] North China Daily News reported, concerning the battle for Tianjin: "The Regiment that trained such brave soldiers would not be one which lacked achievement. ...Those Europeans who witnessed their splendid behaviour all said that Chinese soldiers should be rewarded the Victoria Cross Medal".[52] One of British marines at Weihaiwei wrote in a letter home: "...The 1st Chinese Regiment is a splendid lot of men, and they would knock spots off our Guards at home in drill and marching".[53]

On the way to the North Gate of Tianjin walled city, Captain Barnes and his men saw a horrible scene: "Corpses there were, naturally, in large numbers, most of them in a fairly advanced state of decomposition, and covered with flies. In one place we came upon an entire family, from all appearances, huddled together and almost hidden by a perfect canopy of flies. Most of them, children of tender years, had received wounds of a nature such as to put all hopes of recovery out of the question, even had the victim been a strong man, and from whom the mother, herself badly hit, was striving, in vain, to keep the swarms of noxious flies".[54] It's unknown if this miserable

The Chinese Regiment on parade(1904). These troops were used to suppress local anti–British uprisings and to fight against the Boxer rebellion in 1901

mother realised that those 'foreign soldiers' in front of her were actually sons of similar Chinese mothers. How would she have felt if she knew the truth......?

As one of the only units represented at the actual assault on the City,[55] the Chinese Regiment was allowed to wear a special badge. With the special permission of the British Army, the Regimental badge had a design of the city gate of Tianjin with two Chinese characters, signifying 'Tianjin', inscribed on the top arch. The scroll below the gate contained the name 'The 1st Chinese Regiment' with the name 'Tianjin' in Roman script above the scroll.[56] Colonel Bower, commanding the 1st Chinese Regiment, became one of three committee members of the Tianjin Provisional Government established by the Eight–Powers' Allied Forces, while Captain G. Mockler was appointed the Chief of Police in Tianjin.[57] In 1902, the Chinese Regiment was allowed to send one N.C.O. and 12 men to England to attend the Coronation Ceremony of King Edward VII.[58] In memory of officers and men killed in action, the Chinese Regiment erected a monument inscribed with 23 names of martyrs at Weihaiwei.

After the battle for Tianjin, the British Indian detachment, the major component of the China Expeditionary Force, arrived in northern China, so the Chinese Regiment was no longer required for actual combat, but its members still rendered invaluable assistance to the British forces in collecting and handling transport and other support services [59] before the attack on Beijing as they were very familiar with the local geography and customs. They gathered together 100 large junks and much equipment, and recruited many sailors and coolies within only a few days. On 4th August, when the Allied Forces marched on Beijing, Captain Barnes led 100 men to carry heavy

Lockhart presenting Victoria Medals to soldiers of the Chinese Regiment in 1904.

guns for the International Battery, and during the final rough journey, these guns were carried to Beijing mostly by man–power. At the same time, Captain A. Hill led 30 men from No. 5 Company to escort a team of wheelbarrows filled with provisions northwards. "No matter how bad the roads were, or how great the heat, straight ahead went this column, passing all the other transport, for it never seemed to need a rest",[60] a performance which was envied by the other forces. "It may safely be stated that, of all the different sections composing that heterogeneous army, none was so well supplied with interpreters and means of transport as the British force".[61] Lieutenant General Alfred Gaselee, the Chief–in–Commander of Allied Forces, issued an order of commendation for the Chinese Regiment's splendid behaviour during the march on Beijing.[62]

On 14th August, Beijing fell into the Allied Forces' hands, and the British army became the first one to enter the inner city and diplomatic quarter.[63]

On 28th August, the Allied Forces reviewed their meritorious troops in the Forbidden City to celebrate their occupation of Beijing and to demonstrate their contempt for the Qing Empire. At 7am, the allied forces were on parade in front of Daqingmen Gate, the main gate of the Forbidden City. Afterwards, they paraded from Daqingmen Gate to Tiananmen Gate. Following this they entered the Forbidden City and visited each palace within it in turn.[64] On the way, the cheers of soldiers mingled with crescendos of music, and all present considered themselves unexcelled throughout the world.

That day, the Chinese people suffered a great hurt and humiliation.

The Chinese Regiment led by Captain Barnes was in the allied forces' procession. Concerning this unusual ceremony, Captain Barnes wrote: "It was a glorious sight, that stirred one to the very soul to such a degree that one wanted to hug someone, or shout, or dance, or do something equally insane. I suppose such a sight can never be seen again, unless, indeed, the Chinese repeat their performance". During the parade, those Chinese left to take care of the Forbidden City also made a big impact on him: "Their salient feature was sadness, ... as we neared the living-rooms, you could easily detect contempt and worse feelings in their looks. No doubt they felt far worse than they looked".[65]

It must be difficult for the present day Chinese people to imagine what kind of feelings those Chinese soldiers had when they stood in the very heart of China under the leadership of Captain Barnes.

After the war, on 21st October, 1900, the Chinese Regiment returned to

A memorial for the Chinese soldiers killed in putting down the Boxer rebellion. (1901)

Weihaiwei.[66] This expedition had made the Chinese Regiment well known, so by the end of 1901 it was quickly enlarged into 12 companies consisting of 1, 312 officers and men.[67] In addition to the service for land defence and public order, the Regiment even began to train military personnel for the Chinese government troops.[68] However, a change that would decide the Regiment's fate was also rapidly closing in.

As has been previously stated, because of the huge expenditure incurred during the Boer War and the rapid changes in the political situation in the Far East, the British Government finally regarded Weihaiwei as an unfortified naval port on 20th January, 1902, to be used mainly for Royal Navy's summer recreation and for military exercises. Thereafter, the Chinese Regiment that was costing 30,000 pounds each year [69] became a burden to the military authorities who were eager to get rid of it. On 29th January, 1902, the British War Office issued the Chinese Regiment with a formal order to cease recruitment.[70] In 1905, Japan occupied Port Arthur after the Japanese-Russian War, expelling Russia. In the same year, Britain and Japan signed the second treaty of alliance. The Chinese Regiment now had no useful role to play, so it was proposed that the Regiment should be dismissed. On 1st June, 1906, the Chinese Regiment was dismissed and most of its soldiers were transferred to South Africa where they became policemen. Some other soldiers stayed in the local police force or joined the Chinese government troops.[71] Thereafter, this unique troop disappeared into an unknown corner of history after almost eight years' existence at Weihaiwei.

In 1912, an article written by Mr. Walt, Secretary to the Government and Magistrate for the North Division, was collected in "Shandong - The Sacred Province of China" (published by the Shanghai Christian Literature Society). It wrote: "No account of Weihaiwei would be complete without a reference to the Chinese Regiment, the founding and success of which furnished a signal proof of the genius of the British officer for dealing with Asiatics, and also for the inherent military capacity of the Chinese, when properly led, fed and paid".[72]

In fact, the Chinese Regiment presented one aspect of the miserable Chinese life in those hard days. Thus, these words seem to contain some significance for the present and future Chinese people who want to use the past to know themselves better.

Defence of the land

From the very start of negotiations between China and Britain concerning the lease of Weihaiwei, the British representative MacDonald had the land defence of Weihaiwei on his mind. On 25th May 1898, MacDonald received the detailed lease plan from the British Government, but he was concerned that the proposed leased Territory and Britain's rights within it would not meet the defence requirements of Port Edward. He therefore suggested to London on 27th May that they should request greater rights to station troops, to erect fortifications and other defences within the region east of the meridian 121° 40′ in Shandong Province.[73] Upon gaining permission from the British Government, MacDonald drafted a new convention for the lease and began to negotiate over this with the Chinese Government. After tough negotiations, the Convention for the Lease of Weihaiwei finally stated: "Great Britain shall

The British army drilling in Weihaiwei. (End of the 1920s)

British defence force from Shanghai arriving in Weihaiwei to spend the summer, (1927)

have in addition, the right to erect fortifications, station troops, or take any other measures necessary for defensive purposes, at any points on or near the region east of the meridian 121° 40′ east of Greenwich, and to acquire on equitable compensation within that territory such sites as may be necessary for water supplies, communications and hospitals. Within that zone the Chinese administration will not be interfered with, but no troops other than Chinese or British shall be allowed therein". To MacDonald's surprise, this privilege that he had spent a great deal of effort to acquire soon lost any real usefulness.

In the same year, the British Navy was stationed at Weihaiwei. The newly formed Chinese Regiment began to take responsibility for the land defence of Weihaiwei in 1899. During this time, an Indian expeditionary force belonging to the British army was also stationed there for a brief period. In 1901, the army in Weihaiwei numbered 2663 officers and men.[74] In 1902, the British Navy no longer regarded Weihaiwei as a suitable fortified naval base for the China Fleet, so any defensive measures became unnecessary. They stated: "We do not want a garrison at Weihaiwei – we particularly want to run the place entirely as a non-protected trading station. If the trade comes we will begin protecting it."[75] When the Chinese Regiment was disbanded in 1906, the British Government decided not to send any troops to defend Weihaiwei.[76] After that, a small group of police was in charge of the land defence of Weihaiwei.

The Revolution of 1911 affected the surrounding areas of Weihaiwei such as Wendeng, Rongcheng and Yantai (then known as Chefoo). The situation outside the leased Territory became out of control, so many refugees sought sanctuary within it. This put great pressures on security in the area. In addition, bandits both inside and outside the leased Territory were also causing a deal of concern. A mountain ranger Liu Zhonghai, who was skilled in martial arts, made himself leader of 700 bandits. After killing revolutionaries in Rongcheng, they raided the borders of the leased Territory, in particular seizing and slaughtering men who had cut off their pigtails. At the same time, they slipped into the leased Territory to kidnap people whom they then took outside the Territory, to be used as hostages for the exchange of refugees without pigtails. Liu Zhonghai also threatened that if refugees from Rongcheng were not handed over, he would attack the leased Territory. Though warnings from the British officials foiled his plan and no such attack in fact materialised, people within the leased Territory were much distressed by this situation. As a precautionary measure, Lockhart concentrated virtually all his manpower on protecting the border, by increasing sentries, and blockading the border. However, because the state of affairs had become critical, he requested the British army repeatedly for reinforcement. After countless requests, 100 soldiers who had been stationed in Tianjin were urgently transferred to assist in patrolling and suppressing bandits in the border regions. These soldiers remained until stability had been attained before they returned to their base in March 1913.

During the First World War, almost all of the British army and navy were sent to Europe, so it became impossible to send soldiers or to station them in the leased Territory. In 1915, "Apart from one Royal Marine Warrant Officer, and 18 marines (on Liugong Island) within the 285 square miles of leased Territory, no assistance was obtainable from the local troops if critical situations were to occur".[77]

From 1918, land defence was increasingly strengthened. The main reason was that a progressively more life-threatening situation outside the leased Territory was causing insecurity within it.

In 1918, bandits from Shandong were running wild and unchecked. On the sea, pirates from Dalian not only stole from fishing boats, they frequently committed robberies on land too. As a preventative measure, a detachment of the 18th Indian Infantry of the British Army was transferred to Weihaiwei.[78]

During and after 1928, Chinese warlords were engaged in violent fighting against each other, with the result that soldiers from the losing armies would often flee to Weihaiwei. Because of this, the Scottish Royal Guards were stationed on the west border of Ludaokou to assist local policemen to control army deserters. Due to the shortage of soldiers, sailors from the Royal Navy fleet were transferred to assist in the patrolling of the border region of Weihaiwei. This was also the first time that the British Navy had been involved in land defence activities.

Ever since 1918, land defence had been an on-going affair, but the numbers involved were not large, normally consisting of not more than 100 men. However, during the summers of 1927 and 1928, the number of soldiers increased considerably. The reason for their presence was recuperation rather than military action.

In early 1927, the Chinese National Government regained Hankou and Jiujiang – both British concessions – during its Northern Expedition, which caused Britain some alarm. Because of this, the British government sent a large number of troops to Shanghai in order to protect its own territory, just before the Northern Expeditionary troops attacked. In July that same year, the British army based in Shanghai constructed their military convalescent base in Weihaiwei. Within this base, there were not only facilities for eating, for living, for resting, and for entertainment, but there was also a military hospital that had been constructed to house more than 50 patients.[79] Over the following two years, more than 1000 officers and men arrived each year to recuperate.

Most of the British forces stationed in Weihaiwei came from India. By 1925, most of these were replaced by soldiers from Britain. In general these soldiers remained there for not more than one year and were mostly transferred from Shanghai, Hong Kong and Tianjin. Their barracks were based in Xishawo, Zhaizhi, Zhudao, Tiancun and so on but occasionally temporary camps were set up along the border. Upon arrival on the mainland, soldiers

The military chaplain conducting a service. (1927)

were normally smartly dressed in their army uniforms and would parade along the quays and the main streets. Afterwards, they would sporadically inspect border regions and key towns.

Although the number of soldiers stationed in Weihaiwei was small, and their job was mainly patrolling the streets, it was undeniable that their existence was a major deterrent force to the illegal groups and hostile elements inside and outside of the leased Territory. During this period, public order within the Territory was better than in the neighbouring areas. The Territory therefore became a heaven for various refugees who, however, brought the colonial authorities trouble over the matter of extradition.

In 1901, the colonial authorities had signed an agreement for frontier regulations with Shandong local authorities. Regulation 10 said: "If offenders from within the Territory take refuge without the Territory, the Chinese officials, on due requisition being made to them by the British officials, shall do their utmost to arrest such offenders and hand them over to the British officials, and vice versa. Neither British nor Chinese officials shall, on their own authority, send runners across the frontier to make arrests."[80] After the agreement was signed, both sides cooperated relatively well though they sometimes did not abide by it strictly, but no conflict resulted. Hundreds of criminals had been handed over by each side to the other in accordance with the Frontier Regulations until 1927 by which time, however, the political situation became complex due to the war between various warlords and many people with complex political backgrounds came to the Territory to seek refuge.

At that time, the Commissioner Johnston found there was no strong legal basis for dealing with the question of extradition. The major question was whether the Weihaiwei commissioner had the right to extradite or not? Could the Frontier Regulations be regarded as a legal basis for mutual extradition? Extraditions normally occur between countries, and China and England had no extradition treaty at that time. The Frontier Regulations was an agreement initiated by the former Administrator Dorward and the Chinese Magistrates of Wendeng and Rongcheng, and was created without following strict legal procedures. So Johnston strongly recommended the creation of a Weihaiwei Extradition Ordinance along the lines of the Hong Kong Ordinance concerning the problem of extradition. In view of this, he sought advice from the Crown Advocate in Shanghai, legal experts from the Colonial Office and Foreign Office, Miles Lampson, the British Minister in China, and others.

Their replies were basically the same: the Weihaiwei commissioner and magistrates had no legal right to extradite any Chinese to China, and in view of the brief period remaining for the British occupation of Weihaiwei, it was also impossible to provide the 'statutory authority' which they lacked. However, the Regulations did provide a 'loophole', which might be used in this situation as a political expedient. That is to say, the commissioner could protect those political refugees who deserved help according to international law, but expel other political offenders. This did not help with difficult cases. For example, in July 1930, an attack on the police placed the colonial authorities in a dilemma.

On July 10th, a number of Chinese pedestrians in plain clothes entered the village named Xinzhuang situated about two miles from the territory, and compelled some villagers to provide them with free meals. While partaking of the food, they apparently disclosed their intention of attacking the Buliucun Police-Station in Rongcheng and seizing weapons. Notice of this intention was secretly conveyed by certain villagers to the police, who, when the strangers approached the station, met them with rifle-fire. Some of the marauders made their escape, others were shot, and the remaining 5 were arrested. According to evidence subsequently obtained from the prisoners, they belonged to a party which was acting under the orders of Zhang Zongchang whose object it was to overthrow the existing administration in the part of the province and destroy the power of General Liu Zhennian. The head and a large contingent of Zhang Zongchang's band of marauders, who did not take part in the attempted raid on the Buliucun police-station, were apparently on their way to join the main band in what seems to have been intended as an attack on Rongcheng. They were arrested by the police when some of them tried to intimidate a bus-driver into allowing them to travel in his bus through British territory. Later, of the 21 persons arrested at three different places in the Territory in connection with the affair, six were immediately released by the Magistrate and the remaining 15 were still under arrest.

All those detained in custody would normally be deported without delay. Unfortunately, before they could be expelled, the Chefoo authorities had heard of their arrest and immediately presented a formal demand for their extradition. General Liu also sent an officer from Chefoo to seek a personal interview with the Weihaiwei commissioner, and so the colonial authorities were caught in a dilemma. As General Liu, who had professed to be the staunch ally of the central government at Nanjing, controlled all the north-eastern part of Shandong from his base at Chefoo, if the British authorities refused the extradition, he might take steps to threaten the tranquility of the Territory, provoking conflict between the Chefoo authorities and the colonial authorities. If on the other hand they agreed to extradite them, then those offenders would inevitably be killed.

The British did not wish to offend anyone, so Johnston attempted to treat them as political offenders, because the leader of the men arrested in Weihaiwei, Meng Guangxun, was found to be the holder of a high military commission – the Commander of temporary Division No.104 of the No.2 Allied Army of the Republic of China – issued by Zhang Zongchang. The difficulty was how to differentiate between persons who could reasonably be regarded as belligerents in the present civil war and those who were mere bandits, ready to create disorder wherever and whenever a suitable opportunity occurred. However General Liu insisted that the accused were not belligerents and not entitled to be regarded as political offenders, but were merely bandits, engaged on an enterprise of looting, burning and murdering. Failing to get any strong evidence to prove they were political offenders, Johnston authorized the deportation to Dalian of the fifteen Chinese prisoners on the S.S. "Tun Ho Wan".

Fortunately, General Liu had already left Chefoo because of the pressures of the war, and so did not press the matter of extradition, so there was no further trouble from his side. However, the British action did cause dissatisfaction to the Japanese authorities at Dalian – the Guandong Government. On the 13th of August, an article stating that 14 bandits had been sent to Dalian by the British Authorities at Weihaiwei appeared in the "Dalian Shibao" and "Taidong Ribao". At the same time, the Japanese authorities at Dalian required the British consul there to provide them with the true facts of this incident. On the 15th of August, the British consul, based on Johnston's information, informed the authorities of the Guandong Govern–

A British military band leading the troops marching into town. (1927)

ment of the facts of the case which were briefly as follows: "Some time ago, Meng Guangxun, Song Guangfu and thirteen other Chinese were detected in a plot to overthrow the existing Chinese Government beyond the borders of the Weihaiwei territory. The British magistrate heard the case in the presence of the Chinese magistrate from Weihaiwei city and a representative of General Liu Zhennien. He did not, however, formulate any opinion on the case, but merely took down the evidence, which was then sent to the British legal authorities at Shanghai who ruled that the offence was of a political nature, and that for that reason was not extraditable. They further informed the Weihaiwei government that no evidence existed by which they could try them on a criminal charge and intimated that the only legal course open to them was to banish the men as undesirable characters. Accordingly His Majesty's Commissioner recently authorized the deportation to Dalian of the fifteen Chinese, and the port of Dalian was selected because Meng Guangxun, who held a high military commission from General Zhang Zongchang, had arrived from there the previous June".

On the 22nd of September, the Foreign Affairs Section of Guandong Government made further enquiries because that it did not appear that fourteen companions of Meng Guangxun had originally gone to Weihaiwei from Dalian, so why were these fourteen being banished to Dalian beyond the fact that Meng Guangxun himself had entered Weihaiwei from Dalian? It was evident that gangs of this sort, which were undesirable in the territory of

Royal Marines of the Island Guard on Luigong Island. (1921)

Weihaiwei, must equally be undesirable in the province of Guandong. The Japanese authorities insisted on getting a reasonable reply. The British government was unable to make any immediate reply and it wasn't until November of 1930 after the rendition of Weihaiwei that the British consul in Weihaiwei gave a vague reply in his letter: We had no power to send them to any particular port or to prevent their proceeding to Dalian if they chose (as they did choose) to go there as ordinary passengers. [81]

Whether the colonial authorities had extradition powers or not, it was their consistent policy to protect political refugees according to international law. As a result, during the many years of unrest resulting from frequent civil war in China, various political offenders came to Weihaiwei for asylum, including banished former officials of the Qing Court, high officials of the Beiyang government on the wanted list, defeated warlords from the east of Shandong and the district magistrates of Wendeng and Rongcheng.

Gu Weijun (V.K.Wellington Koo) had sought refuge in Weihaiwei on two occasions. The first time was at the end of 1924 just after the Beijing coup d'etat staged by Feng Yuxiang, when he, as Minister of Foreign Affairs on behalf of the Cao Kun Regime, was negotiating with the British government about the rendition of Weihaiwei. However, President Cao Kun's government fell from power just before the agreement was signed, and the Beijing coup d'etat made Gu Weijun feel he had no future, so he chose Weihaiwei as a refuge. The second time was in July of 1928 when the victory of Northern Expedition ended the Beiyang Government, which was bad luck for Gu Weijun who was then an important official in the Beiyang government. His house and property in Beijing were confiscated by the Guomindang, and his name was placed on the wanted list. After arranging for his wife and children to stay in British territory at Tianjin, he sailed to Weihaiwei under an assumed name on a British merchant ship.

At that time, Yuan Keding, the eldest son of Yuan Shikai, also came to Weihaiwei for refuge. Towards the end of Qing rule, Yuan Keding had been an important official in the Ministry of Agriculture, Industry and Commerce, and also that of Post and Telecommunications After the 1911 Revolution, he was involved in plotting a coup in Beijing to assist Yuan Shikai to become President. After the death of Yuan Shikai, Yuan Keding lived secretly in Tianjin where he helped to finance the Mukden party in their anti-Feng campaign. Thus, he was wanted by Feng Yuxiang (the now victorious "Christian General"). Yuan took his family to Weihaiwei. He seldom went out of his rented house as his health was not good. Johnston would frequently go to visit him.

Cai Tinggan was another refugee helped by Johnston. Cai Tinggan was from Guangdong. He was one of the second batch of children sent to be educated in America by the Qing Court in 1873 when he was thirteen, and he returned to work at the Dagu Torpedo School in China in 1888. Later, he was captured by the Japanese when he fled from Weihaiwei during the Sino-Japanese War 1894-5, and thrown into Osaka Prison in Japan. He was then removed from office after release, but was subsequently appointed head of the Ordnance Dept. of the Navy in 1911. He then worked as a senior military adviser to the President of the Republic of China when Yuan Shikai conferred on him the title of Admiral, later he became Tax Supervisor, and then Minister of Foreign Affairs in the Beijing Government. In July of 1928, Cai was on the wanted list of the Nanjing Government after the Beijing Government fell from the power, and he fled to Weihaiwei where Johnston often visited him and both of them talked widely. Although he seldom went outside his house and most of his time was spent growing flowers in the yard, his presence was discovered by the new government. Some months later, Johnston received a letter from General Liu Zhennian demanding the extradition of Cai. Fortunately, just a few days earlier, Cai had left Weihaiwei for Shanghai, so this did not cause any embarrassment to the colonial authorities. However, Cai's family continued to stay in Weihaiwei and Johnston took special care of them.

Many important persons asked for refuge in Weihaiwei, but not all of them were granted permission. Ex-President Xu Shichang and former Emperor Puyi's refuge demands were both refused by Johnston.

Xu Shichang had stayed quietly in the British concession in Tianjin since he was ejected from the Presidency. In 1928, he was alarmed at the prospect of the British Concession at Tianjin sharing the same fate as the Concession at Hankou, so he wanted to move to Weihaiwei. Johnston and Xu Shichang were close personal friends. In 1918, Johnston became the tutor to Puyi thanks to Xu Shichang's recommendation. However, Johnston refused Xu's present request to refuge at Weihaiwei. The failure of Xu's request seemed to have some connection with Puyi. It was well known that Xu was still loyal to the Qing Court in China.

Before his request, Puyi had enquired from Johnston several times as to whether he might come to live under Johnston's protection in Weihaiwei. However, after the Revolution of 1911, the Qing royal family and its traditional followers continued to carry out restorationist activities, and received support and encouragement from Japan in the late 1920's. But thanks to his rich experience as a colonial official, also as the ex-emperor's tutor, Johnston had much knowledge of Puyi's strong and weak points and was capable of making his own judgment about China's political situation. From his point of view, at that time, most intelligent Chinese were seeking a stable and strong government, and they did not care much about the difference between a republic and a monarchy. Concerning the restorationist efforts made by Prince Gong (Puwei) and his party, Johnston commented, "Their

Indian troops based in Weihaiwei.

aims seem to me very improbable. Any basis of reality they may contain might be nothing more substantial than one of the ambitious dreams in which Prince Gong has been indulging for the last sixteen years". Johnston therefore took the clear-cut stand that he would not become involved in any political actions by the restorationist group.

After 1927, Puwei had invited Johnston to Dalian on two occasions to discuss the question of imperial restoration, but both times he declined. When Johnston heard the news that Japan would take Puyi to Manchuria (three provinces in the northern east of China), he talked of this in his report to the Colonial Office, "If he were to consult me on the subject I should advise him against acceptance, for his own sake, as well as for that of peace and unity in China...... In view of his weakness of character and the conditions under which he would become sovereign of Manchuria, it is quite certain that at Mukden he would be a mere puppet in the hands of the Japanese". Johnston knew clearly what the consequences would be if he permitted Puyi and his followers to take refuge in Weihaiwei. He stated in his report, "I felt that to do so might easily lead to a situation embarrassing to the British Government; especially as among the ex-Emperor's relatives and constant attendants there are several persons who cling to the belief that they can make use of him for their own political or pecuniary advantage, and whose machinations are always liable to make him a centre of intrigue". Therefore, although Johnston had a deep affection for Puyi and Xu Shichang, he, as a representative of the British government, still politely refused their requests.[82]

50,000 Chinese labourers depart from Weihaiwei to take part in the First World War

On 4th August, 1914, the First World War broke out in Europe. In the course of the war, the belligerent countries involved suffered severe losses of soldiers and thus there arose an acute shortage of manpower. In order to extricate themselves from a difficult position, Britain, France and Russia simultaneously turned towards China in the hope of recruiting Chinese man-power to fill the gaps. That resulted in a large export of labour to the western countries on a scale unprecedented throughout Chinese history. As a result, Weihaiwei became closely involved with Europe once again and was the biggest recruiting place for the export of Chinese labourers to Europe during the First World War.

Recruiting depot for Chinese labourers. (1916)

Indeed, at first the Entente countries intended to urge China to take part in the war,[83] which would not only strengthen the those countries and eliminate the German threat in the Far East, but would also help maintain and even enlarge their interests in China, because China, if she really became involved in the war, would have to depend on western assistance in financial, military and other areas due to her weakness. At that time, the downfall of the Qing Court and the birth of the Republic of China, the separatist warlord regimes and the foreign invasions had all brought China to a turbulent situation. However its major foreign enemies were greatly involved in the war in Europe and lacked the strength to interfere in China, which thus offered an opportunity for China to enter international society again. Therefore, urged by the progressive representatives of the new generation, China actively requested to take part in the war in 1914 and 1915,[84] intending to take this opportunity to regain German privileges in Shandong and thus taking the first step towards smashing the fetters of colonialism. Unfortunately, Japan, which regarded the First World War as a favourable opportunity to occupy first China and subsequently the whole Far East,[85] recognized that the participation of China would improve that country's position in the world, so it was strongly opposed to that participation and finally succeeded in keeping China neutral. Furthermore, Japan opposed the suggestion that Germany should return Qingdao directly to China and tried every possible way to join the Entente and declared war against Germany. On 7th November, 1914,

Japan occupied Qingdao, assisted by British troops.[86] Around that time, the Jiaoji Railway was also seized by Japanese troops. On 18th January, 1915, Japan quickly submitted its Twenty-One Demands to the Chinese Government as part of its plan for the domination of China.[87]

However, this Japanese act of aggression did not intimidate the Chinese people, but strengthened their resolve to participate in the war, because China knew very well that it would have no right to attend the Peace Conference after war unless it made some contribution to the war effort, thus the Shandong problem would be left unresolved, and China would even be reduced to becoming a dependency of Japan. On the same day that Japan proposed its Twenty-One Demands, the Foreign Ministry of the Beiyang Government sent confidential letters to ministers stationed in various European countries asking them to sound out European opinion on the matter of China's participation in the war.[88] Liang Shiyi, Chief-Secretary to the President and one of the war party, also drafted a detailed scheme to send labourers rather than soldiers to Europe[89] in order to gain the right to attend the Peace Conference.

Liang's scheme happened to meet the Entente countries' needs and was accepted initially by France. As the main battlefield in Europe, France had suffered heavy casualties and the northeast part of the country was almost ruined, and thus recruiting foreign labourers became an urgent necessity. In the beginning of 1916, following the suggestion of the French envoy Monsieur Conti, Liang Shiyi and Ye Gongchuo, senior officials in the Transportation

C. Maguire, the manager of the Recruiting depot . (May 1917)

Ministry sent Liang Rucheng, Li Jianshan and others to represent China in negotiations with the French representative, Colonel Georges Truptil, regarding the recruitment of Chinese manpower. In order to avoid German intervention, Liang Shiyi established the Tianjin Huimin Company to undertake the whole recruitment, and this was registered in the Foreign Ministry on 6th May that same year.[90] On 14th May, both sides signed an agreement to recruit 200,000 Chinese labourers, and as a result, recruitment centres were established in Tianjin, Hong Kong, Pukou, Qingdao and other places.[91] Although France's recruitment scheme was ambitious, only part of it came to fruition in the end, because there were various problems concerning the methods of recruitment, management, salary-distribution, and cooperation with Chinese companies, furthermore, there was also the negative reaction to France's clumsy diplomatic performance in Tianjin. On 20th October, the authorities in the French Concession in Tianjin enforced the demolition of the Chinese Police Station in the Lao Xikai area and arrested Chinese policemen, in order to occupy the Lao Xikai area. As a result, on 25th October, more than 8,000 Tianjin citizens assembled to pass 6 anti-French resolutions including the winding up of the Huimin Company and the prohibition of French recruitment in China.[92] In addition, the death of President Yuan Shikai and the resignation of Liang Shiyi both caused France to lose the direct support of Chinese politicians in positions of power. Therefore, only about 50,000 Chinese labourers had been directly recruited by France by the end of the war.[93]

Although Britain's recruitment got off to a late start, it surpassed other countries in numbers and efficiency. In fact, Liang Shiyi first discussed his scheme with the British side, but Britain firmly rejected it as soon as she realized that China's true purpose was to take this opportunity to improve its international position,[94] because Britain enjoyed the biggest foreign presence in China, and would never wish to lose her many privileges there. However, as an ally of France, Britain not only sent troops to fight in France, but also transferred a great number of men to support the front. Britain also suffered heavy casualties, especially on the first day of the Battle of the Somme when the total number of the killed and wounded, lost and captured, reached 57,470. This total figure had even reached 400,000 by the autumn of 1916.[95] Both the front and the rear still required men continuously, but very few people of the appropriate age were still available in Britain that time. How to ensure a continuous supply of manpower[96] became the biggest problem for Britain. Although the situation was very grim, there was still much difference of opinion inside the British Government regarding this matter because the British working class was strongly against importing foreign labourers into their homeland.[97] The War Committee finally decided to send foreign labourers rather than British labourers to France.[98] Considering where best to recruit such labourers, Britain then turned toward the Chinese who could 'work endlessly without rest'.[99] In August 1916, the British Army Minister was under an obligation to contact France to discuss the recruitment of Chinese labourers.[100] At the same time, the British Foreign Office also began discussions with its envoy in Beijing concerning the recruitment requirements of the British Army authorities.[101]

In view of China's neutral status at the time, the British government initially selected Hong Kong as the base for recruitment and also demanded secret collaboration from the Hong Kong authorities.[102] However, the plan was opposed by the British Envoy in China, John Jordan, who thought that the people of South China were both too slim and too short and would fail to cope with the cold weather found in Europe. The British military attach é, David Robertson, also doubted whether there were sufficient suitable labourers available in Guangdong. In fact, in August 1916, David Robertson preferred to use Weihaiwei as the recruitment base.[103] The reason lay in Britain's experiences in recruiting a great number of Chinese labourers mainly from Shandong for the Transvaal gold mines in 1904, also their successful experience in forming the Chinese Regiment in Weihaiwei. In their eyes, Shandong men were strong and hard-working, had a placid nature and were easy to manage. In addition, Weihaiwei was both a coastal town and a British leased territory. Another was that barracks for labourers and lots of other basic facilities had been left by the Witwatersrand Native Labour Association of Johannesburg and the Chinese Regiment, and were still in good condition. Therefore, Shandong was considered the best recruiting ground[104] and naturally Weihaiwei was the best recruiting depot. John Jordan even hoped that the recruited labourers would mainly consist of those who had been former members of the Chinese Regiment or had worked in South Africa.[105] Both John Jordan and David Robertson suggested that recruitment should be undertaken directly by the British Government, using the same procedures as the ones employed for the recruitment of the Chinese Regiment. With no recruiting agency involved, costs would be minimised. Jordan also said that it would be unnecessary to offer any explanations to the Chinese Government.[106]

Robertson, in the name of the British Legation, submitted a recruitment proposal to the British Government and soon obtained its approval. On 8th October, 1916, Thomas Johnstone Bourne of the British Munitions Department was appointed the War Office's representative for the purpose of recruiting labour in Northern China to join the British Expeditionary Force in France. He was placed in charge of the whole of the recruitment in Weihaiwei.[107] On 15th November, Lieutenant Colonel Bryan Charles Fairfax was appointed to be responsible for the Chinese Labour Corps established in France on 21st February the following year.[108] In the same year, the British War Office set

The Chinese Police at the Recruiting depot. (1917)

up a "British Government Recruitment Agency for Weihai" consisting of the police station, the administrative office, the army supplies section, the hospital and so on.[109] Within the walled city of Weihaiwei, an agency was also set up to recruit people. Mr. Bourne was in charge of the recruitment personnel, the registration and salaries of the Chinese labourers, packing and transport. The ships were supplied by the British Navy stationed in China and the clothes for the labourers were provided by Messrs Forbes and Co who also had the responsibility for local recruitment in Weihai. Interpreters were also employed at the same time. Most of interpreters who worked in Weihaiwei were young people from Beijing, Tianjin, Shanghai and Hankou.[110]

Once the Chinese labourers had arrived in Weihaiwei from far and wide, they were sent to the recruiting depot, where they had their health checked and other formalities performed before signing the official contract. Those who passed the medical test successfully were each immediately assigned an identification number, which became their identification for the duration of their contract. This number was used to identify each individual in China and in Europe; also to record payments and other allotments of food, clothing and tasks assigned to him. It was entered, together with its owner's name in English and Chinese, into what was called an identification paper and was also placed upon the recruit's wrist in the form of a light brass bracelet. This was not removable until the expiry of his contract. Once he had been assigned this number, each man had a photograph taken, with his hands holding a small slate in front of his chest with that number written upon it.

This photo would then be pasted into his salary book to provide a means of verification when he claimed his wages.[111]

Under the contract made with the British authorities, each labourer would be engaged for a period of three years, but this could be terminated by his employer, the British Government, at six months' notice at any time after the first year. He could be called upon to work ten hours per day on the railways or roads, or in factories, mines, dockyards, or any other sphere of a non–military character. His wages were divided into two portions. One portion would be given directly to the labourer himself while in Europe and the other would be sent to his family (or other nominated person) in China every month. The amount of these wages was dependent on the actual position and job the labourer held. The lowest–level unskilled labourer was only paid 1 Franc daily, and even the most hard–working never earned more than 5 Francs daily.[112]

After all these formalities were completed, the labourers were organised into quasi–military units. There were fifteen per squad with a leader; three squads formed a platoon; three platoons formed a company; and three companies formed a battalion. Each battalion had a British commander and two interpreters. This done, they commenced daily training in order to improve their stamina, undertaking marching, and other exercises. Once there were sufficient recruits to fill a ship, they embarked on a British or French merchant ship destined for Europe.[113]

Initially the British authorities recruited few labourers in Weihaiwei – there were only 100 recruits up to December 1916.[114] This was partly due to the inability of large ships to anchor alongside the port of Weihaiwei, also the shortage of a reliable rail or road link with the inland cities, but also because of Germany's interference and the Chinese public's opposition to the western recruitment campaign as a result of the Lao Xikai Incident in Tianjin. In order to ensure sufficient labourers, the British envoy suggested, based on a recommendation from the Jinan Consul, John Pratt, that the recruits should be transported by the Jiaoji Railway, then under the Japanese control, from inland locations to Qingdao, then shipped to Weihaiwei by sea.[115] Pratt also suggested appointing missionaries along the railway as recruiting agents within the inland regions. This method proved effective. About one month later, on 18th January 1917, 1,083 Chinese labourers left Weihaiwei for France.[116] Because China protested several times at the Japanese occupation of Qingdao and the Jiaoji Railway, Britain only used Qingdao as a transfer station before March 1917, in order not to offer any excuse for Chinese intervention. However, China broke off diplomatic relations with Germany in March, so Qingdao became an independent depot for exporting labourers and Mr. Pratt was placed in charge of this.[117] The recruiting headquarter was also moved from Weihaiwei to Qingdao in the middle of 1918.[118]

Although the British Government did not inform the Chinese Government in advance about its recruitment activities at Weihaiwei, its actions were still supported secretly by China. In order to aid the allies' recruitment, the Foreign Ministry of the Beiyang Government, on 30th January, 1917, sent confidential letters to governors of coastal provinces and northeast provinces, demanding that the foreign recruitment should be handled only by the local chamber of commerce, and not any Chinese government officials, to avoid objections being raised by the Germans and their allies.[119] When two Britons were arrested by the local authorities because of their recruitment activities outside the Weihaiwei Territory, the Chinese Foreign Ministry immediately requested that they should be freed. Even Mr Bourne, who was in charge of the recruitment, was directly assisted by the Weihaiwei Office of Overseas Chinese Affairs.[120] During that time, in order to encourage China to enter the war earlier, Britain, France and Russia, each signed a secret agreement with Japan to support it in assuming Germany's privileges in Shandong.[121] The Allies also promised China that it would recover its nation status and other rights.[122] China was unaware of these secret deals between the Allies and Japan, but it nevertheless broke off relations with Germany on 14th March, 1917 to ensure that status and those rights. China subsequently joined the Allies and declared war against Germany on 14th August, but its obligations to the war were limited to the supply of raw materials and labourers, which was most useful contribution that China could make to the Allies' war effort in view of the country's poverty and backwardness. After this, the whole of China became an endless source of labourers.

During the First World War, the Allies, including Britain and France, but excluding Russia recruited in all about 150,000 labourers in China,[123] including more than 54,000 labourers who boarded ships in Weihaiwei.[124] These Chinese labourers comprised a great number of poor peasants or the jobless from North China and a few peasants from South China. They had little education and had to sign a contract to earn their living in the distant, strange and war-ridden Europe. A song popular at that time amongst the Chinese labourers revealed their bitterness and

Wage levels for Chinese labourers.

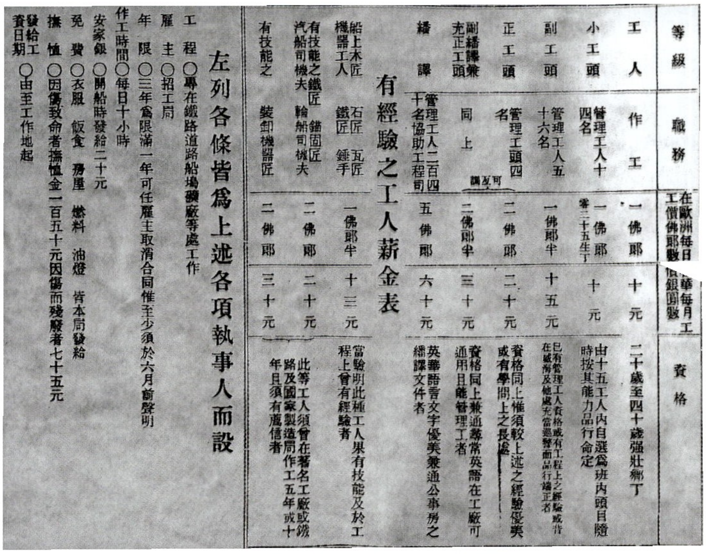

等級	職務	在歐洲每日工價佛郎數	在華每月工價銀圓數	資格
工人	作工	一佛郎	十元	二十歲至四十歲強壯鄉丁
小工頭	管理工人十四名	一佛郎零二十五生丁	十元	由十五工人內自選爲班內頭目隨時按其能力品行命定
副工頭	管理工人五十六名	一佛郎半	十五元	已有管理工人資格或有工程上之經驗或昔在威海及他處充當巡警而品行端正者
正工頭	管理工頭四名（可互調）	二佛郎	二十元	資格同上惟須較上述之經驗優美或有學問上之長處
副繙譯兼充正工頭	同上（可互調）	二佛郎半	三十元	資格同上兼通尋常英語在工廠可通用且能管理工人者
繙譯	管理工人二百四十名協助工程司	五佛郎	六十元	英華語言文字優美兼通公事務之繙譯文件者

有經驗之工人薪金表

船上木匠 機器工人	石匠 瓦匠 鐵匠 錘手	一佛郎半	十三元	當驗明此種工人果有技能及於工程上曾有經驗者
有技能之鐵匠 汽船司機夫	錨固匠 輪船司機夫	二佛郎	二十元	此等工人須曾在著名工廠或鐵路及國家製造局作工五年或十年且須有薦信者
有技能之	裝卸機器匠	二佛郎	三十元	

左列各條皆爲上述各項執事人而設

工程〇專在鐵路道路船塢礦廠等處工作
雇主〇招工局
年限〇三年爲限滿一年可任雇主取消合同惟至少須於六月前聲明
作工時間〇每日十小時
安家銀〇開船時發給二十元
免費〇衣服 飯食 房屋 燃料 油燈 皆本局發給
撫恤〇因傷致命者撫恤金一百五十元因傷而殘廢者七十五元
發給工資日期〇由至工作地起

Newly recruited Chinese labourers. (1917)

sadness in Europe.

The Chinese labourers were at the risk of their lives at all times throughout the long sea journey and while they were in Europe. For example, on 24th February, 1917, the French ship "Athos", loaded with Chinese labourers, was attacked and sunk in the Mediterranean by a German submarine. 543 Chinese labourers lost their lives[125] and the following ships were forced to make a detour. Because it was permitted for the Chinese to be packed in the ships fairly tightly,[126] this made their journey even more arduous, and often some of them could not endure the suffering and committed suicide on the journey by jumping into the sea. After arriving in Europe, the Chinese labourers would be immediately assigned to the most difficult and arduous work. For example, they excavated trenches, loaded and unloaded ammunition and provisions, constructed railways, roads and bridges, made bullets, rescued the wounded, buried the dead and undertook mine clearance. In the severe cold, or under the burning sun, the endless hard labour, the bad wartime living conditions, as well as epidemics of disease, and injuries resulting from their work, caused the lives of these Chinese young people to be of poor quality and frequently threatened. The agreement that they were not supposed to work directly at the front became a mere piece of paper. Zhang Bangyong, the interpreter for No. 13 Battalion, recalled: "The places where we dug trenches were within the range of fire of the enemy, and some points were only 50 yards away from the enemy trenches, so in reality we worked mostly at the front". Sometimes during snowy weather, they would resemble snowmen. After the snow had melted, the mud in the trenches would cover their lower legs, so that during their rest periods they were often forced to sleep standing up. However, the British Officers and machine gunners were comfortable, as their trenches had ceilings, so they could sit or lie down at any time, even play cards.[127] After the war started, modern weapons, especially the bombs from planes threatened the Chinese labourers' lives. They regarded these flying monsters (i.e. planes) in the air, which they had never seen before, as some demons from a Chinese myth. When they first experienced bombing, the Chinese labourers were often frightened out of their wits, and would flee in all directions, so even if they were not killed by explosions, they would be driven insane. Mrs Salle once saw such insane Chinese labourers at Noyelles-sur-Mer near the Somme River where the British headquarters of the Chinese Labour Corps was located. Many years later, she still remembered deeply the sad and shrill cries: "Sinimama, Sinimama"[128] although she never understood what they were crying about.

It was a bitter disappointment that not only must they endure such heavy labour, but the Chinese labourers also had to suffer racial discrimination, a humiliation which they felt deeply. Because Britain and France recruited Chinese labourers to assist them to fight against Germany, those men – especially those recruited by the British – would be placed under military control as soon as they arrived in France. A British Officer, E. Manico Gull, who accompanied the second batch of Chinese labourers to France once observed: "Westerners in China, especially those in the treaty ports, only saw the Chinese from the windows of their offices and clubs, thus, they would tend to regard Chinese labourers as a group of unthinking machines that sought nothing but food and money, and they forgot that they were people who possessed the usual human characteristics of dignity and family affection."[129] Unfortunately, the above opinion was held by most of the British officers who were responsible for the recruitment.[130] Therefore, under their control, Chinese labourers were not allowed to enter various coffee bars,[131] and were even prohibited from using the toilets which were designated for Britons.[132] Their personal freedom was strictly limited, so they were very like prisoners. In the case of any dispute, British officers frequently did not bother to determine right or wrong, but inflicted corporal punishment indiscriminately, even opening fire to suppress unrest.

Studies by a number of scholars have revealed that Chinese labourers under French control obtained better treatment and wages and also more freedom than those under British control. Mr Jiang Ting, an eminent scholar of history, who graduated from Colombia University in America, once worked as an interpreter for Chinese labourers in France during the war. He referred to the British racist attitude with deep feeling: "In my view, Chinese labourers were relatively satisfied with their treatment by the French. Apart

from the difference in the way they were controlled, one main reason was the matter of attitude. The French officers displayed less racial discrimination towards the Chinese labourers than did the British who were always sedulously striving to uphold the white officers' dignity and sense of superiority."[133]

In the memory of Mrs Salle, the degree of British maltreatment and amount of corporal punishment which were inflicted upon the overseas Chinese labourers, were not far behind the later brutalities inflicted by the German Gestapo upon their victims.[134] Many Chinese labourers could not bear their cruel treatment under the British and would flee to the French controlled Chinese labourers' camp. However, the British military authorities didn't consider improving their treatment; instead, they complained that the French were too friendly towards Chinese labourers and strongly urged the French authorities to prevent any contact between the Frenchmen and Chinese labourers.[135] What is more, once the fighting had started, British officers would often disappear without giving any warning to their Chinese labourers, who had no fighting experience. For example, on the eve of Christmas Day in 1917, No. 13 Battalion of Chinese labourers, who were excavating trenches in Arrass, were suddenly attacked by German tanks. When their Chinese interpreters wished to report this to their British officers, they found that all of their officers and overseers had vanished, so the Chinese labourers had to withdraw in confusion by themselves. Upon arriving back at their camp,

Labourers carrying out physical exercises on the beach. (1917)

Chinese labourers on their way to Europe (1917)

they found that the Britons were preparing for bed. Faced with the infuriated Chinese labourers, British headquarters explained that the cause of this incident was their unlucky unit number, so they decided to change it from No. 13 to No. 64 Battalion.[136]

Chinese labourers who had lost their lives were even unworthy of consideration in British eyes. For example, the largest Chinese labourers' cemetery in Europe is located at Noyelles-sur-Mer on the Somme, where some of the fiercest battles had occurred, and where 842 Chinese labourers who were killed during the First World War are buried. Mrs Salle recalled: "At first, they were carelessly buried just like animals and some heads were even left uncovered in the ground because they were buried vertically! Later, the British returned to create the present cemetery in order not to leave a unpleasant impression in the eyes of later generations……"[137]

In order to survive and to cope with this strange environment, and to protect their interests, these lonely Chinese labourers would often attempt to learn a difficult foreign language with the help of their young Chinese interpreters. Many university graduates in the camp were deeply moved by the labourers' remarkable ability to cope with hard work, the way they would help each other during those difficult times, and their strong desire to acquire knowledge. Yan Yangchu, a graduate of Yale University, worked to eliminate illiteracy among Chinese labourers in France at that time. He recalled later that he had planned to go to France to educate Chinese labourers, but unexpectedly he found himself learning from them, which made him realise that the Chinese common people were not incapable of being educated, but had simply been deprived of any education. From that time on, Yan Yangchu began to devote himself to educating the common people and improving the lives of the villagers. As a result, he, together with Einstein and others, was honoured with the title of "The Ten Greatest Revolutionalists of our Time" by the American Congress's Commemoration of the 400th Anniversary of the Death of Copernicus in 1943. Of these ten, he was the youngest and the only Easterner.[138] Of course, Yan Yangchu was not the only talented intellectual working in the Chinese labourers' camps.

In spite of their extremely unfair treatment, thanks to their superior endurance and sacrifices, the Chinese labourers completed their civilian war services and even many combat missions in an extremely severe environment, and paid the price in that more than 20,000 of them were reported killed or missing. Their contribution to Allies' final victory is well worth mentioning. As Dr Xu Guoqi, Assistant Professor of the History Dept, Kalamazoo College, commented: The arrival of 150,000 Chinese labourers at least made it possible for that same number of British and French young people to be released to participate directly in the war at the front. From this point of view, the 150,000 Chinese labourers were equivalent to 150,000 soldiers although they failed to enjoy the same treatment as those soldiers. British and French authorities also spoke highly of the wonderful performance of Chinese labourers. Marshal Ferdinand Foch, Commander-in-Chief of the Allied Forces, praised them in the following words: "Chinese labourers are 'the finest workers in the world and have excellent potential to become soldiers. They can endure any bitterness and finish their tasks guaranteeing both quality and quantity.'" Chinese labourers under British control also performed wonderfully though faced with many problems and with racial discrimination. A Briton, H.R.Wakefield, pointed in his report on the Chinese labourers that every Chinese labourer was "the most versatile person, could endure unendurable pain, work in all weathers, cold or hot; was good at studying, dealt with the various demands of the British Expeditionary Forces with ease". The British War Office also regarded Chinese

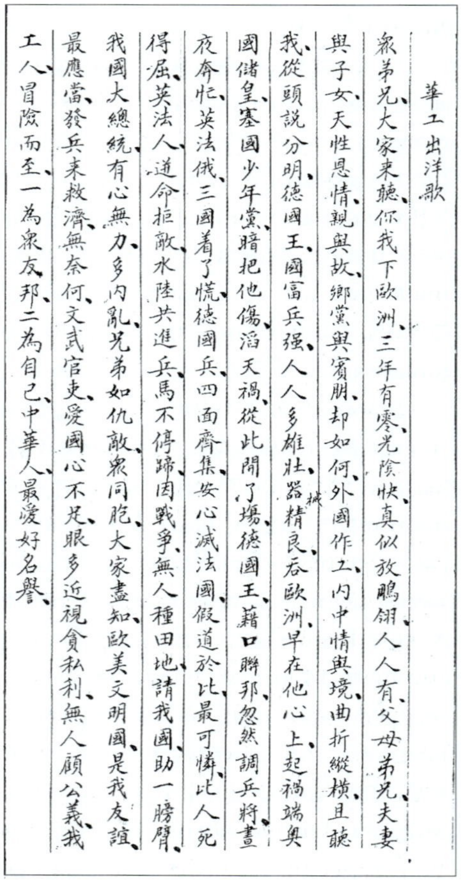
華工出洋歌

衆弟兄、大家来聽、你我下欧洲、三年有零、光陰快、真似放鵰翎、人人有、父母弟兄、夫妻與子女、天性恩情、親與故、鄉黨與賓朋、却如何、外國作工、内中情與境、曲折縱横、且聽我、從頭説分明、德國王、國富兵强、人人多雄壯、器械精良、吞欧洲、早在他心上、起禍端與國儲皇、塞國少年黨、暗把他傷、滔天禍、從此鬧了場、德國王、藉口聯邦、忽然調兵將、晝夜奔忙、英法俄、三國着了慌、德國兵、四面齊集、安心滅法國、假道於比、最可憐、比人死得屈、英法人、道命拒敵、水陸共進兵、馬不停蹄、因戰爭、無人種田地、請我國、助一膀臂、我國大總統、有心無力、多内亂、兄弟如仇敵、衆同胞、大家盡知、欧美文明國、是我友誼、最應當、發兵来救濟、無奈何、文武官吏、愛國心不足、眼多近視、貪私利、無人顧公義、我工人、冒險而至、一為衆友邦、二為自己、中華人、最愛好名譽、

A song written for the Chinese labourers.

The largest cemetery for Chinese labourers at Noyelles-sur-Mer in France. 842 were buried there. In 2002, a public memorial service was held, in which both Chinese and French people took part, the largest ever, when they were regarded as the pioneers of Sino-French relationship by the French government (2002)

labourers as "the best ones" out of all the foreign labourers.[139]

Germany formally surrendered on 11th November, 1918 and the First World War was over. The Allied countries exploded in jubilation. As one of the victorious nations, China also held grand governmental and non-governmental celebrations, and the whole country was gripped with dreams of future prosperity. On 16th November, Lockhart received a special telegram from the Colonial Secretary of State: "On the happy occasion of the cessation of hostilities, I desire to convey to Weihaiwei my congratulations on the successful issue of the struggle and my thanks for the assistance rendered. The Labour Force, recruited through the efforts of the staff at Weihaiwei, has performed services of great value, and the loyal support of the Government by the Chinese community is highly appreciated".[140] Europe was at peace once again. Britain and France and their politicians had succeeded. But what reward was awaiting the Chinese labourers, and their country, who had painfully contributed to that victory, often with their lives?

It was bitterly disappointing that, shortly after the war, the American nurse and writer Ellen N. La Motte should have claimed, to everyone's surprise, that the Chinese labourers had been harmful to the Allied countries because they had brought the Spanish Flu with them to Europe. During the Paris Peace Conference in 1919, Arthur Balfour, Foreign Secretary, in collaboration with the Japanese representative, proclaimed that China had made no contribution to the First World War and it didn't "pay a single shilling or lose a single person" for the war.[141] Moreover, unexpectedly the Western Powers jointly supported Japan's claim to inherit German privileges in Shandong. The Chinese representative Gu Weijun angrily stated: During the war, China sent more than 140,000 labourers to Europe. They were deployed over all the battlefields and fought just like any soldier of the victorious countries, bleeding and sacrificing themselve…… for what? Just in order to win the war and

restore the peace? If the Shandong problem was not settled fairly, thousands of souls would cry out in heaven and the world would still be in disorder, because most of those Chinese labourers came from Shandong.[142]

Ultimately, the Chinese representatives' efforts failed to arouse any sympathy from Britain, France, America or the other powers. This was a world in which no one but oneself could win fair treatment and justice for oneself. The Chinese became completely disillusioned with the Western powers when the news reached China, and this led to the emergence of the May Fourth Movement in 1919 which had epoch-making significance in Chinese history. China finally refused to sign the Peace Treaty, which was the first time it had said "NO!" to the Western Powers. Two years later, the Chinese Communist Party was born and the Chinese destiny was rewritten.

Regarding those Chinese labourers retained in Europe after the end of the war in order to fill the trenches and clear the battlefields, Britain and France sent them back to China as soon as possible on the pretext that they were disturbing local order.[143] These Chinese labourers who had been involved in the many bloody battles in Europe just disappeared from the scene after the last batch of them had boarded ships back to China – but not before they had poured wine over their fallen comrades' tombs. Except for about 3000 Chinese labourers who chose to settle down in France, or elsewhere in Europe, the only trace of those many thousands of men is to be found in the more than ten cemeteries for Chinese labourers scattered throughout France and Belgium. It is most important for a filial son not to abandon his parents

During World War I the allies also purchased large number of horses and mules from the surrounding area of Weihaiwei for the war in Europe. The photo shows the horses together with Chinese labourers waiting for boarding the ships to Europe in the depot at Jinxianding.

and forget his hometown in China. To comply with this requirement, all the Chinese labourers' tombs in Europe faced towards the east. Meanwhile, those Chinese labourers left behind in Europe continued to make a difficult living. They worked hard and some started their own small businesses. They gradually melted into French society thanks to their diligence and persistence. Some of them even re-enlisted in the French army again to fight against Germany during the Second World War. As the earliest Chinese to settle down in the mainland of Europe, they also initiated the history of immigration from China to France. They not only made a significant contribution to the development of France, but also laid the foundation for the participation in the mainstream of French society of those Chinese who arrived later. Over several decades after the war, they and their descendants never stopped fighting for the historical recognition of the participation of the Chinese during the First World War. Thanks to the continuous efforts made by the Chinese people in France, the history of those Chinese labourers during the First World War resurfaced in the minds of ordinary people and gradually attracted the attention of the French public and leading political circles.

On the eve of the Qingming Festival in 2002, the overseas Chinese held the greatest memorial ceremony in the cemetery at Noyelles-sur-Mer for those Chinese labourers who had sacrificed themselves for the victory of the First World War in France. French President Chirac and Premier Jospin sent special letters to show their respect for those Chinese labourers. Chirac wrote: "Nobody will forget these brave warriors that came from far away and shared a common fate with France in a brutal war, they had safeguarded France's territory, ideals and freedom with their own souls and human bodies." France, the earliest major western nation to establish diplomatic relations with New China, had finally acknowledged the Chinese labourers' contribution to France during the First World War. But it was too late for any such acknowledgement to have the slightest practical significance for the deceased. Maybe what would console those dead Chinese labourers, who once led a wretched life far from home, was the statement by Wu Jianmin, the Chinese Ambassador to France, that what might comfort the souls of the deceased was that, compared with their own times, the Chinese people had not only stood up, but moreover their country had made huge progress, which was merely a start, and the future would be even happier.[144]

It is often said that the people who have seen the light should not forget those who fell down in the darkness. Today's people not only have the duty to understand, keep firmly in mind and ponder that phase of history, but also need to carefully examine this modern world and our future from the perspective of those young overseas Chinese workers.

Difficult to realise the dream of a "Second Hong Kong"

4

Fervent hopes followed by disillusionment

As indicated in many historical documents, at the time that the British leased Weihaiwei the fervent hopes of British merchants were greatly stimulated. They were eager to take advantage of Britain's administrative power over Weihaiwei to exploit their commercial advantages. In February 1902, the Times newspaper's comment on this matter represented the attitude of the British merchants of that time: "Just as Hong Kong is the commercial centre of Southern China, it is highly probable that Weihaiwei may become the commercial centre of Northern China. During the early years of the British occupation, Hong Kong used to be deemed as a useless burden. Although it was less useful than Weihaiwei in certain respects, it has become one of the biggest commercial harbours in the world."[1] English newspapers and magazines published in China also held the same view. They all considered the commercial prospects for Weihaiwei to be very bright. Even some of the British colonial officers stationed in Asia were optimistic about the shift in British Policy regarding Weihaiwei that was likened to "a change from Portsmouth to Margate"[2] (i.e. from a naval emphasis to a touristic one). It was under such historical conditions that a number of foreign merchants and companies appeared in Weihaiwei soon after the start of the British lease.

In 1898, a Briton, Duncan Clark, established "D. Clark & Co." on Liugong Island. This was the very first company with foreign capital in modern Weihai. Duncan, the founder of this company, was born in Scotland in November 1856. His father died early, and as a result, Duncan started working while still rather young in order to support his mother. After his arrival in China, he worked in the Chinese Imperial Maritime Customs at Shanghai and Chefoo (now named Yantai). In 1892, he participated in the efforts to rescue the crew of the London Commercial Liner "Stanfield" for which he was awarded the gold 'Sea Gallantry Medal' by the British government. In April of the next year, Duncan married the daughter of Edward Newman, the owner of the 'Family Hotel'. In the same year that the British leased Weihaiwei, Duncan left his job in the Customs and moved

After the British leased Weihaiwei, western merchants started to open import and export businesses in the port area. This effectively ended the embargo on western trade. (1904)

H.D. CHING

his family to Weihaiwei where he gradually founded an independent company for managing commercial trading.

D. Clark & Co. in its early days mainly dealt in supplies for the Royal Navy and colonial officials. With the development of commerce and tourism in Weihai, the company expanded to meet the interests of ordinary people. It invested in tourism, ferry transportation, house building, education, etc. In the 1930s, the management of D. Clark & Co. became more conservative. Except for its involvement in hotels, all its other business basically stopped. During the period of the British lease, thanks to its long experience, its stable relations with the local officials and its management of the postal service as an important government organization, it had occupied an important position in all sorts of economical and social activities within Weihaiwei. Within the area of commerce and trade, D. Clark & Co. was mainly engaged in the export business. It had many shops and storage houses on Liugong Island and in the commercial district of Port Edward. Apart from importing large quantities of general merchandise, it imported materials such as coal. In fact, it was one of the biggest wholesale merchants in coal and foreign goods in Weihaiwei at that time. At the same time, it was the biggest supplier to the navy in Weihaiwei. Especially during every summer, when the British China Fleet came to Weihai for the vacation, this company managed to supply almost everything needed by the fleet. As to the commercial service side, it was the only agent in Weihai for the Hong Kong postal service and managed the post offices both on Liugong Island and in the commercial district of Port Edward, which included the postal business of the whole area. In the sphere of tourism, D. Clark & Co. was the biggest hotel company in Weihaiwei. The Island Hotel was founded on Liugong Island in 1898 and the King's Hotel, which was a mainland hotel and was eventually taken over by D. Clark & Co. (and later renamed the Eastcliff Hotel), were the greatest in size and quality. Additionally, on the island of Liugong, the company owned an aerated water factory that could produce 1500 dozen bottles a day and a bakery that had a capacity of 1000 pounds of

The founder of D. Clark & Co., Mr. Duncan Clark with his wife Anne. (early 20th century)

During the British occupation, merchants from Britain, Korea, the US and Japan came to Liugong Island to open-up various businesses to supply the British forces, which promoted economic prosperity on the island. (1933)

bread an hour. As regards their shipping business, D. Clark & Co. set up a lighter company, which offered the rental of boats both for pleasure and for commercial use, also a company which supplied filtered water to all the ships coming to Weihaiwei. Two piers were built especially for the support of tourism. It was also the earliest company to develop the ferry business plying between Liugong Island and the mainland in Weihai. In addition, the company managed the planting of fruits and vegetables, specializing in foreign varieties, partly for the local market, some for export. In 1904, D. Clark & Co. established a free school called King's School on Liugong Island, teaching Chinese students English and commerce.[3] As the founder of the company and its chief manager, Duncan Clark was very active in various political as well as social circles. He was not only one of the important members of the consultative team advising the colonial government, but was also one of the most influential members of many of the Weihaiwei clubs and entertainment societies.

Lawers & Clark Co. was another well-known company with British capital in modern Weihaiwei. Its founder Ernest Clark also

King's Hotel, near the present East Hill, was the most modern hotel in Weihaiwei, and was run by Astor House, later transferred to D. Clark & Co. The Japanese destroyed it by setting fire to it on 17th August 1945 while withdrawing. (1933)

British naval officer and a Chinese man outside the entrance of the International Savings Society on Liugong Island (1923)

established companies in Shanghai and Hong Kong. After 17th March, 1899, when the Lawers & Clark Co. was founded in Weihaiwei, the development of its business progressed quickly. Its position became more and more prominent. During the period of British rule, it managed part of the economic affairs for the colonial government, almost taking on the role of economic spokesman. The annual reports from the colonial government to the British government were all totally drawn up by this company. In business affairs, Lawers & Clark Co. acted mainly as an agent. Firstly, it was the agent in Weihaiwei for the British Hong Kong and Shanghai Bank, in charge of depositing all sorts of tax–income for the colonial government, paying military expenses to the troops stationed there and supplying banking services to the foreigners who came to Weihaiwei on commercial business or as tourists. Secondly, it was the agent for the maritime business of the Taigu and Blue Chimney Shipping companies, importing foreign cloth, rice, flour, bean–cakes, cigarettes, medicine and other general merchandise, and, in addition, exporting peanuts and peanut oil from Weihaiwei as well as certain marine products such as sea cucumbers and salt fish. Thirdly, it was the agent for official land exchange affairs. At that time, all official property exchange had to go through the Weihaiwei Land Property Co. Ltd. that belonged to Lawers & Clark to obtain the official price and to carry out the related procedures. Fourthly, it was the agent for passenger transportation by sea at Port Edward and also the peanut export business. It formed a barge (or lighter) guild that was respon–

Former premises of the Fock Tai & Co (Fu Tai), agency for foreign goods, founded by Mr. Zhou Tianquan, the manager of the Lawers & Clark Co.

WHWLCO No 23
D. CLARK & Co

D. Clark & Co. at Liugong Island. (1905)

sible for all loading and unloading of goods and determined the charges for such services. Furthermore, it also formed a guild for the export trade in peanuts in order to control the management of this product. Peanuts were the major export of Weihaiwei. Apart from all these agency businesses, Lawers & Clark Co. was the largest industrial company amongst the few such in Weihaiwei. During the early period of British rule, almost all the important buildings in Weihaiwei belonged to this company's Land Property Co. Ltd. Additionally, dozens of Western-style summer vacation homes were built by this company in the seashore areas of Half-moon Bay and Weihai Bay. The company collected the rentals for long or short periods from families or individual tourists.[4]

Apart from commercial and monetary capital, a considerable amount of industrial capital was invested in Weihaiwei during the early period of British rule, particularly investment in mining. In 1898, British merchants had already started to investigate the mineral reserves of Weihaiwei. They analyzed the quality of the minerals there and handed in a "Report on mineral resources in Weihaiwei." In this report, the British merchants thought that there were deposits in the area of gold "of very good quality and in huge quantities" and there were also other minerals present. They requested that the colonial government provide support towards their investigations. This report stimulated the British merchants' passion for exploring for minerals. In the same year, British merchants proceeded to purchase a land of about 6.6 acres along the ridge area of a mountain called Gold Peak to the northwest side of the Fanjiabu Village, with the intention of mining for gold.

In 1903, the government proclaimed "The Weihaiwei Concessions Ordinance No.1 of 1903" concerning mining management, and issued 73 mining permits to British merchants. The British controlled Weihaiwei Gold Mining

Co. Ltd. was formally established in 1902 and started mining along the ridge area of Gold Peak within the same year with a registered capital of US$600, 000 and with all the necessary equipment ready. Their engineering technical personnel were mainly Japanese and Korean, with more than 400 local miners. The yearly production of ore in sand form of ten thousand tons was transported by sea to places such as San Francisco. Due to insufficient capital, the mining company went bankrupt in 1906.

Apart from the above-mentioned foreign companies, there were more foreign companies opened by British, German, and Danish merchants. But other than the British companies, none of these had much success in Weihaiwei, because of their lack of management capital or simply because they were established too late.[5]

Generally, during the period of British rule, foreign companies owned by Western merchants developed rather slowly. There was nothing spectacular in their achievements. Compared with other commercial sea-ports there was insufficient foreign capital moving into Weihaiwei, almost all in the form of commercial capital, with very little industrial and financial capital. Thus "if it is to be reviewed in the future, from the point of view of those involved in Weihaiwei, the British lease period would only have a beginning without

Clearing the mining pit.

any conclusion, and would be a record simply of plans on paper without any concrete actions. It's rather a story of hopeless wishes, delayed endlessly."

Originally, there was an urgency in the British capitalists' intention to make good use of Weihaiwei to expand their commercial rewards. The many advantages they enjoyed in Weihai were vastly superior to those of other commercial ports. But why was the outcome of investment eventually stagnant? The answer could only be discovered by considering the fundamental attitude of the British government's management of Weihaiwei.

At first, the intention of British rule in Weihaiwei was simply to plan and build a modern port in order to keep a military balance with Russia. When this intention proved no longer necessary, many British merchants hoped to be able to develop their businesses in Weihaiwei. But because of the original military intentions the lease of Weihaiwei was without any definite deadline. Thus the expectations of the British merchants became rather vague and uncertain. The motive of the British government in occupying Weihaiwei was to strengthen its influence over the Qing government, thus protecting the overall British position in China. As for Weihaiwei itself, in the eyes of the British government, its role was only that of a "political hostage", nothing but "a useful little pawn on the international conference table." As a result, the British government's attitude greatly influenced the amount of foreign

Grinding ore.

Miners transporting ore. (1904)

capital moving into Weihaiwei.

In modern times, when foreign capital entered into China, foreign merchants made the commercial ports their first choice for their investments. This was mainly because in these ports they could enjoy certain privileges such as long term lease of land, and freedom from taxation. Most importantly, these privileges were also protected by the unequal treaties. However, as for

Later stages in panning for gold. (1904)

Later stages in sieving out gold. (1904)

Weihaiwei, although foreign merchants enjoyed just as many privileges as in the other ports, in the absence of any definite deadline for the lease, such privileges were not at all secure. The question of the deadline became a constant shadow in the minds of foreign merchants during the period of British rule of Weihaiwei. This was especially the case for industrial investors, whose timescales for investment and return on investment were so much longer. This difficulty first arose shortly after the start of British rule.

According to the "Rendition for the Lease of Weihaiwei", the deadline for the British lease of Weihaiwei was only as long as that of the Russians remaining in Port Arthur. Consequently, after the Japanese occupied Port Arthur and expelled the Russians in 1905, foreign merchants in Weihai immediately expressed their worries concerning the future political situation of Weihaiwei. They urged the British government to negotiate with the Qing government to clarity the leasing period so they could invest in Weihaiwei on longer–lasting terms. The Colonial Office, in order to block China's claim for its return, decided to make Weihaiwei a subordinate of Hong Kong.

The British Hong Kong government was required to make preparations for the hand over. Not long afterwards, the Chinese requested the return of Weihaiwei as anticipated. The British Foreign Office considered the decision of the Colonial Office would cause great international anger which might even affect more important considerations than those of keeping Weihaiwei. As a result, the British Foreign Office decided not to make any change. Certainly nothing was done to clarify the deadline of the lease. The vagueness of its terms might well allow for more alternative choices for future action. The Colonial Office consequently gave up its original plan, but offered an answer that puzzled all the foreign merchants: "The British government considers that the British lease of Weihaiwei will not or cannot be influenced by the current affairs in the Far East." However, according to the lease conditions, unless both China and Britain could agree to revised conditions, Weihaiwei would definitely be affected by the Russian action of giving up Port Arthur and Dalian. On 24th March, 1906, all the foreign merchants signed an appeal to the colonial government, requesting the British government to make up its mind regarding its attitude towards Weihaiwei, and asking the British government to promise to bear any losses in case of any damage to investments caused by the return of Weihaiwei.

On 18th December of the same year, the Colonial Department's response was quite clear-cut: the British government would not discuss any hypothetical situations. Whatever happened in the future, there would be no way in which they would be prepared to bear the losses of those who had invested in Weihaiwei. This response clearly implied that the British government would not support any foreign merchant who had invested in Weihaiwei. From then on, British merchants in China halted investment in Weihaiwei. Those few factories which were already opened for business closed one after the other. Some foreign merchants withdrew their capital from Weihaiwei. Only a few foreign companies that were engaged in trading still carried on with any enthusiasm, hoping that more favourable times might come eventually.

In 1919, during the Peace Conference in Paris, the Chinese representatives put forward their rightful requests to claim for the return of the leased lands from all the big powers. First of all they wished to get back from Germany, a defeated nation, all its privileges in Shandong. This made the foreign merchants who had invested in Weihaiwei feel uneasy again. They thought this would have an impact on the future of Weihaiwei. Once again, they hoped that Britain and China would revise the lease according to the Sino-Japanese "Treaty of South Manchuria" signed in 1915, with its related regulations, to prolong the leasing of Weihaiwei to 99 years. The foreign merchants once again appealed to the British government, together with the request for the government to bear the losses in case any changes happened. Of course they did not get any satisfactory response. It was during the later Washington Conference that the British, after weighing the benefits and losses, formally decided to return Weihaiwei to China. Both sides soon started negotiations. This caused the Western merchants and foreign companies' tiny glimmer of hope to become thoroughly extinguished. From then on, the economy of Weihaiwei gradually declined.

The beginning of national business and the expansion of foreign trade

The time during which Weihaiwei was leased to the British, was the period during which national capitalism was starting to develop in China. After the first Sino–Japanese War, the Qing government began to put into effect business strategies, and encouraged the development of national industry. The financial strategy changed quickly from a state of "making do" to one of "seeking wealth". At this time a number of Chinese entrepreneurs started to "build factories to advance themselves", and "to seek prosperity through business" was a highly popular topic. This "self–help in seeking prosperity" exercise, that eventually involved the whole country, took the first difficult step towards capitalism. This resulted in the continual emergence of entrepreneurs. Most of these businesses consisted of developments from traditional manual industries. Even though they were few in number, and not big in size, nevertheless they represented the birth of a new economic power. This represented a new beginning in Weihaiwei, the start of the long process of transformation from a traditional farming industry into contemporary commercial enterprises.

At that time, the textile trade became the earliest and the most developed public capitalist industry. Traditionally, Weihai women were capable of employing numerous different techniques of embroidery for various types of decorative items. After the British invasion and the leasing of Weihaiwei, nuns from Roman Catholic Church organised women into weaving lace trimmings and embroidery. From then on, the imported art of lace weaving was merged with Weihai's traditional embroidery, and eventually developed into a specialised industry, with its own unique style. From 1912, after Chong Shuhan had established the Yifeng embroidery factory, other national embroidery factories began to follow suit. By 1927, there were about 12 such factories. Businesses that specialised in hair nets for export took off in 1913. Chinese hair was sent to Germany for special treatment, and was then imported back to Weihai to be made into hair nets for export. During the first half of the 20th century, this business was at its peak. According to statistics, by 1921 the number of women involved in this business reached 623 and the value of the export of hair–nets reached HK$70.78 million. The cloth manufacturing industry began to develop also. In 1919, there were 8 silk manufacturing factories throughout the whole region. They possessed 80 machines for the weaving of cloth and boasted an annual production of 7000 pieces of cloth. In 1928, Zhu Xiru established the Yongzeng cloth manufacturing factory outside the north gate of the walled city. He had 20 wooden weaving machines and was considered one of the largest cloth manufacturers.[6]

In 1928, Ping Chengli and other persons of the Yantai Changxing Match Company formed a partnership with businessmen Wang Yingzhi from Liu village in Weihaiwei, to form the Dewei Match factory. In 1930, its construction was completed in the north part of Weihaiwei with a capital of $4 million. It manufactured brands such as "Xianlu" and "Taiji" matchsticks. The production facilities were imported from Japan. About 70.168 million boxes were produced daily and were sold widely from Jiaodong Peninsula to the three North–east provinces in China. It became the main match supplier to these areas. It broke the monopoly of foreign match makers. However, after the establishment of the puppet Manchurian government, the factory

Fruit stalls in front of the Royal Naval Canteen. Liugong Island (1937)

Girls in the countryside making embroidery for export to Europe. (1930s)

started to face a loss in profits and gradually went downhill.[7]

The manufacture of soy sauce and vinegar was gradually transformed from production as a family business into small factory production. There were ten factories in total and among these, the Yuan Xindong Sauce Factory was a big production company set up by Dong Baiyong in 1918. The products from his factory were well-known far and wide, and not only were they popular in Shanghai, Tianjin, Dalian, Hong Kong and Macao, they were also exported to Korea, Japan, Singapore and the Philippines.

In June 1929, Meng Zhaoqian and some others from Weihaiwei established the Zhong Wei Rubber factory outside the East Gate. It was the biggest machinery business in Shandong at the time, and was also the oldest rubber industry in the Province. Its main products were "Twin Lion Ball" Wellingtons and gym shoes. It produced more than 200,000 pairs a year and these were sold within the Jiaodong area and the other three northern provinces.[8]

At the end of 1920's, two small power plants appeared. One was the Nightless Power Ltd, which was situated in the walled city of Weihaiwei. It was set up by Qi Xiaotian in 1926. This power plant had one 15h.p. diesel engine and one 7,000kW generator. It could only supply a limited amount of electricity to certain parts of the walled city.

Another power plant was Guangming Power Ltd at Port Edward. It was established on the 23rd of March 1929. The chairman was Li Yizhi, and Sun Xintian its general director. Power was mainly supplied to Port Edward. The total installed capacity reached 310kW, and the transmission line was 75km long. This power generation was essentially for domestic lighting, two cinemas and one cotton factory.[9]

These modern national industrial enterprises in Weihaiwei developed slowly. The level of investment was small, the equipment simple and crude, and the technology not very advanced. The products were not of the highest quality. One of the main reasons for these problems was the limited experience of business practice and also a severe shortage of funds. Due to the colonial government's maintenance of traditional systems, small-scale peasant production and the feudal system remained stable. This feudal economic relationship severely impeded government and private funds from moving into the development of modern industrial enterprises. Land, money lending at a high rate of interest and commerce had for a long time been the primary areas of investment for wealthy people in Weihaiwei. At that time, nearly all the industrialists and businessmen were also landlords. Regardless of whether they were rich businessmen or ordinary people, once they obtained money, they would purchase land. It was very difficult to persuade local people to accept new concepts, unless they were able to profit from them immediately.

Compared with industrial enterprises, trade was flourishing.

At the beginning of the British occupation of Weihaiwei, local industry and commerce did not flourish, and transportation was poor. However, following the example of Hong Kong's free port system, the British declared

Carpentry workshop. (1917)

A salt storage area near the port. (1904)

it would open up Weihaiwei to other countries, imposing duties on neither imports nor exports.

Weihaiwei's free port status attracted plenty of foreign businessmen. They arrived to do business. The number of enterprises at Port Edward increased to 700 at its peak. In the walled city, more than 200 shops were established. After 1909, due to the increase in exported products from Port Edward, foreign shipping and financial agencies moved from their original base on Liugong Island. These firms were primarily interested in import and export, though some were involved in trading seafood, shipping, cigarettes, wine, groceries and tourism. Several firms with abundant funds opened up new branches in Hong Kong, Tianjin and Dalian. The main exports were agricultural and sideline products. The main imports were flour, cotton yarn, rice, kerosene, cigarettes and leather. These imports mostly came from Europe, America, Japan, Southeast Asia and Hong Kong.[10]

With the development of the import and export trade and the entrepot trade, Weihai's traditional businesses, such as farming and fishing, began to serve the needs of foreign trade, thus resulting in a steady improvement in their commercialization.

During this period, there was a big increase in the export of peanuts. In 1918, the volume of peanut exported amounted to 40% of the export trade. This increase led to the expansion of the planting area. Until 1928, peanut planting in the whole region reached about 6500 acres, amounting to 13% of the total farming area. Before 1914, the main buyer of peanuts originated from Hamburg in Germany. Subsequently, all peanuts were transported via

Roadside repair shop that fixed everything. (1902)

Metal-worker, his specialty was repairing woks. (1902)

Hong Kong into Europe. However, this trade was under the monopoly control of foreign firms. Until 1922, the peanut industry guild, which was organized by the British company Lawers & Clark consisted of 92 members. They were not only responsible for setting the standards of package weights, trading dates, but were also accountable for supervising peanut quality inspection and foreign sales.

The fishing industry flourished due to the great demand of seafood, and it became an industry second only to farming. In the earlier days, fishing was reliant on sailing boats. However in 1925, the Weihai Fishing Industry purchased wooden fishing vessels with diesel engines, and began to fish using motor-driven vessels for the first time. By 1929, there were 21 motor-driven vessels. Rich fishing resources and a good environment for trade also enticed fishermen from surrounding regions According to the statistical records for 1929, 227 wooden sailing boats were locally licensed, but 1139 sailing boats and 9 diesel vessels originated from other regions.

In order to meet the demands for export, the technology for salting fish and freezing fish became much improved. Most seafood was dried, preserved or frozen, and was then transported to Shanghai, Tianjin or Hong Kong. The number of firms dealing with the purchasing, selling and processing of sea food had reached more than 50 by 1930.

The increase of the shipping trade stimulated the rapid development of sea transportation. In 1902, there were only 146 ships of 151,809 tons moving in

A flour mill developed by the Yimin Mill company. (1926)

An indoor market of fresh produce in Port Edward. (1902)

and out of the region of Weihaiwei. However, by 1929, the total tonnage had increased to 1,307,015 tons, with 1139 ships.

These ships belonged to approximately 20 countries, from Europe, America and Asia. The income for the colonial government increased from ¥1,067 in 1903 to ¥210,558 by 1929. Shipping taxes became the biggest source of revenue for the colonial government.[11]

Over this period, Weihaiwei's financial sector became developed as well.

The goods yard in Port Edward. (1908)

A Chinese tailor's shop on Liugong Island. (1938)

A silk firm founded by Yantai merchants in Weihaiwei. (1902)

A market at Port Edward. (1933)

Street trader at Liugong Island. (1924)

Soon after the British occupation of Weihaiwei, the HSBC and Macaulay banks set up branches in Weihaiwei. Foreign firms in Weihai acted as agents for these branches. At that time, currencies circulating in the Weihai market included silver dollars, copper dollars, Mexican eagle dollars, paper money from foreign banks, and banknotes issued by Shanghai and Tianjin. There was also an abundance of banknotes emanating from local, traditional Chinese private banks.

In 1888, the Qing Army stationed in Weihaiwei began to establish banks in the walled city. These dealt with the salaries of soldiers and provided basic banking services. From that time, Weihaiwei's Chinese banks had started to increase in importance. After Britain leased and occupied Weihaiwei, these private banks continued to be influential.

Within the leased territory, the old and new banking systems existed side by side, causing currency chaos which affected business. This situation improved only after the chamber of commerce was established to sort things out. The earliest professional bank in Weihai was the Weihai Agriculture

Market day. (1935)

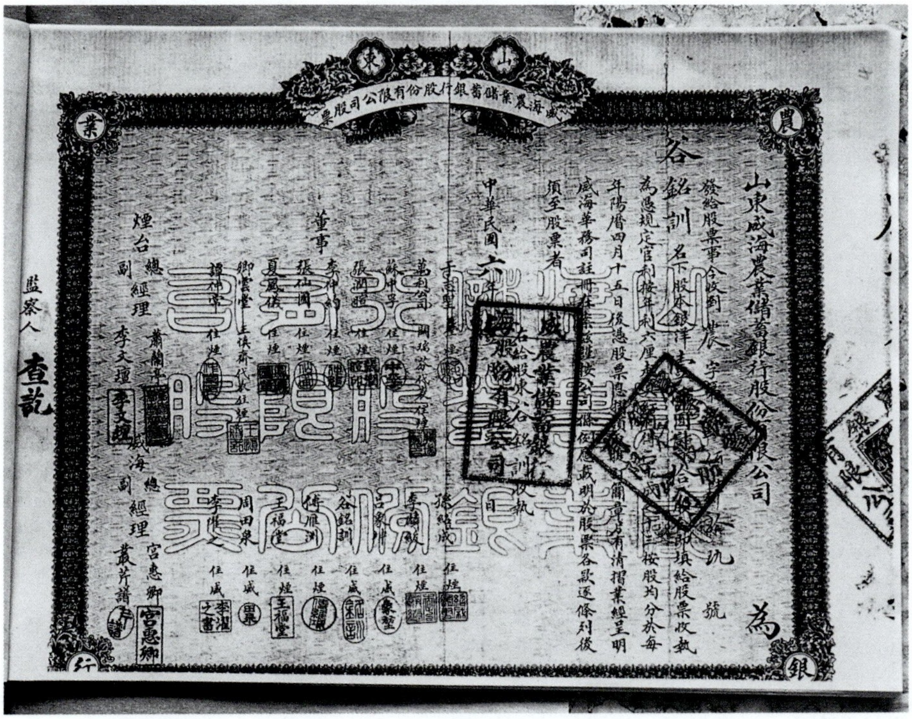

Share certificate for the Weihaiwei Agricultural Savings Bank.

Savings Bank, which was established in 1915 by Lin Siting, Gong Huiqing and twenty other leading citizens, who raised capital by floating shares. They set up a branch in Yantai. As a result of two reforms in 1916 and 1917, its total capital multiplied from ¥100,000 to ¥250,000. It used British sterling as the standard rate and dealt with the collection, saving, loaning, and issuing of paper currencies. In 1925, as a result of the inability of the branch in Yantai to cope with a sudden massive withdrawal of funds, the bank was unable to continue operations.

The entrepot trade that had been developed to support the free trade policy remained prosperous for a while, but due to the lack of strong support from manufacturing industry, it became too dependent on the world market, domestic and foreign political situations and financial instability as time went on. Any external disturbance or trouble became a threat to Weihaiwei. The victims were not only business firms but also the ordinary people, who suffered most directly. This illustrated the weakness of a single transit port economy.

Tourism prospers

The tourist industry in Weihaiwei prospered rapidly after the lease to Britain. It developed into an ideal holiday resort in the eyes of Europeans. During the end of spring and the beginning of summer, Weihaiwei became a lively location to which tourists from far and wide flocked looking for their favourite forms of entertainment and to enjoy its sunshine, and natural beauty. There were many attractions, both natural and man-made which encouraged Weihaiwei's transformation from a military port into a holiday resort.

Traditionally, Weihaiwei was renowned for its extraordinary landscapes and enchanting sights, as well as for its perfect weather conditions. Due to

Hunting was popular with the British in the countryside of Weihaiwei. (1902)

its proximity to the ocean, it was warm in spring, cool in autumn, not excessively hot in the summer and there was no merciless cold weather in winter as in other inland places. Many Britons full of colonial dreams were enchanted by the excellent weather conditions.

In 1902, Mr C. E Bruce–Mitford of Weihaiwei School, late English Master and Lecturer in Classics at the Queen Elizabeth Grammar School and the Municipal Technical School, Blackburn, Lancs, had written in his book entitled "The Territory of Weihaiwei" that "Weihaiwei is universally acknowledged to possess a climate of the first order. Naval and military experts differ as to its value as a place of arms; politicians have wrangled over its commercial potentialities, but one and all are agreed as to the excellence of its climate... there is no time of the year when its climate is not invigorating and agreeable, and there is no reason why it should not be frequented as a health resort all the year round"[12] In a report of the colonial government, it was suggested that: "Weihaiwei's weather is second to none, it is one of the best places in the world for perfect weather, and possesses the potential for the development of tourism as well as being the best place for establishing homes for convalescence for the people from Britain".

Realizing that Weihaiwei was a unique location for tourism and convalescence, the British navy constructed on Weihaiwei as well as on Liugong Island various forms of entertainment and facilities for convalescence. In 1927, the British army stationed in Shanghai constructed convalescent

Bathing huts on the beach at Liugong Island. (1910)

Lockhart and Johnston accompanying Mr. Yang Shixiang, the visiting Governor of Shandong, to Baoquantang Spa (Japanese-owned) in Weihaiwei on 11th July 1905.

A poster advertising the Queen's Hotel in Weihaiwei.

British naval officers in the walled city of Weihaiwei. (1924)

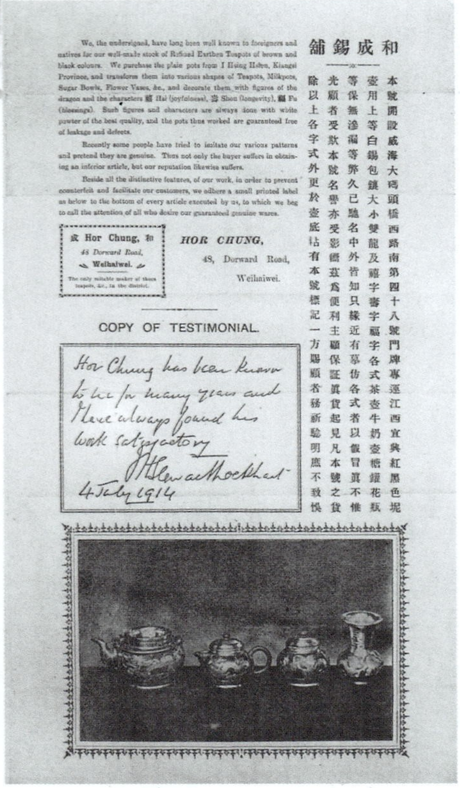

和成錫舖

本號開設威海大碼頭橋西路南第四十八號門牌專運江西宜興紅黑色坭壺用上等白錫包鑲大小雙龍及囍字壽字福字各式茶壺牛奶壺糖鑵花瓶等保無滲漏等弊久已馳名中外皆知只緣近有摹仿各式者以假冒眞不惟光顧者受欺本號名譽亦受影響茲爲便利主顧保証眞貨起見凡本號之貨除以上各字式外更於壺底粘有本號標記一方賜顧者務祈驗明庶不致悞

We, the undersigned, have long been well known to foreigners and natives for our well-made stock of Refined Earthen Teapots of brown and black colours. We purchase the plain pots from I Hsing Hsien, Kiangsi Province, and transform them into various shapes of Teapots, Milkpots, Sugar Bowls, Flower Vases, &c., and decorate them with figures of the dragon and the characters 囍 Hai (joyfulness), 壽 Shou (longevity), 福 Fu (blessings). Such figures and characters are always done with white pewter of the best quality, and the pots thus worked are guaranteed free of leakage and defects.

Recently some people have tried to imitate our various patterns and pretend they are genuine. Thus not only the buyer suffers in obtaining an inferior article, but our reputation likewise suffers.

Beside all the distinctive features, of our work, in order to prevent counterfeit and facilitate our customers, we adhere a small printed label as below to the bottom of every article executed by us, to which we beg to call the attention of all who desire our guaranteed genuine wares.

成 Hor Chung, 和
48 Dorward Road,
Weihaiwei.
The only reliable maker of these teapots, &c., in the district.

HOR CHUNG,
48, Dorward Road,
Weihaiwei.

COPY OF TESTIMONIAL.

Hor Chung has been known to me for many years and I have always found his work satisfactory
4 July 1914

A local advertisement for pewter earthenware made by the Hor Chung company. (1920s)

homes in Weihaiwei. Apart from the British, fleets from other countries also anchored at Weihai to convalesce. Diplomatic officials and other foreigners, including businessmen, frequented Weihaiwei for vacations too.

To meet the demands of all these British and foreign tourists, Weihaiwei reinforced, preserved and improved its environment as well as its entertainment facilities.

After 1914, a large-scale forestry project was begun in Weihaiwei with the planting of many trees. The colonial government imported different trees and flowers from Japan, America, Germany, Canada and so on. There were species such as black pine, locust tree, French parasol, American poplar, silver pine, and flowers such as roses. Most of these plants were cultivated on Liugong Island and around the docks. However, the largest amount of tree planting took place on Liugong Island, and in only 10 years, from 1907–1917, more than 3,000,000 trees were planted there. Public hygiene and ecological protection became a matter of concern. The building of factories and shops that might cause pollution was forbidden. At the same time, the disposal of sewage into the surrounding sea and onto its beaches was prohibited. In 1907, "The Wild Birds and Game Preservation Ordinance" became effective and periods of hunting were being restricted and it was necessary to apply for permits for hunting. Besides, colonial government and the army established various sports and entertainment facilities which enriched the

Two European girls boating near the beach. (1918)

In front of the King's Hotel. (1920's)

lives of tourists.

In order to satisfy the needs of tourists in Weihaiwei, the service industry was expanded. Businessmen such as Sun Qinxuan, Gu Shanyi, and 50 others, collaborated in the setting up of the Weihai Club for tourism. Gradually more than 30 businesses had been established, such as the Donghai restaurant, the Weihai Hotel, Qingho Lou, Anleyuan, Xinheju and other restaurants. The King's Hotel was the biggest, grandest hotel and was owned by Mr. Duncan Clark. This hotel was situated in the convalescent area in the eastern hill region. It possessed 80 big bedrooms, and also had such facilities as a pool room, tennis court, ice–making room and other attractions, such as a pro–

A picnic on the beach (1921)

fessional band which would entertain guests with performances of western music. The hotel could also ferry guests between the eastern hill and Liugong Island. This hotel became the most popular meeting place for high ranking British officers and important guests. Not only did the government establish facilities on Liugong Island, but businessmen from 11 other countries and regions were granted special permission to set up hotels, restaurants and other businesses to provide for British officers. The Island Hotel which was built in 1900 by the D. Clark & Co. became the most prestigious hotel. Photographic businesses developed rapidly as well. In 1918, the Shanghai Zhaofang Photo Studio established two branches, in Port Edward and on Liugong Island. Flourishing business led to the opening of another two photo studios – Yifang and Datong.

The flourishing tourist industry triggered handicraft production as well. During that time, silver, alloy, tin inlaid products and models of sailing boats etc, proved so popular that they were also exported. Products that were of cultural interest, especially those tin inlaid products and the delicately carved wooden boats, were popular with foreigners. The craft of making tin–inlaid products started at the end of the Qing Dynasty, and their development was the result of British peoples' appreciation and purchase. In the beginning, craftsmen only produced teapots whose lip was inlaid with tin alloy as the British adored these, but this later developed into the use of tin–alloy casting, forging, engraving, and welding into all kinds of patterns, and inlaying these within various

Souv

English schoolboys visiting Weihaiwei for the summer. (1921)

Visiting European church school children meeting up with children from the local Catholic Boys School. (1940)

ceramic products. The last stage involved polishing them to produce exquisite artifacts. Foreign merchants and tourists in Weihaiwei began to purchase these artifacts in bulk. Weihaiwei thus became renowned for producing tin inlaid products and this was the period during which this art reached its peak. The carving of wooden ship was a speciality of Qi Qingsu and others, pioneers in this craft, whose shops were situated at Port Edward. They employed more than 30 people. Following this, Dongya, Taihua, Wenhua, Baolong and other firms also began business in this trade. In the early days, most artifacts were models of small sailing boats, and apart from supplying these to tourists, some were sold to fishermen or ocean liners that used them to bless the "Dragon King" and "Queen of Heaven" to ensure their safety. The perfection of this art and the increasing demand encouraged these businessmen to produce models of other types of craft, including cruisers, speed boats, and submarines. These artifacts became most popular with the tourists.

Another tourist attraction was hot spring baths. Weihai's hot springs were discovered during the Song Dynasty. These hot springs contained positive sodium (Na) and chlorine (Cl), radioactive and trace elements. Mineral springs were a rarity along the China Sea. They had therapeutic effects on patients suffering from anxiety, poor digestion, problems with the heart and blood vessels and breathing, as well as skin problems. After the Sino-Japanese war, Weihaiwei was occupied by the Japanese who utilized these hot springs by extending them into pools. When the British leased Weihaiwei, the Health Authority in Hong Kong conducted a detailed investigation into the beneficial effects of these hot springs. Their curative effects were confirmed. After 1903, with the agreement of the British colonial authority, Japanese businessmen began to develop these hot springs on a large scale. They imported building materials from Japan, and they adopted a Japanese style in their construction of hot spring pools. These were luxuriously decorated for the exclusive usage of Europeans.

The growth of the Chamber of Commerce

The Chamber of Commerce was established by the Qing government in 1903 for the development of industry and commerce. In the following year, "A Simplified Agenda for the Chamber of Commerce" was issued, which stipulated that branches of the Chamber of Commerce should be established at all local levels, including those of provinces, districts, and counties. Thanks to the support from local government at all levels, Chambers of Commerce soon spread throughout the whole nation.

Responding to this nationwide popularity, businessmen in Weihaiwei began to set up their own commercial organizations. In 1906 Mr Sun Fushan united more than 80 shops and set up the "Dock Commerce Society" in which he assumed the position of Chairman. However the society employed only traditional methods, which resulted in a lack of communication between its members. There were too many failings and its organizational abilities and activities, as well as its influence on society, were very limited. Thus whenever Weihai businessmen negotiated with modern commercial organizations, they could never do so from a position of strength. Local businessmen finally realized that it was necessary to be united as an organization in order to protect their own interests. This realization enabled them to adopt modern ways of conducting their business and to establish a modern Chamber of Commerce. Under the influence of Mr Sun Fushan, Mr Gu Mingxun, etc, the Dock Commerce Society was officially re-established as the "Port Edward Chamber of Commerce" in July 1916, with 20 board members at its head, who were elected by its members. The leaders were initially known as Minister and Deputy-Minister, but these titles were subsequently changed to Chairman and Vice-Chairman. Mr Sun was the first Chairman and he was succeeded by Gu Mingxun, Li Yizhi, Sun Xintian,

A notification from the Chinese Chamber of Commerce announcing the reforming of the financial market. (1910)

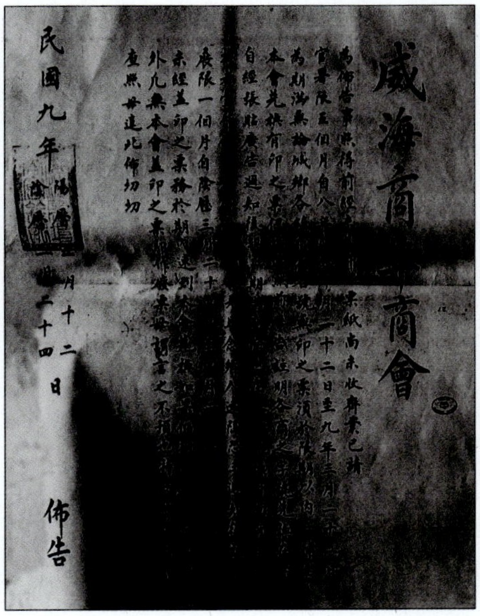
威海商會
民國九年
佈告

and so on. After the City Commerce Society was established, other professional associations began to follow suit, such as an "Association for the Hotel Industry", a "Guild for the Fishing Industry", a "Tailor's Society" and so on. At the same time, Weihai city also set up the "Walled City Chamber of Commerce". After Weihaiwei was returned to China in 1930, these two organisations merged into one which was named the "Weihaiwei Chamber of Commerce".

The Port Edward Chamber of Commerce motivated the development of Weihaiwei in both economic and social directions by uniting diverse businesses into a single organisation.

The foremost tasks for the Port Edward Chamber of Commerce were to reorganise businesses and to rectify certain improper guild regulations to encourage the prosperity of the economy. Due to inadequate business regulations, banknotes were being issued recklessly and this became a very serious problem. According to the statistics of 1910, about 119 companies who had been authorized to issue banknotes needed to be investigated. "Small businesses that were recklessly issuing banknotes caused the depreciation of these notes as they became worthless and lost credibility. It became a common occurrence for many of the businesses which issued banknotes to face bankruptcy. This affected the credibility of banknotes as well as damaging the interest of the public". So in 1917, the Port Edward Chamber of Commerce issued rules and regulations to "systematize banknotes, maintaining order in the public domain" and also produced "precise rules for the issuing of banknotes". According to these "precise rules", businesses issuing banknotes must possess certain prerequisites such as capital and collateral security or other forms of guarantee. There was required to be a judicious match between the number of banknotes issued and the actual business capital, and in addition, a certain fee had to be paid to the Chamber of Commerce to receive its official seal of approval to be allowed to operate. With the adoption of these procedures, the Chamber of Commerce became responsible for all the financial risks that might befall its members. Soon after, the Chamber of Commerce brought out its "business rules" and other regulations, and continued to perfect these rules. The rules and regulations set up by the Chamber of Commerce brought a positive boost to Weihaiwei's economic progress.

A great deal of effort was put into protecting the interests of local businesses. In the Committee's "regulations", it was declared that the Committee would take as its motto: we "act as an intermediary in disputes between two parties". Within the Committee, there were evaluation and accounting departments to elucidate commercial discrepancies and disputes related to money matters. In order to protect the interests of businesses, the Committee established an "Investigation Department" especially to inspect and study the daily activities in the realm of business. If they discovered any

Opening ceremony of the Victory Pier built with financial support from the Chinese Chamber of Commerce. (18th November 1918)

"improper and unfair behaviour", the Chamber of Commerce would automatically act as arbitrator. In August of 1925, the Chamber of Commerce established a new department called the "Business Arbitrator" and also produced the "Accounting Management Regulations" to assist in the resolution of disputes in a more uniform fashion. According to historical records from the period that Weihaiwei was leased by the British, most business disputes were dealt with by the Port Edward Chamber of Commerce and hardly any went before the Courts. To protect businessmen's interests the Chamber of Commerce played a positive role. For instance in 1924, when Weihaiwei's fishing industry was threatened by unlawful fishing boats from other areas, this Committee hired boats at its own expense to patrol and provide protection after failing to receive any assistance from the Colonial Government. When the Colonial Government perceived that the salt business was prospering and wanted to increase its taxes, the Chamber of Commerce immediately negotiated with the Colonial Government to protect the interests of the salt industry. The Chamber of Commerce protected the interests of local businesses by

In honour of Lockhart prior to his retirement, a stone tablet was erected by the Chinese Chamber of Commerce for his beneficiary policies. (1921)

Members of the Chinese Chamber of Commerce. (1930s)

restricting the expansion of foreign companies. Take the electrical industry for instance: the British company Lawers & Clark Co. had been authorized to invest in electricity in Weihaiwei but the Chamber of Commerce objected strongly and threatened not to use their electricity. This led to the withdrawal of the special agreement between the colonial government and Lawers & Clark Co. In 1928, at the instigation of the Chamber of Commerce Committee, a national electricity company known as Guangming Power Ltd was established.

Thanks to the rapid growth of the economy, the Chamber of Commerce's activities expanded. They became involved in public services, becoming the main investor in education, municipal works and charitable work, and sponsored and participated in all kinds of important social reforms. For instance, the Chamber of Commerce raised a significant amount of money known as the "Gulf Construction Fund" to construct the largest Victory Pier in Weihaiwei, also the excellent Johnston Road, and the installation of the first street lights. As for education, the Chamber of Commerce instituted a modern system of teaching and was involved in the construction of the first girls' school in Weihaiwei, known as the Shude Girls' School. They sponsored the construction of the first secondary school, Qidong Middle School, and independently started a night school for the public, to promote education, create a new social environment, and obliterate backward customs such as the binding of feet and opium smoking. To this end they set up the "Natural Feet Association" and the "Give up Smoking Centre".

Another important task for the Chamber of Commerce was the implementation and promotion of charitable activities. One of the most important charity acts was the provision of help to people suffering from natural disasters. In 1920, due to continuous drought, about 40,000 people were threatened by starvation. In order to protect these people from death, the

Members of a charitable organization founded and financed by the Chinese Chamber of Commerce.

Port Edward Chamber of Commerce, together with the village elders took on the tremendous task of rescuing the sufferers. With the assistance of the Colonial Government, they succeeded in developing a relief centre, aided by Chinese and foreign businessmen in Weihaiwei. Telegrams were sent, donations were sought and food was collected. A remarkable degree of support was received from both international and national charitable organizations in which money and materials were generously donated. In particular, the Hong Kong Chinese Commerce Society and the Donghua Hospital donated up to 11, 000 American dollars. The provincial government also exempted all relief crops from taxes. The statistics show that, during this calamity, approximately 65,730 American dollars were received to protect the livelihood of 10, 000 victims for four months free of charge, and about 30,000 victims received relief payments. This assisted nearly every victim in the territory and was considered a great achievement at that time.

After the 1920s, the power and influence of the Port Edward Chamber of Commerce was renowned and had spread throughout all aspects of social life and became a very important force in society. The Port Edward Chamber of Commerce took part in politics and played a very extraordinary role at the time. Due to the Chamber of Commerce's activities in industry, commerce, municipal works and charities, the colonial government's financial expenditure was reduced. So the colonial government supported the Committee in its policies encouraging the development of industry and commerce. The Chamber of Commerce's involvement in politics brought about changes, especially in the colonial government's economic policy making. However, they could merely act as consultants in the political sphere, and the main decision maker was still the colonial government. For this reason, the Chamber of Commerce's political career did not run as smoothly as it hoped. For instance, during the May 4th Student Movement (1919), the Chamber of Commerce wanted to

Members of the Chinese Chamber of Commerce marking Armistice Day. (1927)

maintain law and order within the Territory, and proposed to recruit local factory workers, shop assistants, etc to form a militia group. The Chamber of Commerce would provide funding for the purchase of weapons as well as for military training. The colonial government accepted their proposal, but refused to allow the Chamber of Commerce to exercise any control over this military group. In 1922, the Chamber of Commerce criticized the over-centralized system and made demands for autonomy, but this was rejected. The Chamber of Commerce continuously met with refusals in response to their pleading, for example for an increase in the provision of public expenditure. It is obvious that the aim of the colonial government's support for the Chamber of Commerce was purely to assist the government itself and its own interests, rather than granting much political power to the Chamber of Commerce. Once the Chamber of Commerce showed signs of becoming stronger than the government expected, the British authorities would adopt all kinds of measures to obstruct and suppress it. However, the Chamber of Commerce, as representatives of national industry, in spite of its conflicts with the colonial government, still had close relations with that government in the realm of politics and economics. Most of the top personnel in the Chamber of Commerce had had dealings with foreign businesses and agencies in the past. In reality, they were merely hoping that the colonial government would be more open-minded in their rule, so that the Chamber of Commerce could become involved in policy making as a means of protecting its own interests. Thus, it was necessary for them to rely upon foreign investment and colonial authority. Whenever the colonial authority tried to interfere in the activities of the Chamber of Commerce, the response was to compromise.

Ripples in stagnant water: Western ideas spread into Weihaiwei society

5

A blend of Eastern and Western cultural activities

A Christmas dance at the at the Theatre on Liugong Island held by the British Navy and expatriates (1908)

Ever since the British leasing of Weihaiwei, there had been several changes to festivals and customs in the area. Some British annual customs were adopted in Weihaiwei. These became gradually systematized. According to an ordinance proclaimed by the colonial government in 1903, holidays in Weihaiwei would fall into two different categories: public holidays and bank holidays. The exact dates were decided by the British Commissioner and

announced within a government official gazette: the Commissioner was allowed to regulate these festivities and holidays at any time. He had the right to designate specific dates as public holidays or bank holidays. The public holidays in Weihaiwei included Western religious festivals such as Christmas, Easter, Whit Sunday, etc. and important dates such as the birthday of King George V and his Coronation Day, also Victoria Day, etc. If any public holiday should happen to fall on a Sunday, then the following Monday would automatically become a public holiday. On the other hand, bank holidays were of two different types, official and unofficial. These had no set dates and had no connection with public holidays. For example, during 1921, the holidays declared by the colonial government included only six days as public holidays, while the number of bank holidays was as high as 12 days. During bank holidays, all bills for payments would be delayed until after the holiday. Furthermore, observance of bank holidays was not limited to the banks. The whole territory would also be on holiday.

Among all the British festivities and customs in Weihaiwei, the most important and most characteristic ones were those celebrations organized by the colonial government. These activities attracted lots of people to witness their impressive and solemn ceremonies. They became part of the important content of festival life for any foreigners stationed in Weihaiwei. When it was

Weihaiwei people attending the celebration for the King's Birthday on the parade ground outside of the east gate of the walled city. (1920's)

The parade to celebrate the King's birthday in 1905.

HMS Alacrity, the Commander in Chief's Despatch vessel dressed overall with flags and firing 21 gun salute to celebrate the King's birthday (1920s)

the King's birthday, the local colonial authorities would send a congratulatory telegram on behalf of all the residents. In addition people would be summoned from among the various military, political, commercial and educational organizations to a meeting on the large parade ground outside the East Gate. After the raising of the flag, a military parade would take place before the commanding officer, followed by a concert of military music and a firework display. As for the British fleet on the sea of Weihaiwei, as long as they were at anchor, they would be decorated with coloured flags and ribbons from 8am. At 12 noon, there would be a 21 gun salute to celebrate this special day.

After the end of the First World War, Armistice Day became another important date for celebratory activities. The colonial authority established a monument in order to commemorate those British soldiers who had formerly served in Weihaiwei and who had died in the First World War. According to the usual British custom, each year at 11am on 11th November, people from all organizations would be summoned to this monument for a memorial service to be held there. After the ceremonial performance of the British National Anthem "God Save the King", there would be two minute's silence, followed by presentations of wreaths by the Commissioner representing the colonial government. In the meantime, all the traffic would come to a halt for two minutes, and all the fleets at sea would sound their horns to show their respects to the dead.

There was one important feature of the content of all these ceremonial activities. Generally, all of them would be combined together with some sort of political activity. For example, the Commissioner would award medals to members of the local gentry or merchants and to colonial officers, and in addition Chinese people from every walk of life would present gifts to the colonial authorities, all this taking place during the ceremonial activities. In 1910, when the Accession of King George V was celebrated in the Queen's Club on Liugong Island, the Governor of Shandong (Sun Baoqi) was also invited to attend.

Unlike the minority of the local gentry and merchants, the ordinary people of Weihaiwei were not so impressed by these colourful Western festivities and noisy ceremonial activities. To them these were only additional novelties and nothing much more. Due to the protective attitude of the British colonialists towards traditional customs and social structure, Weihaiwei con-

After the First World War, a War Memorial was built in Weihaiwei to commemorate the war dead. On 11th November each year a ceremony to remember the dead was held in common with all British territories. The photograph shows Johnston laying a wreath at the memorial in 1927.

tinued to function as a closed and conservative society. In their daily lives and normally observed customs, the most important events for the ordinary people were still the traditional Chinese festivals such as the Spring Festival, Lantern Festival, Dragon Boat Festival, Mid-Autumn Festival, and Lunar New Year. During these festivals, there were various customary entertainments. Although they were very simple affairs, the degree of enthusiasm and the numbers of people taking part were well in excess of the ceremonial activities sponsored by the colonial authority.

During the British colonial period, the most popular artistic activities were theatrical performances. Among these, the traditional Peking opera occupied the leading position. In the city area, there were many travelling dramatic troupes. Even in the countryside, the larger villages would also get together amateur troupes for performances. During any traditional festival, family celebration, opening ceremony of a business and on winter days when it was too cold to work in the fields, they would display their special performance skills in both the city and in the countryside.

Early in the 20th century, the first commercial theatre was built outside the North Gate of the walled city. This could hold five to six hundred people, although the facilities were rather basic. In 1918, the Tongle Theatre was also established on the south of Dihua Street. Later, this was renamed the Mingxing Theatre and contained stalls, side seats and balcony seats. It could hold an audience of up to one thousand and became the largest professional modern-style theatre in Weihaiwei. In order to attract audiences, famous troupes and singers were invited from other locations to come and

British soldiers in Weihaiwei hold wreaths for dignitaries to lay at the Armistice Day Ceremony. (1927)

The open-air theatrical performance at Zhang Jiashan Village. (1904)

On the occasion of the Chinese New Year, or major Chinese festivals, there would be a number of travelling troupes to entertain the villagers in comparatively big villages. (1915)

The open-air theatrical performance at Zhang Jiashan Village. (1904)

Land-boating dance. (1906)

The peep show newly introduced to Weihaiwei was then very popular with children, just are modern computer games today. (1938)

perform there. The level of performance of these troupes was generally of quite a high standard. They were very much appreciated by the general public.

Western theatre and social dancing was imported into Weihaiwei during this period. However, at that time, these artistic activities mainly took place within the European community and in some of the more open-minded new

A puppet show held on market days. (1921)

Members of the newspaper reading room at Weihaiwei. (1907)

A large open-air performance in Cisheng Temple, Zhang Village. (1933)

schools. The general public had no opportunity of joining in, nor had they much interest. 1921 saw the very first silent movie in Weihaiwei. After 1925, many silent movies came to be shown at the Mingxing Theatre, but due to the low level of audience attendance, the cinema business never became wide-spread.

The establishment of a modern news press was the one important cultural event which occurred in Weihaiwei during the period of British rule. The earliest newspaper, Weihaiwei Lyre (published daily), was first published by the British in 1900. This newspaper contained mostly news from the British Isles, international news and news about important events happening in Weihaiwei. It was mainly intended for the British personnel stationed in Weihaiwei. Since it was written in English, it did not have much influence on the Chinese community there.[1] However, as time went on, Chinese newspapers also started to appear and provided a new means for spreading information concerning recent events in Weihaiwei. In August 1923, the Weihaiwei News Press was started by 17 Chinese people including Fu Tingyu and Miao Woming, in order "to promote education and to enlighten the people's minds". They published the very first Chinese newspaper in Weihaiwei, the Weihai News. But it was soon closed down by the colonial authority. In December 1927, Sun Hanchuan started the Midday Post of Wei-Hai-Wei. An introduction for the launch of this newspaper was written by Johnston.[2] This newspaper attracted enormous attention at the beginning, but the articles it published were mostly critical of the confused conditions in Weihaiwei and the darker side of its society, while endlessly praising the colonial rule. Thus it caused dissatisfaction amongst progressive readers and closed down in 1929. Later on, in March 1930, people from Yantai including Xu Zhenjiang and Zhang Mingqi started up Weihaiwei Daily News. This newspaper contained eight pages every day. Its objectives were to "enlighten people's minds and instill ideas of progress" and it contained strongly expressed revolutionary ideas about racialism and democracy. The quantity of its information and quality of its printing were far better than the earlier newspapers.[3] The Weihaiwei Daily News published a lot of articles promoting progressive ideas, attacking corruption, and spreading knowledge of science.

During the colonial period, several bookshops appeared in Weihaiwei. Among these, the earliest and largest was the Jishengchang Bookstore located on the eastern side of the Tianhou Palace. This bookshop not only sold books but was also in the business of printing. In 1907, the business people of Weihaiwei also founded the "Weihaiwei Newspaper Reading Society" within the same building. Sunday meetings were held where public speeches would communicate the new ideas of the time. This turned out to be the starting point for the modern library business in Weihaiwei.

Foreign schools and modern education

The period during which Weihaiwei was under British rule was one in which China suffered humiliation year after year, and the whole nation was striving with great determination to make progress. At that time large numbers of schools were established to cultivate talents which were much needed to achieve social change, and would be the chief means of strengthening the nation. After the Reform Movement of 1898, China's old-fashioned education system had started upon its difficult road towards modern education. It was not until after the 1930s that there was any well developed modern education system in China. At the same time, several positive changes also occurred in the educational situation in Weihaiwei. A number of modern schools appeared one after the other. The earliest modern schools were mostly established or controlled by Westerners in the area. Among these, the more

The Weihaiwei School. (1904)

well-known ones were the Weihaiwei School, the Anglo-Chinese School, the Huangren School and the Mingxing Girls' School.

The Weihaiwei School was founded in 1901, and was a preparatory boarding school for boys. The first principal was an Englishman called Herbert Beer. Initially it was located on Liugong Island and subsequently moved to the mainland in 1903. This new school was totally managed according to the British style of teaching. All its teachers were recruited from Britain, and all its staff members were Europeans. Its curriculum was maintained in parallel with the school system in Britain. In 1901 it had only 4 students, and normally about 50 thereafter. All of these were overseas European children living in the Far East. Weihaiwei School was once regarded by the British as the best European-style school in the Far East. But due to its refusal to accept Chinese students, its presence had little impact on the development of education in Weihaiwei. In the early 1920s, owing to the likelihood of the imminent return of Weihaiwei to China, both students and staff members fell rapidly. It was forced to close in the autumn of 1925.[4] Later on, it was became the Eastcliff Hotel. It also ran short-term summer schools for those European students who came to Weihaiwei as a summer resort.

The Anglo-Chinese School was founded in 1902 by an Anglo-Chinese Episcopal Church missionary, Mr Browne.[5] Its location was on the west side of the Tianhou Palace (inside the Experimental School of today). Its curriculum was not fixed, but biased towards English, typing, applied commercial courses and western natural science. All of these were practical subjects that were lacking within the traditional education system. In its early years, this school forced its students to take part in religious activities, which was repugnant to many of them. Consequently, it found it rather difficult to attract students. In order to overcome the resistance of traditional culture, the school was forced to change its attitude. It also strengthened its Chinese language course, following the Chinese traditional way of education. Chinese teachers were employed to teach traditional Chinese classics, history and philosophy. Gradually, it expanded and became widely accepted by the local community. At that time, most of the students entering this school were the sons and daughters of wealthy families within the colonial area, or Christians. The quality of teaching was higher than in other schools. It raised a group of modern students who met the needs of Chinese society. Among these were a number of professionals and experts.

The Mingxing Girls' School was founded by Catholic sisters in 1908. Its location was inside the St. Mary's Convent. The objective of this school was not to promulgate basic education, but rather to enable girls to learn embroidery and lace-making, and acquire the skills of spinning and weaving. Its cultural courses were quite simple, and limited to Christianity, the Chinese

The Anglo-Chinese School was established by the Anglican Church in 1902. In 1930 its name was changed to the Yuhua Private Junior School. The photograph shows the 7th graduation class of 1939.

classics, mathematics and geography. The school required that its students should spend half of their time on cultural courses; the other half learning professional skills. Students not only obtained a basic level of cultural knowledge, but most importantly, they acquired an expertise that could earn them a living. Therefore, the school was welcomed by the general public within the colonial area. Gradually it became the largest girls' school in Weihaiwei. After graduation, students from this school mostly became the backbone of the business of spinning and weaving in Weihaiwei. Since the objective of Chinese traditional feudal education was to train students for the civil service examination system, there were previously no vocational schools. The Mingxing Girls' School can thus be regarded as the first of Weihaiwei's vocational schools.

In 1904, the colonial authority opened the one and only official school in Weihaiwei, named the Huangren School.[6] Its curriculum was set up to satisfy the requirements of the Chinese educational authorities. In addition, it provided some English language courses, but basically, it resembled a Chinese primary school. After graduation, students could continue their studies in a Chinese middle school outside the colonial territory. Due to its basic Chinese traditional education and the fact that entrance was free of charge, the school continuously expanded. In 1919, the colonial authority divided it into two parts. One part was the Huangren Free School, and the other was the Huangren Public School which charged a certain level of fees.[7]

Although they were relative latecomers to the educational scene, in comparison with the foreign schools, those modern schools founded by the people of Weihaiwei eventually became the main source of modern education in Weihaiwei. According to the official records, more than 70% of all schools during that period in Weihaiwei were founded by local people. Among them, the most noteworthy were the Shude Girls' School, the People's Night School, and the Qidong Middle School.

The Shude Girls' School was founded in 1908 by the Weihaiwei branch of the Natural Feet Association. It provided a three-year course of education, and was completely free of charge. There was a strong aspect of feminism in its objectives: "To enable women to achieve their true potential; to encourage their natural abilities; to educate them morally and intellectually, as well as physically; to enable them to become self-supporting"[8]. The curriculum was rather different from the Chinese traditional one. It consisted of nine courses, including home economics, moral values, art and crafts, Chinese language, mathematics, science, history, geography, and letter-writing. In 1920, music and calligraphy were added to the courses. A number of these would still fall within a modern curriculum. The Shude Girls' School was the very first girls' school in the history of Weihaiwei.

The Catholic Boys School founded by the French Catholic Mission in 1902. The photograph shows the school buildings built in 1934.

Ever since the May 4th Movement, many organizations had appeared in China with the objective of raising the educational level of the people. As part of this trend, the Weihaiwei City Commercial Association established the Weihaiwei People's Educational Association on 16th September 1923. Soon afterwards, this organization became engaged in collecting donations for the funding of People's Night Schools. On 15th October that same year, an opening ceremony was held at the Tianhou Palace. These evening classes were mainly held inside schools, public meeting places and temples. They

Johnston presenting the Government Free School with a scroll written by the abdicated Emperor Puyi. (1927)

were for farmers and labourers aged between 12 and 50. All the study material and tuition fees were free of charge. The teachers were also volunteers. All the finance came from donations. Teaching materials came from Shanghai, using the "Common People's Thousand Words" published by the Nationwide Association. Complete in 4 books, introducing one thousand commonly used words, this course could be taught in just 4 months. Upon graduation, students were given a diploma. Afterwards, each one would receive a free

The Government Free School, the only one set up by the British colonial authorities. (1908)

Children reading their essays aloud for Lockhart on Graduation day at the Government Free School. (1921)

copy of a monthly newsletter reviewing what they had learned. Initially, there were 20 schools containing 551 students. In 1924, six more were added, in addition to a few girls' schools. These people's night schools provided an opportunity for education to many poor members of the general public. This became the starting point of community education in Weihaiwei.

The Qidong Middle School was the first secondary school founded by the people of Weihaiwei. It holds a special place in the history of education in Weihaiwei. On 20th December 1926, Sun Qichang and others used the original Chinese military base as a school building to found Qidong Middle School, in order to solve the problem of secondary education for the students of Weihaiwei. This school advertised courses for students between the ages of 13 and 18. Its curriculum included more than 15 courses, which were comprehensive in their nature and practical in their aims. All the teachers it employed were university graduates. Thanks to its emphasis on providing vocational training to meet the needs of the community, students could enter into their chosen career straight after graduation. Consequently, the school was welcomed by the community. Its classrooms eventually became too small to meet the needs of the gradually expanding student intake. As a result, in 1928, the school applied to the colonial governor to build a new school on

威海齊東學校招生廣告

民國十五年陰曆正月廿二日

中華民國十四年陰曆十一月

詳細本校印有招考簡章
可隨時向各報名處索閱

A student recruiting advertisement for Qidong Middle School. (1926)

an official site with the aid of a grant. The Governor agreed and promised 5, 000 yuan in financial aid, but requested that the school should collect a comparable amount in donations. In a comparatively short time, nearly 20, 000 yuan in donations were raised. On 14th August 1929, the new school was opened and its name was changed to the Weihai Middle School[9].

All these new modern schools appeared in Weihaiwei during the period of British rule. No matter how much they might differ in their curriculum, class teaching methods or target student intake, they all achieved significant progress in comparison with the old fashioned privately-operated village schools. Yet the number of these new schools was very small, and almost all were concentrated within Port Edward. The vast number of villages still continued to follow the traditional education style of the private village school, employing simple equipment and ancient teaching methods. The content of their learning was limited to ancient Chinese poetry and the

Teachers and students of the King's School, a free school, founded by the British businessman, Duncan Clark, on Liugong island in 1904, providing English, business studies and other modern courses to Chinese students. (1904)

traditional Four Books and Five Classics. After the 1920s, some of the larger villages began to introduce a modern education system, but due to the difficulty in finding qualified teachers, more often the private teachers still continued with readings from the Confucian Classics. The new schools were new only in name and nothing else. Even in most new schools, readings from the Classics still continued until the early 1930s, although they had already been abolished by the Revolution of 1912 in other places. Thus during this period new education did not emerge with a unified system and syllabus. This was quite different from the development of modern education elsewhere in China during the same period and was a direct result of the colonial authority's educational policy.

Lockhart, the first civil Commissioner, had never been very enthusiastic about promoting new education. He was content with the status quo and didn't want to interfere with the schools. After the Huangren School was established he would often present awards to its outstanding pupils. However,

Local people saying farewell to Duncan Clark when he left Weihaiwei for Britain. (1920)

On the occasion of the first anniversary of the Weihaiwei Student Federation, set up after the Jinan Massacre in May 1928.

A leaflet distributed by the Weihaiwei students calling for the continuation of the boycott of Japanese goods on the first anniversary of the starting of that boycott. (1920)

he didn't make much effort to develop an educational system. Not only was there no educational administrative organization to deal with education and to improve methods of teaching, but the old-fashioned style of education was actually encouraged. In 1905, the Qing government abolished the civil service examination system and promoted Western style education, yet the colonial authority considered that the people of Weihaiwei had no need for the new education that was being promoted outside the territory. They even adopted active measures to maintain and encourage traditional education within it.

After the 1911 Revolution and the May 4th Movement, modern educational developments went from strength to strength. New style education spread quickly throughout China. The people of Weihaiwei also increased their demands for new schools. Petitions were written to the colonial authority appealing for the founding of more new schools. There were several instances of donors offering money and land for schools. Yet, as Lockhart said at the time: "Among the people there is a strong demand for British style education. Still, it must not be encouraged too much." With this kind of leadership, very little attention was paid to education by the colonial government. It was not until 1928 that Johnston, the Commissioner at that time, with the permission of the Colonial Department, included education for the first time as one of the items of expenditure in the

A poster denouncing the 1928 Jinan Massacre, an atrocity committed by the Japanese.

financial budget of the colonial government, in order to save face for the British. Even so, this was limited mainly to the few schools run by the church. This colonial education policy seriously hindered the development of education in Weihaiwei. According to the records in the official files, in 1921, the literacy rate of people in Weihaiwei was 9%. Of these, only 227 were female. Even up to 1930, the literacy rate was still only 10%.[10]

In November 1929, a letter from Johnston to the British Minister in China contained this description of the educational situation in Weihaiwei: "Owing to the urgent necessity for stringent economy, we can do nothing whatever – except to a very limited extent in the case of the Government school just mentioned – to supervise the course of education, to plan or carry out any definite educational system, or to improve and develop the numerous private schools established in the villages. We have no Inspector of Schools or Director of Education; and the state of the village schools in particular, with their old-fashioned methods, their out-of-date curricula, and their general inefficiency, certainly reflects little credit on the British administration. Unfortunately, therefore, it is an undeniable fact that educational system of Weihaiwei – or rather the total lack of a system – exposes us to much adverse criticism; and if we were called upon to explain to the Chinese educational authorities the precise nature of the steps taken by us to provide the children of Weihaiwei with a sound education on modern lines, it would be extremely difficult for us to furnish a statement which would deserve to be accepted as satisfactory."[11]

Modern medical treatment and public health

Prior to British rule, there had been no consideration paid to modern medical treatment and public health in Weihaiwei. People in the region mainly depended on privately established Chinese herbal medicine shops or quack doctors. In the countryside, there was a quite serious lack of doctors and medicines. In 1900, when Swettenham made his investigation of Weihaiwei, he thought there were too many poor people living there. He considered that if the government were to invest capital to build a hospital, it could easily

The Civil Hospital set up in 1902. (1921)

Royal Navy Hospital on Liugong Island. (1938)

become a free hospital for poor local people. This would be too much of a financial burden for the British to bear. Thus he suggested that there was no need to build a hospital in Weihaiwei, and that the responsibility for medical treatment should thus depend mainly on the Chinese herbal medicine shops in the area.[12] Due to its tight budget and the small numbers of Westerners who lived for any considerable period in Weihaiwei, the colonial authority considered that only a few basic health improvement measures were required during this early period. As Weihaiwei became a base for British fleets stationed in China, and a centre of tourism and recuperation for overseas Europeans, the arrival of Westerners increased year after year. The demand for improved health facilities began to increase. With the expansion in trading activities Weihaiwei became more threatened by infectious diseases from outside. Therefore, the colonial authority changed its attitude and adopted a series of measures to strengthen the provision of medical treatment. Consequently, health conditions in the territory were greatly improved.

In 1902, a medical officer was appointed to manage public health throughout the whole area and to quarantine any ships from foreign countries. The rank of this medical officer was rather high. He, the Senior District Officer and the Junior District Officer became the three senior officers subordinate to the commissioner.

In 1902, the government established temporary hospitals for Chinese people both in Port Edward and also on Liugong Island. During this initial period, the facilities were rather simple and basic. Treatment was mainly similar to that of an out-patient clinic. The hospital in Port Edward was managed by a Chinese doctor who had studied Western medicine and had only two other employees. Its equipment included 15 stretchers. Liugong Island temporary hospital, located in the East Village, was named the Civil Hospital. This was managed by an English doctor. In order to attract Chinese people to come for treatment, both these hospitals were free of charge.

In 1908, the government proceeded to extend and renovate the hospital in the City commercial district. It became known as the Civil Hospital and was the largest hospital within Weihaiwei. It was more comprehensive in its medical treatment, and was capable of accepting fifty to sixty residential patients at the same time. In 1916, a village hospital was added at Wenquantang making use of freely donated land there. This was comparatively small in scale and conditions there were not so good. At this time, including the Civil Hospital on Liugong Island, there were a total of three Chinese hospitals in

A night soil collector. Times of collection were very strictly controlled. (1918)

the whole area. The total number of beds was over 70, which means there were about just 4 beds available for each ten thousand people throughout the population of the whole territory. Due to the fact that the environment and facilities of these Chinese hospitals could not meet the demands of the Westerners, those who came to Weihaiwei would mainly turn to the Liugong Island Royal Navy Infirmary for medical treatment and diagnosis. At the time that was the hospital which possessed the best facilities in Weihaiwei, and had the highest standard of medical treatment. However, from its very beginning it refused to accept Chinese patients. In 1929, the Civil Hospital built two high quality wards with the aid of donations from the Port Edward Chamber of Commerce. From this time the hospital was able to offer medical treatment to Westerners.[13] Meanwhile, the management of private medical services was also strengthened. According to the regulations, private medical services must be subject to a relevant department investigation to demonstrate that they could meet the necessary standards of medical service. Otherwise, they would be closed

A street scene on Liugong Island. (1930s)

down.

The government paid particular attention to the improvement of public health. To achieve this, the colonial authority selected officers from amongst the police inspectors to become Health investigators responsible for supervision and management of public health in Port Edward and on Liugong Island. From 1902, the government built up a series of facilities such as public toilets, drains and tap water wells. In 1903, the "Public Building and Health Ordinance" was proclaimed. From the angle of health these stipulated very detailed requirements regarding all sorts of public and private buildings such as slaughterhouses, milk factories, bakeries, pigsties, cattle sheds, and food shops. In addition a rigorous system of investigation was established. For example, with regard to slaughterhouses, the government specified that all domesticated animals used for food must be tested by the medical officer within 24 hours prior to slaughtering. After slaughtering, all the refuse must be cleared away within three hours. No blood stains should be left. No meat was allowed to be sold or exhibited outside before it had been checked by the medical officer or health investigator. The slaughterhouse and its attached building must be washed with sea water once every day, and they must be painted with lime water at least 4 times a year. A health investigator inspected the slaughterhouse once a day. Throwing out garbage was strictly forbidden. Because the outdoor toilets at the time were extremely unhygenic, from 1903, a series of regulations on the management of toilets was imposed to ensure improvements to existing, or newly-built, toilets which must be built according to standard specifications.

In order to strengthen the awareness of public health issues, in 1909, the Department of Heath published a whole batch of Health Promotion leaflets to be dispatched to the villages and schools. In 1910, another batch of 400 guidelines for the prevention of cholera were dispatched free of charge to the villages.14 Starting in 1915, a health course was instituted within the schools, and an examination based on this course would often take place. By way of encouragement a certain amount of prize money would be awarded to those whose achievements were excellent.

Furthermore, the government also paid special attention to the prevention of diseases. During the early period of British rule, smallpox was very common in Weihaiwei, and the death rate was relatively high. In order to prevent smallpox from occurring, the colonial government instituted a programme of vaccinations. However, many difficulties were encountered in the execution of this programme. Mainly due to superstitious beliefs, the people considered vaccination to be unlucky. Some also expressed doubts as to whether vaccination was the best preventive measure against smallpox. In addition, their prejudice against foreigners also created a barrier to the acceptance of vaccination. To counter this, the government launched a wide-scale propaganda exercise

W. M. Muat (first left) was appointed Senior Medical Officer in 1906. The photograph shows Muat receiving his CBE on the occasion of his retirement in 1923.

in support of vaccination by distributing health leaflets. In 1905, an annual scheme of wholesale free vaccination was initated. In order to make this convenient for the residents, the Department of Medical Treatment trained a group of vaccinators from among the local people. Each spring, under the guidance of medical officers, these would go to different villages vaccinating people from door to door. In order to encourage its acceptance, competitions were sometimes organised. Vaccination gradually became widely accepted. According to the statistics, in 1929 alone, there were 13209 people who accepted vaccination.

Black fever was also one of the most common diseases in Weihaiwei at that time. Those affected were mostly children under 5 years of age. In 1900, firm measures were taken to combat this disease. To prevent the occurrence of black fever, free inspection and treatment would be provided twice weekly in the villages, under the control of the medical officer. Later on, black fever clinics were also established.

Another medical measure to be adopted by the colonial government for disease prevention was the fight against plague carried by rats. In 1911, such a plague broke out in the North East. After that, it spread to Yantai and quickly spread from there. On being notified of the outbreak, the government immediately added a quarantine post at the border. People both inside and outside the territory were forbidden to leave or enter. Anyone returning to Weihaiwei from Yantai was forced to get an injection for plague prevention at the Civil Hospital. In the meantime, a rat–catching association was established inside the border, offering rat–catching equipment free of charge to the local residents. To encourage rat–catching, the colonial government offered prizes according to the number of rats' tails that were presented. Thanks to these effective measures, the spread of rat disease in Weihaiwei thus came under control.

Generally speaking, because the government's medical treatment concentrated on the Westerner residents in the commercial area of the City and on Liugong Island, the relatively poor condition of medical treatment available throughout the village areas did not change a great deal. Health conditions in the villages were still quite poor because of the serious lack of equipment and medicines. Grave infectious diseases such as typhoid fever, scarlet fever broke out at various times. For instance, in 1918, during October to November, influenza spread throughout the whole area resulting in the deaths of at least 900 people. Within just one family of 8 there were even 6 deaths! Still more serious results were caused by cholera within the villages during 1919. According to the colonial authority's General Census Report, about 5000 people died from an outbreak of cholera. In some villages half of the total population was wiped out. Other sources indicate that the number of deaths at the time was actually much higher more than that reported.[15]

The introduction & development of western sports

During thousands of years of development and change, China had accumulated considerable cultural riches in the area of sporting activities, but because of the traditional emphasis on seeking perfection in the literary arts rather than the martial arts, the social value and effects of sport received far too little consideration and development. In the modern age, Western sporting activities rapidly spread far and wide, whereas Chinese sports had stagnated, without any advancement. Towards the end of the 19th century and the

A soccer match at the Queen's Hotel. (1911)

本館開設威海碼頭天后宮街 星期六

威海午報

中華郵政特准掛號認爲新聞紙類 每日出一張

OF WEI HAI WEI

總經理孫漢川

第五十一號

本報價目 廣告價目

本隊定於今日下午三句鐘與後營英兵足球隊合賽茲將本隊之運動員列後
李百鈞 孫華農 谷新秀 谷源璨 孫文序 劉希玉 成光烈 楚金福 鄭道宏 谷源洪 林心之
威海足球聯合隊啟

公平交易協和隆
本號開辦以來信用昭著資本豐厚專以買賣生米爲業或鄉人來本號售賣或本號在鄉間收買皆以公平交易童叟無欺但有高貨不惜重價從無許減分量勒當價目等情且本號之貨行銷外洋信用早爲中外人所共知今爲擴張營業計特登報聲明如有上等之貨可到本號售賣不勝歡迎之至
天主堂路東協和隆號謹啟

請吸國貨美耶牌香烟
中國三友廠 美耶香烟好 請君樂購吸
爲的價錢少 敬請經理家 及時推廣銷
金錢不外溢 愛國以爲寶 每箱得贈品
年終鴻利早 利權最優厚 獲益定然高
欲想經理者 面洽速爲妙
威海成興東總經理啟

武術研究會實行開幕
本報館內附設武術研究會定於三月十五日開幕每生徒每月納費洋兩元
願學武術者莫失良機實於身體大有裨益

進口貨

出口貨

昨日銀市

善戒鴉片嗎啡

Advertisement of a soccer competition between Chinese and foreign teams, published in the Midday Post of Weihaiwei. (1928)

beginning of 20th century, "The Sick Man of East Asia" even became a nickname for the Chinese nation during the Qing Dynasty. However, sporting activities in Weihaiwei succeeded in developing rapidly with the introduction of Western sports.

Ever since the British leased Weihaiwei, they introduced a number of sports to the territory. Generally speaking, these sports could be divided into 4 types: ball games, seasonal sports, track and field events, and recreational sports. Of these types, the most popular were ball games, which included football, tennis, golf, cricket, basketball, baseball, volleyball, croquet, squash, billiards, and bowls.

Modern football started in Britain in 1863, and was termed "The First Game of the World". Soon after Weihaiwei came under British rule, the game of football was introduced. On 26th December 1900, a competition took place on the United Services Playground of Liugong Island between the sailors of the British Cruiser "Orlando" and the garrison of the island.[16] This was the earliest record of a football game in Weihaiwei, and marked the introduction of football into the territory. Five football grounds were constructed by the British authorities and foreign schools. Gradually, football became the most frequent, most popular, and most influential sport in Weihaiwei during that period.

Tennis originated in France during the 12th to 13th centuries. After the Westerners came to Weihaiwei, they soon built tennis courts near their offices and residences. Immediately, tennis courts spread all over the City area. Even on a small island like Liugong, there were more than ten of them. At first, the only people who played tennis were Westerners or a minority of wealthy Chinese people. Ordinary local people would seldom visit a tennis court. Later on, following the wider accessibility of tennis courts, the game started to become popular amongst young Chinese students in Weihaiwei. During the final period of British rule, tennis even became a formal competitive activity in Chinese sports events.

Traditionally, golf originated in Scotland. It was fashionable in Europe during the 14th to 15th centuries. In 1902, the colonial government established the Weihaiwei Golf Club to organize and develop the game. In 1907, the Port Edward Golf Club was established in association with British merchants settled in Weihaiwei. Any Overseas British person in China could become its member. Among the guest members, there were nearly one hundred from Shanghai alone. In the same year, a golf course was constructed outside the East Gate of the walled city. Meanwhile, the British Navy founded yet another golf club on Liugong Island, and established a golf course there as well. Later on, two more golf courses were established in the west and south villages of Weihaiwei. As a typical upper class game, only foreigners and a very few rich Chinese merchants could take part. The general public could only be on-lookers. The British naval golf course was particularly exclusive. Not until the 30th of November, 1930, were its rules revised to permit Chinese officials and foreign cruiser officers to become accepted as honorary members. Before that, people of Weihaiwei were excluded except for those who were responsible for the maintenance of the course and young children who retrieved the balls. The main duty of these children was to carry the players' balls and clubs around the golf course, and also to retrieve the lost balls.

In Weihaiwei, the seasonal sporting activities included sailing, boat racing, hunting and horse racing. In 1918, the government and Western merchants formally established a sailing club in the port of Weihaiwei to develop European-style competitive sailing boat activities. During the summer tourist season, races would occur every Saturday afternoon at 3pm, over a triangular course of about five miles, starting on alternative weeks from either Liugong

The golf course on Liugong Island. (1938)

A caddie in Weihaiwei. (Early 20th Century)

Island or Port Edward. Horse racing was another popular Western competitive sporting activity and was associated with gambling. During its period of rule, the colonial government had intended to establish a race course near Jinxianding, and a casino in the style of the French Monte Carlo within another area. Due to the lack of sufficient capital, neither project was realized. Instead, foreigners who visited Weihaiwei would make use of the village roads and fields, after the autumn harvest was over, for horse racing activities. This development was quite popular. Sometimes, they would go to Yantai race course to satisfy their enthu-siasm for this sport.

The establishment of sports sites in Weihaiwei increased to meet the expanding demand for these activities. Apart from those grounds dedicated to one particular sport, two general purpose sports fields were constructed. One was the Royal Navy United Recreation Ground on Liugong Island. The other was the Parade Ground located outside the East Gate. This Parade Ground used to be the military show ground during the Ming and Qing Dynasties. Towards the later period of the British rule, golf courses, cricket grounds, football fields, volley ball grounds, basket ball grounds and running fields were all to be found there. Apart from competitive sports, this also provided a place for meetings as well as for British military training and troop reviews. It was the biggest comprehensive public sports field in Weihaiwei during that period.

In 1907, a Sports Association was organized in Weihaiwei by a number of Chinese people including Zhang Fulai and Li Huae, in order to encourage research into sports and physical activities. In their application to set up this Sports Association, they stated that sport could not only strengthen a person physically, but was also able to influence them psychologically and spiritually. It was pointed out that: "The way of education must be threefold, including

The cricket pitch on Liugong Island (1921)

intellectual, moral, and physical aspects. Then it would become a complete education." This was the very first time that such a threefold education project was proposed in Weihaiwei, and it represented a new trend in which education was to be combined with physical exercise.[17] In 1929, some members of the Port Edward Chamber of Commerce who included Sun Qinxuan went even further by raising sports to the status of an influence on social behaviour and a force that could improve social manners. In order to promote "high standard entertainment" and to enable the public to cultivate the habit of healthy amusements in sports and games, the Weihaiwei Club was established to organize and develop social sporting activities.

As time went on, the introduction of modern sports from overseas became

A sailing race organised by the Weihaiwei Mandarin Ducks Sailing Club. A sailing race was a must for British fleet and foreigners at Weihaiwei in the summer. (1918)

The start of the Marathon. (1915)

more and more acceptable to the general public of Weihaiwei and steadily increased in popularity. Some of these sports became well established and a high standard of performance was achieved. Take football for example. As early as 11th February 1901, local people were already engaged in organised contests against those foreigners stationed in Weihaiwei.[18] After that, the sport of football developed in Weihaiwei very rapidly. In particular it became widespread throughout the local schools. Many of these established amateur football teams. Within the community many football lovers appeared and so football teams were organized. These Chinese football teams often competed

A photograph of referees and winners of the first Weihaiwei Sports meeting. (1929)

Horse racing at Weihaiwei. (1905)

against the foreigners visiting Weihaiwei, also the British sailors, and frequently won. This reversed the usual situation in which the Westerners were normally the winners in Weihaiwei's football games. During this time, there appeared plenty of talented footballers, and when these people moved to other locations, they spread their enthusiasm for the game and soon became the football organizers in that area. As a result, Weihaiwei football became famous for some considerable time.

On 9th June 1929, the first Territory Games took place in Weihaiwei. On 17th May 1930, another Spring Sports took place there. In addition to track and field events, football, tennis, and basketball, as well as a three-legged race, and egg and spoon race, were included. According to the 1930 report of the Weihaiwei Daily News: "It was well known that Qingquan School was paying great attention to its preparations for the event. Apart from attending Classes, every student spent most of their time in sports training, so that there was often not enough time for them to eat their meals." This typifies the strong enthusiasm for sporting activities in Weihaiwei during that period.

Missionaries enthusiastic but impotent

Christianity came very early to Weihaiwei. According to the earliest records, it was back in the 1830s that Christian missionaries first appeared in Weihaiwei. In the autumn of 1889, a British Christian sect, the Plymouth Brethren, sent a Scottish preacher Mr Stephen and his wife to Stone Island as missionaries. They quickly established a church. In the summer of 1892, the Brethren sent an English preacher, Dr J. Norman Case, from Shidao to Weihaiwei to do missionary work, and in the autumn of the same year, Mr and Mrs James Dawson also came to live in Weihaiwei.[19] Following this, the number of missionaries coming to Weihaiwei increased continuously. Weihaiwei also began to have formal church organisations. However, these missionary activities met with only little success. First of all, the concepts of Christianity were in conflict with those of Confucianism in China. It was thus rather difficult for the general public to accept them, and so it was not easy to initiate missionary activities. Secondly, the local officials and gentry, in common with Chinese officials in other areas, had been worried for long time that the spread of Christianity would result in "great confusion in public morality", which might upset the present social order. Therefore, there were many obstacles placed in the way of missionary activities. In 1896, when some missionary preachers tried to rent houses in Weihaiwei, this was not allowed. Thirdly, under the protection of the unequal treaty, missionaries sometimes acted in improper ways. This provoked strong antagonism among the local people when those missionaries insisted on pursuing a course which finally led to the following "church incident at Weihaiwei".

In February 1897, a British preacher rented for a second time a house from the widow Mrs. Wu to convert it into a place of worship in order to expand the influence of his church. The local district magistrate Li Zunian received a report from the Weihaiwei foreign affairs committee member Wang. He immediately ordered the sub-district deputy magistrate of Weihaiwei to force the owner of the house to take back the contract. When the owner asked for it to be returned, this was angrily refused. This news infuriated the

Weihaiwei Catholic Church founded by the French Franciscan Order. (1960s)

A statue of the Virgin Mary. (1960s)

local people. On 5th of March, about 700 anti–church people gathered together and greatly damaged the house. The case was delayed for half a year before any decision was made. On 1st November, a similar incident occurred in the west part of Shandong Province. After that, the British Minister MacDonald sent a demand to the Zongli yamen requesting that the Chinese local authorities should issue official notices proclaiming protection for missionaries who rented houses under contract, and demanding that the damaged house be repaired; furthermore the local district magistrate Li should be removed; and local people must not be allowed to interfere in church affairs. After repeated pressure from the Qing government, Magistrate Li was dismissed. The official notice protecting the church was also posted on the front door of the British missionary.[20]

The religious world of Britain became quite excited when Weihaiwei was leased to Britain in 1898. They considered this action would be helpful in sweeping away obstacles to missionary work. Immediately, the Chinese Episcopalian Church and the Plymouth Brethren established themselves in Weihaiwei, and an Anglican Church was constructed there in 1898. After that, St. James Church, the United Chapel and two other churches were also built on Liugong Island and in other villages. The Plymouth Brethren also acted as publishers for printing Gospel Sheet Calendars each year as well as printing official documents for the colonial authority. Furthermore, during

St James Church on Liugong Island. Circa (1910)

A Canadian Catholic Priest of Weihaiwei. (1930s)

the summertime, when the British fleets came to visit, printing services were also offered to them.

French Catholics followed shortly after the Protestants had arrived. In 1900, the French priest Father Luo Hanguang came to Weihaiwei from the Catholic headquarters in the East region of Yantai. He built St. Joseph's School within the walled city and commenced missionary activities. In 1902, after he had gone back to Yantai, the British priest, Father Lang Binghua, came to organize missionary work. In the same year, he purchased a plot of ground in the Triangular Garden and built a Catholic church attached to the Haixing Primary School. In 1908, a Catholic nunnery (which later became St Mary's Orphanage) was built to the west of Haixing School, together with the Mingxing Girls' School. In 1931, the churches in Weihaiwei became independent. After that, their sphere of influence expanded continuously. From 1931 to 1936 was a prosperous period for the Catholic Church in Weihaiwei.

In order to extinguish barriers and misunderstandings between the Protestant and Catholic churches and Chinese traditional thoughts and culture, missionaries took all kinds of opportunities to propagate Christian doctrines, and, to gain the local people's support, carried out educational, medical, publication and various other charitable projects which also promoted the

A cardinal from the Vatican with the teacher and children of the Catholic Boys School. (1930s)

development of Weihaiwei. It's especially worth mentioning that, as a result of the Catholic Church's efforts, the industry of embroidery in Weihaiwei developed quickly. It remained an important export industry for some time.

However, the enthusiasm of the missionaries was not very well rewarded. This was very disappointing for them. The local people's attitude towards the charity businesses developed by the Western churches was relatively welcoming, but they were not really interested in the Christianity that the missionaries really wanted them to accept. During the whole period of British rule, the practice of Western religion was basically limited to those Westerners who were stationed in Weihaiwei. It had little influence upon the thoughts and lives of the local Chinese people. Although Weihaiwei's coastal location meant it was remote from the centre of Chinese government throughout much of its history, and the educational level of the local people was low, Shandong Province was the place of origin of Confucianism. Everyone there was aware of the ethical values of Confucius which were a fundamental influence upon people's behaviour. Under the lasting influence of the teachings of Confucius and Mencius, local people in Weihaiwei did not easily accept any outside influences. Within the region, all sorts of religious superstitions were also very common. However this did not mean that the people of Weihaiwei were

A Catholic Church ceremony in Catholic Boys School. (1931)

Catholic Church school students taking part in religious activities. (1930s)

all devoutly religious. In fact, there were many more irreligious people in Weihaiwei than religious ones. Traditional belief systems, based upon a strong historical cultural foundation, were not easily shaken. For instance, Buddhism and Taoism had been popular in Weihaiwei for nearly a thousand years, but even the devotees of these beliefs became fewer by the late Qing period, let alone those of the "Western religion" that had been introduced only recently by Westerners. After 1898, missionaries encountered all sorts of difficulties, and there still was little progress in converting the Chinese to

The Young Men's Christian Association at Weihaiwei. (1906)

Missionaries in the countryside, Weihaiwei. (1930s)

Christianity. What is more, the minority who did become Christian found it rather easy to abandon their new faith. According to documentary records, one of the preachers in Weihaiwei managed to convert up to twelve people to Christianity in one village. However, after the preacher left, these twelve all reverted back to their traditional religion. This proved strength of the power of tradition.

Rather unexpectedly for the missionaries, their work also failed to receive much protection or blessing from the colonial government. The stratagem of the British rule in Weihaiwei was actually to conserve the old systems and traditional customs. As a result, the principle of religious freedom was observed by the colonial governors one after the other. As for the class of

Missionaries at Yangting Village during their missionary work in the countryside. (1930s)

Catholic nuns with orphans in their charge. (1938)

Orphans saying prayers. (1930s)

ruling officials, Johnston, the person who had shouldered the most important position in Weihaiwei for such a long time, was famous for his anti-missionary inclinations. He considered Confucianism to be the cultural root of the Chinese people. He thought it to be unique to the Chinese people and that for them it was the most suitable religion in the world. He believed that China might manage without Buddhism or Taoism, but it couldn't manage without Confucianism. Lockhart, another long term administrator held the same view and firmly supported Johnston's opinions. For instance, the school founded by the British Episcopalian Church in Weihaiwei had been subsidized each year by the government since its inception. But in 1905, when Lockhart became aware that Chinese students in this school were forced to become Christians, he cancelled its government subsidy from 1906. In 1911, when the government

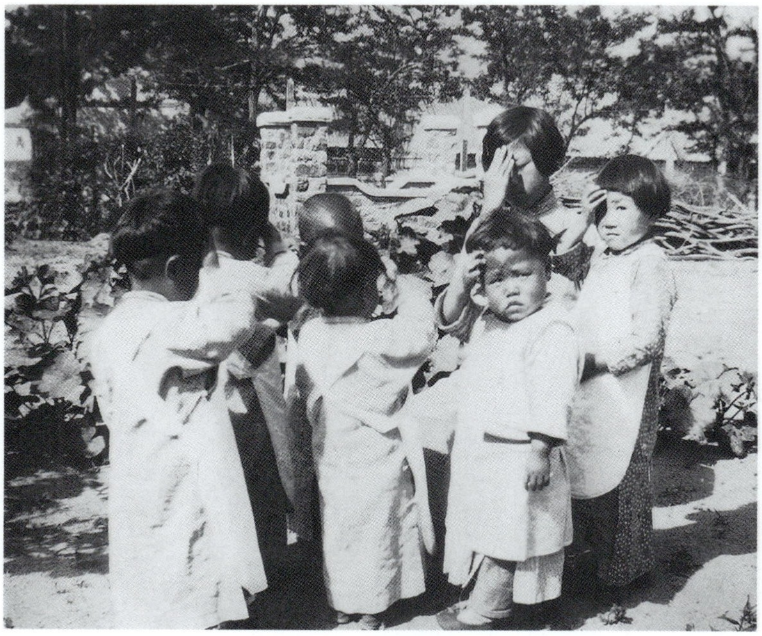

conducted a population census, among the many kinds of question asked, only religion was excluded. This was in order to prevent the people considering the census to be a government propaganda exercise for the spread and encouragement of Christianity.

Hand in hand with this went the government's protection of traditional religious beliefs among the local people of Weihaiwei. After the Revolution of 1911, traditional faiths were seriously attacked, and radicalism raised its head within the region. The government immediately took measures to counter this. For example, anyone damaging a temple or its statues would be put in prison for two years or fined 500 yuan. This was a very severe punishment. During that period some people suggested that the property of temples should be impounded and used to help the schools. This suggestion was firmly opposed by the government. Within the region, a number of Christians also proposed to the government that certain temple property could be converted to build a school for spreading Christianity. The government's reaction was also relatively unsympathetic. Even up to 1933, of the 200,000 people in the region, only 205 people were believers in Protestantism and Catholicism. To quote the words of the colonial authorities: "As regards public welfare and family life, Christianity had no significant function."[21] During this period, the people of Weihaiwei mostly went along with their traditional religious faiths and customs.

Traffic changes and development

Animal drawn carriages only became popular in 1909. The photograph was taken in 1903. At that time a few families could afford this form of transport.

At the beginning of the 20th century, the amount of traffic in Weihaiwei expanded quickly. This change became most obvious in the area of road traffic, and meant that traditional means of transportation started to change. Many kinds of vehicle began to play more and more important roles in people's social life.

The wheelbarrow was the most widely used vehicle, and the most

popular and most primitive means of transportation. Although it existed in various forms, the basic structure was always the same. Its uniqueness was its simplicity of construction; it was convenient to push; and was less demanding on the road surface. This vehicle had been in continuous use from ancient times. It didn't lose its popularity even after the introduction of more modern means of transportation. During the First World War, when the British in Weihaiwei were enlisting Chinese labourers, the wheelbarrow was used as an important means of military transportation and went on a "long march" with Chinese labourers to European battlefields.

{note: (or is there a picture?) In China one wheel was in the centre of the wheelbarrow rather than at the front, as in Europe. With the weight of the load on either side of the wheel, it was a very efficient means of transport}

In later times, the earliest modern means of transportation introduced to Weihaiwei were rickshaws, bicycles, and animal-drawn carts. At that time, there were generally two types of rickshaw in Weihaiwei: one for private usage and the other for commercial transport. The private ones were bought by rich families for their personal use only and pulled by hired men. The commercial vehicles were also divided into two subcategories: those which could be rented together with their driver for long term usage; and those which drove around the streets to be hailed by passengers. These latter were mostly concentrated on Liugong Island to do business with the British military there.

1902 was the earliest year in record of bicycles appearing in Weihaiwei.

Cargo Junk. At a time that steam ships were under the control of foreign companies. (early 20th Century)

During that time, Westerners stationed in Weihaiwei would organise cycle touring clubs. Those bicycles were mainly imported from England and Germany. At first, their use was not all that widespread. Their owners were mostly foreigners. The bicycle was still far from being a regular part of the daily lives of the general public. It was only after the 1920s that the introduction of bicycles started to increase. According to the statistics of 1924, there were 368 bicycles with registered plates within the region. After only ten years, this number had increased to 2200.

The introduction of vehicles drawn by animals was an important event in the history of modern transportation in Weihaiwei, and had become very widespread there by 1909. At that time, there were mainly two kinds in the region: two–wheeled, and four–wheeled, horse–drawn carriages. As the conditions of the roads improved, the two–wheeled carriage spread very rapidly. After the 1920s, it became the most important means of mainland goods transportation. According to the records, Weihaiwei contained 1692 of them in 1920, and this increased to 2110 in 1921. By 1930 the number had exceeded 3000. The four–wheeled horse–drawn carriage originated in the West. It was introduced into Weihaiwei during the early years of British rule. This sort of carriage was only employed for transporting people. In

The mule–litter was popular for local weddings and outings. (1909)

Laying an asphalt road at Weihaiwei. (1902)

those days, the general public had not got into the habit of travelling by carriage. Lots of carriage owners tried to promote the business, even advertising travel free of charge to washerwomen. But these measures were not very effective. It was only in the 1920s, following the increase in the numbers of tourists visiting Weihaiwei, that the transport business began to prosper. In 1920, there were 38 four-wheeled horse-drawn carriages in the region. These had reached 61 in 1921 and further increased to over 200 by the end of British rule. Around 1930, this expanded to become the most important form of short-distance transport for people in the commercial area.

During the period of British rule, the greatest novelty was the appearance of mechanical transportation in the mainland traffic of Weihaiwei. Owing to defects in the quality of the public roads, mechanical vehicles had been forbidden in Weihaiwei. In 1927, when Weihaiwei became a base for convalescence of British troops stationed in Shanghai, the government introduced two motor trucks and one ambulance. Thus the motor vehicle appeared in Weihaiwei for the very first time. In 1928, the government formally repealed the regulations against motor vehicles and allowed them to be introduced and purchased by private persons. Within that same year, 27 vehicle dealers' shops were established by Chinese merchants. In the same year, short-distance routes for transport were opened up to the main villages within the region. In 1929, three long-distance routes were opened up to other regions. By 1928, the total number of all kinds of mechanical vehicles, including motor trucks, had reached nearly 50.

Regarding control over the various forms of transportation, their management by the government was very strict. All vehicles, including even the man-powered mono-wheel cart, had to be issued with a permit. Even the drivers needed to obtain a licence. Every vehicle had to display a registration number in a prominent position. Regulations required that lights must be installed and switched on from sunset to sunrise; these regulations further required that vehicles for transporting people were strictly forbidden to carry animals, sick persons with contagious diseases, and goods other than hand luggage; passenger vehicles with vacant seats were strictly forbidden from refusing to take passengers. Drivers should dress suitably and maintain their vehicles in a tidy condition. If a vehicle for transporting people encountered a group of animals on the road, it had to stop immediately and remain stationary until the animals had passed. Moreover, there were many detailed regulations concerning vehicle routes, their timetables and prices charged for travelling, etc. The big difference between traffic then and now was that Weihaiwei in those days followed British practice, i.e. both pedestrians and vehicles travelled on the left side of the road.

The improvement and development of transportation in Weihaiwei went hand in hand with the modernization of road construction. From 1901, a few road–building projects had already started. However, the 23 miles of village road constructed during that time were mostly very crude and simple.. Many sections of the road were destroyed by flooding in 1902. In that year, the government created an engineering team which was made responsible for road

Rickshaw boys waiting for business on Liugong Island. (early 1930s)

building and maintenance. After that, road construction gradually became more regulated. That same year, the government invested and started building the high road from Half-Moon Bay to Stone Pier in Port Edward. This was completed on 31st May, 1903, and had a length of 3 miles. This was the very first modern highroad in the Weihaiwei mainland area. During this period, the government constructed eight major high roads and fourteen minor ones. Their total length was 50 miles. At the same time, a total of 255 bridges and tunnels were also built.

In addition to all this, the maritime business was also developing quickly. This included both the introduction of scheduled steamship transportation of passengers and mail, and also the rise in cargo transportation by steamer. In 1903, in order to further develop the postal service, the government signed a contract with the government signed contracts with two British-owned merchant steamship companies. which allowed them to open a scheduled steamship service to Shanghai and Tianjin. This was the very first such scheduled steamship transportation in the region. Ever since that time, Weihaiwei has possessed a steady and reliable maritime service. Under the stimulus of a free harbour policy, a modern maritime business rapidly established itself in Weihaiwei. Steamship arrivals in the harbour increased year after year.

Cargo-passenger sampans at the pier of Liugong Island. (1938)

The first cars reach Weihaiwei. (1927)

The first police motorcycle was purchased by the colonial government. (1927)

About 100 came in every month, an average of more than 3 each day. The yearly average quantities of goods transported reached 590,000 tons. At that time, this business was almost entirely in the hands of non-Chinese merchants. Of these, British steamer companies managed the routes to Shanghai, Tianjin, Yantai and Hong Kong; while Japanese companies managed the others to Qingdao, Dalian, Andong, Haizhou, etc., whereas there was only a single Chinese company, which managed just one route to Yantai. Chinese investment was mainly concentrated on the sailing vessel transportation business. In 1919 alone, there were 4535 sailing vessels arriving at the harbour.

As a part of public transport within the territory, the short-distance ferry transport between mainland Weihaiwei and Liugong Island also continued to expand ever more rapidly. Ever since 1898, the British Navy had provided one steamship for ferrying

The wheelbarrow was the most popular form of transport in the rural areas.(1902)

passengers. In 1903, the authorities purchased another two small passenger ferryboats to make it more convenient for tourists to travel to and from the island. The British commercial King's Hotel also provided its own sailing boat to travel between East Hill and Liugong Island. Owing to the limited space of the wharf and the depth of water along the coast, large sized ships could only be anchored in the gulf. This provided a great opportunity for the traditional sampan to do business in the ferrying of passengers and goods.

Villagers going on a trip by mule. (1902)

The Weihaiwei through modern western eyes

6

"An evil den of monsters" – The walled city of Weihaiwei

According to the "Convention for the Lease of Weihaiwei", the concession granted for British rule did not include the walled city of Weihaiwei which was part of Wendeng County and thus still under Chinese rule.

During the period of British rule in Weihaiwei, the Qing government set up a sub-district deputy magistrate's office there as a subordinate organization of Wendeng to execute administrative management power within the walled city. The rank of the administrative official there varied over time. Before the British concession, it was 9th rank. After that, the British who dealt with local businesses complained that this level was too low, and suggested the Qing government should dispatch a higher ranking official to manage the city. In the summer of 1899, a more appropriate 5th rank official from Dengzhou was transferred to the city of Weihaiwei, "mainly for inspecting and strengthening the coastal defences and water conservancy as well as for planning and handling Sino-British negotiations." A little later, again in response to a British request which was agreed to by the Zongli Yamen, any questions concerning the concession settlement would be discussed directly between the British Commissioner of Weihaiwei and the Chinese Governor of Shandong Province. Thus the 5th rank official lost any real importance and was removed to Yantai. In May 1906, the walled city of Weihaiwei came under the control of a 7th rank sub-district deputy magistrate. After the Revolution of 1911, the deputy magistrate's office changed into an administrative office which dealt with Weihaiwei walled city affairs. The area of the walled city was not large, only 0.55 square kilometres; and its population was less than 2000 during this initial period. However, thanks to its location at the centre of the leased territory, its position was unique and important politically, economically, and culturally.

From an early stage, Britain wanted to occupy Weihaiwei. As early as 1900, the Governor of Malaya, Frank Swettenham, who had been sent by the Colonial Office to investigate Weihaiwei pointed out: "It is a mistake that the right of legislative rule over the city of Weihaiwei should still belong to

China. This situation must be revised immediately." He went on: "While this small and backward Chinese city still maintains its autonomy, this 'nation within a nation' actually becomes an asylum for all sorts of bad characters and a focus for rebellion." He suggested, "on the pretext of the Chinese mob's attacking British boundary commissioners, this walled village should be placed under the same legislative control of British rule [as the Weihaiwei concession]."[1] There were also many people in Britain who suggested that the British government should employ the same measures that it had done in the case of Kowloon, and simply occupy Weihaiwei City by force. The British government, which was afraid of condemnation from international public opinion, did not accept this suggestion of outright occupation, but preferred a policy of indirect control. During the discussions on the handover of power, the British side suggested that the appointment of the Chinese administrative official in the city of Weihaiwei should require the prior agreement of the British. Although this opinion was not accepted fully by the Chinese side, it did form an unwritten agreement. That is to say, whenever a sub-district deputy magistrate or committee member was appointed, the first thing to be done was to obtain the recognition of the British colonial authorities. In order to achieve its goal of control, from 1900 onward the colonial authorities offered those Chinese officials a monthly allowance of 40 yuan. Those who accepted this British salary all did their best to maintain a good relationship

with the British side. They would make the greatest effort to comply with any requests from the British. Likewise, the British also did their best to satisfy any requests from the officials of the City of Weihaiwei. That included offering protection for their personal safety and guarantees of political asylum. For example, during the Revolution of 1911, the colonial authorities made every effort to protect the sub-district deputy magistrate Zhao Dingyu.

On 18th January, 1911, revolutionaries in Wendeng drove out the district magistrate Yue Baoshu and formed an interim military government. On 23rd January, this interim government sent Zhang Suian to arrest Zhao Dingyu. Zhang Suian soon succeeded in capturing Zhao Dingyu. Zhao Dingyu had worked in Weihaiwei City for many years and had been on good terms with British officials such as Lockhart. Having got news of the capture of Zhao Dingyu, Johnston led his men in driving out Zhang Suian and reinstated Zhao Dingyu in his office. Qi Yutan, the Chairman of the walled city Chamber of Commerce was punished severely for helping Zhang Suian to enter the city. Qi Yutan had been in conflict with Zhao Dingyu over the sharing of benefits and so had asked the interim government in Wendeng to arrest Zhao Dingyu. The colonial authorities blamed Qi Yutan for Zhao Dingyu's capture and later expelled Qi Yutan from the leased territory using as an excuse his action in arresting other people outside his jurisdiction. Qi Yutan had to remain in the walled city for four years and was not permitted

The walled city of Weihaiwei. (1933)

Unrepaired streets near the East Gate in the walled city. (1924)

to leave it.

After the commencement of British rule in Weihaiwei, the British opened a trading area within Port Edward. The whole of the city's trade development centre was shifted from the walled city to Port Edward. What's more, due to the unstable situation of the Chinese government, the walled city felt uneasy and insecure. Most businesses moved out. Those remaining comprised only a few small shops with little capital. The economy of the walled city sank into a state of stagnation. However, there were still a number of prosperous industries, namely opium, gambling, and prostitution. Within this small city, opium dens, brothels and gambling houses were everywhere.

What's more, local villains and hooligans caused trouble, and law and order was unenforceable. Consequently, the city was referred to as "An Evil Den of Monsters" by the British.

It was an indisputable fact that opium was as great a disaster as a flood within the city. After the British settlement, the colonial government saw only the profit from taxing opium and forgot about their proper duty, and in 1902, they proceeded to take the sole monopoly of that trade.[2] In 1904, they allowed British colonial merchants in Hong Kong and Southeast Asia to engage in opium enterprises within Weihaiwei. What is more, they even established an opium plantation within the settlement. In September 1906, the Qing government passed a law banning opium in order to rid the country completely of this poison within ten years. In January 1909, the government proclaimed the Order against Opium again, repeating its earlier resolution. Under pressure from the public and international opinion, the colonial government was forced to abandon its monopoly, and in June of the same year it too proclaimed an ordinance banning opium. However this ordinance still allowed smokers to purchase a certain amount of opium if they registered themselves as addicts and they could obtain a licence for that purpose. This

West Street within the walled city. (1927)

made the situation even worse, because the corrupt local officials in the City, under the incentive of the profits that could be made from the high tax on opium, played games with the law, and so many opium addicts from outside swarmed into the City. As a result, the opium business, already prosperous in the city, boomed. According to statistics, in 1928 registered opium houses numbered 42 within the City, and at their peak exceeded 60.

Another undesirable phenomenon in Weihaiwei was the habit of gambling. The British occupiers were opposed to gambling. They made quite an effort to ban it. Soon after the hand-over to British rule in Weihaiwei, they posted an order to this effect everywhere in the area. In August 1906, The Gambling Ordinance was proclaimed. According to this ordinance, anyone opening or managing a gambling den, and all those who took part in, as well as those who were involved in supporting, this activity, would be punished with fines or imprisonment. The maximum fine was up to 100 yuan, and the longest term of imprisonment was 6 months. In the case of under-aged boys, they were beaten with a whip. In order to ban gambling, detectives were sent in secret to visit suspected gambling dens; constables were sent on sudden raids; organized teams would be sent to make an inspection. A lot of determined efforts were made to stamp out gambling. The earliest record of a gambling raid was in 1902 quoted from the Acting Magistrate's case book, "on the night of the 16th inst: (16th October 1902) I raided a large gambling establishment in Yangting consisting of 4 booths and a shop, capturing 10

South Street within the walled city. (late 1920s)

Scene at the crossroads in the walled city. (1898)

gamblers, 2 ingots [of] value taels 19, plus a quantity of cash, and confiscating the tents"[3]. Although the attitude of the British in banning gambling was a positive move, the habit could not easily be eradicated within China, where it had been formed over several centuries. Historical documents indicated that during the period of British rule, cases of gambling were still high and showed little sign of decreasing. For example, during the three years from 1924 to 1926, the total numbers of criminal offences were 567, 702 and 579 respectively, and of these the corresponding gambling cases numbered 148, 173 and 167 in each year. Their proportion of the total criminal offences was thus 26%, 24%, 28% respectively. That was the highest level, but it was still growing. In fact, these statistics only reflected those cases actually being prosecuted and were only the tip of the iceberg. Considerably more cases were undetected by the police. In order to avoid capture by the police, gamblers devised many sly tricks. Some concealed themselves in underground rooms or remote abandoned houses; some even hid within ancient tombs. Due to the lack of effective measures for banning gambling in China at that time, the area outside the leased territory became a haven for gamblers. Those living close to its boundary went outside to gamble; those living near the walled city went inside to gamble. Consequently, the profits from gambling inside the walled city were becoming ever higher.

Inside the city, the activities of prostitutes were also very blatant. The British attitude was to allow registered prostitutes but ban all the others. There were a number of brothels outside the East Gate area, where both brothel owners and prostitutes obtained licences from the colonial government. In the early days of British rule, illegal unlicensed brothels were concentrated mainly near the Stone Pier within Port Edward. According to official statistics, there were more than 20 such establishments. Their business was booming. Many British sailors and disreputable individuals with no proper occupation would visit them. This phenomenon attracted the attention of the colonial government. They were worried that whenever the Chinese got together, there would be gambling. What's more, they might start plotting some actions against the colonial government. Therefore, from 1902, the government started to investigate and ban these establishments, which caused the unlicensed prostitutes to flood into the city. The walled city did nothing to stop this phenomenon. As a result, prostitution became widespread. In addition, there were many waitresses serving in the opium houses who, apart from serving tea, lighting the clients' pipes, providing opium and massaging their backs, were also in the habit of offering sexual favours. Thus the opium dens also became illegal brothels.

In the opinion of the British, this state of chaos in the city was due to the corruption of the Chinese officials. In fact, there were many regulating organisations in the city. There was the Police Office for keeping law and order; the Tobacco Customs House for collecting tax revenue from tobacco sales; the Opium Prohibition Bureau for banning opium and gambling. However the real function of these organizations was not to ensure the orderly running of society, but to maximise the financial gains which those officials could enjoy. Most of the minor officials serving within these organisations set their eyes on squeezing profits from them. For example, a good way for producing wealth for the Opium Prohibition Bureau was to resell what they had confiscated to the opium dens at a much higher price than the market price. This "official" opium was called "official earth". According to the regulations, for each pipe in the opium house it was necessary to buy a certain amount of "official earth". Initially this was 8oz(250g) and later on this was increased to 16oz(500g). Likewise, the tax was also increased from 4 yuan per pipe each month to 8 yuan. If no purchase of "official earth" was made or no tax paid, then the pipes would be confiscated and the opium houses investigated and closed. Those officials who were meant to ban gambling would forget about their real duty once they had got their hands on this money. On the contrary, they would even open gambling houses for profit. Consequently, it was not surprising that the city of Weihaiwei was in a state of chaos.

Old and new look for town and country

The city area of Weihai was founded many centuries ago, following its establishment as a military district, which led to the arrival of immigrants and the start of its commercial development. It was in the 31st year of the Emperor Hongwu (1398) that the Ming Dynasty started to station soldiers here as a military district, and it was known as Weihaiwei (Weihai military district, the second 'wei' meaning a military district). During the first year of EmperorYongle of the Ming Dynasty (1403), the walled city of Weihaiwei was built by the labouring people of Wendeng and Mouping. It occupied 0.55 square kilometres, and was in the form of a square, according to the

The South Gate of the walled city. (1938)

traditional architectural concept of a "round heaven and square earth". The city wall was just over 30 feet in height and 20 feet in thickness, with a total length of three kilometers. Four gateways were constructed to the north, south, east and west. There were two main roads for traffic linking the East/West and North/South gateways. Shops and firms were built along these main roads.

The walled city of Weihaiwei during the period of British rule was not regarded as a city in the British sense, but rather as a "village with walls". This was firstly because it was "small", a small place with a small population. Its scale was more or less that of a village. Secondly, because it was "rustic": the whole city consisted of single storey buildings in a dilapidated condition, without any buildings in good shape, in no way different from a village. Thirdly, because it was "dirty": public health facilities were not good. In a certain sense, health conditions there were even worse than in some of the better villages. It was the case that during the 32 years of British rule, this city didn't develop. On the contrary, it gradually became even more dilapidated. Most of the buildings had been beyond repair for many years. Broken roofs and walls were everywhere. Among all the houses, only one, the "Wang Family Residence" was unique and had some style. It occupied an area of more than 1.7 acres, with nearly one hundred rooms. In addition, it had an established garden as well as a theatrical stage. It had once been the home of a retired high official and was built in the grand style. Alas, following the

The East Gate of the walled city, an important gateway. (1902)

decadence and fall of the official class there, it could never display the full dignity of its early splendour again. However the Temple Theatre had preserved the traditional grand architectural style although it stood at the centre of a crossroads and thus caused some trouble to the traffic. In the South Street a stone archway for women who were faithful to their husbands after death proved an unexpected attraction to many foreigners. The four historical gateways were still in existence, but after more than five hundred years of the effects of wind and sunshine, they were already badly weathered.

What the British were most proud of were the changes taking place in the commercial district outside the City. In reports to the colonial government, and publicity documents produced to attract business and tourism, there was always much talk of these changes, in order to publicise and praise the achievements of the British. In comparison with the walled city, here everywhere was clean and tidy, fresh, and full of vitality. The public works of the colonial government were mainly concentrated in the coastal area to the northeast of the city. Here were to be found the government administration concentrated in the Northern Camp, the commercial trade district concentrated near the shipyard, the summer sanatorium in the East Hill area, and the residential area concentrated in two villages near the Stone Pier.

Although construction within the territory did not develop very rapidly, even so, after over 20 years of effort, from the south to the east, the commercial area constructed along the bay was just beginning to take shape. Within this area, there was a single main road along the coast linking the south and the north, with a cluster of more than twenty side roads at the north end around the docks. The surface of the road was very smooth, and consisted mostly of gravel, forming its foundations, with cement or asphalt on the top. Stone ditches were built to conduct the surface water into the drains, so that no rain water was left to make road muddy. After daily cleaning and tidying, the road was always clean. Along the roadside, were planted lines of trees, with willows and poplars growing abundantly; whilst in the street garden near the docks, shrubs grew luxuriantly, festooned with many beautiful flowers. Although there were no tall buildings on the streets, you could see many Western-style houses. These were mainly elegant detached courtyard garden houses with flowers and lawns, situated amongst beautiful trees. The most attractive of these buildings was the King's Hotel located on East Hill. It stood on the high cliff overlooking the beach, in a green and hilly area. Owing to its attractive geographical location, it looked very stylish. Sadly, it was deliberately destroyed by Japanese bombardment in August 1945. The Haixing Primary School building, established by the Catholic Church, was the one tall building existing at that time. It was renovated during the mid-1970s. Although the main structure of the building still exists, its appearance is no longer the same as the original. The summer

City centre temple theatre. (1898)

Commercial Street on Liugong Island. (1938)

Seymour Street in Port Edward. (1930)

house for the Admiral of the Royal Navy was also the pride of the British. It was built in 1904. Because of the two pairs of rounded windows on the front of the building, which rather resembled four eyes staring towards the sea, people commonly called it the "Four-eyes building". This building had a unique style. The staircases rose up to the second floor; the outside corridor was supported by wooden pillars; the roof displayed the artistic craftsmanship of its designer. (This house remains the best maintained building in Weihai up to the present day). Apart from these, other outstanding buildings were the Lawers & Clark company building near the pier, the official residence at Beicang, the official building of the Senior District Officer, and four bungalows at the south of the bay. All of these were characteristic of the traditional European architectural style.

The pride of the British in their achievements was not only evident in these beautiful and elegant buildings, but also in the use of British names to boast of their power and to display their ownership. The names of local places were changed to include the names of eminent British persons, ranging from those of British monarchs down to important government officials and merchants. For example: the Port of Weihaiwei was renamed Port Edward, using the name of the British King Edward VII, following the example of

The Triangle Park, the first park in Weihaiwei. (1936)

Victoria Harbour in Hong Kong. The coastal street on Liugong Island was named Seymour Street, after E. H. Seymour, the British Commander-in-Chief of the international force, or Eight Nations' Alliance against the Boxers. The main roads in Port Edward were also renamed after the Commissioners and other British officials such as Dorward Road, Lockhart Road, Browne Road, Blunt Road, Johnston Road, and Lampson Road. Even some of the hills that had no connection with the British had their names changed to British ones such as Mount MacDonald and the Fitzgerald Range.

In the first few years after Weihaiwei's return, the city reconstruction was also appreciated by the remaining westerners.

After the return, the newly established Weihaiwei Municipal Government abolished the separation between the inner and outer city, and treated them as one single place in their regulations and overall planning. In 1931, the East and North Gates were demolished. The Temple Theatre at the cross roads was also demolished, and direct roads into the city were constructed, thus opening up the city that had been enclosed for over five hundred years. Later, the other gates and walls were gradually demolished.

At the same time, in the course of the demolition of walls and construction of new roads, the Weihaiwei Municipal Government also developed many scenic spots within the city, by reconstructing and extending certain buildings and parks there.

The Huancui Temple located on the west side of the City was first constructed in 1489. It was renovated and rebuilt three times during the Qing

Official residence of Naval Officer in Charge, Liugong Island (1938)

Dynasty, the last time in 1757. During the period of British rule, this building had become somewhat dilapidated. In July 1931, the Municipal Government renovated it and proceeded to tidy up the surrounding area to form a park. The renovated building was supported by twelve square pillars. Inside it was spacious and bright. The lower floor was surrounded by corridors; the upper floor was very elegant, with beautifully carved flying eaves. Two pavilions were added. The upper one was to the south, and called the Moon-watch Pavilion; the lower one opposite the main building, which was a little smaller, was called the Sea-view Pavilion. The scale of the main building was not large, but it was located high up and overlooked the surrounding area, with its excellent natural scenery. It was beautiful enough to delight any visitor. (It was burned down by Japanese troop in December 1944. The present building was re-built in 1977-80).

Wukou Garden, a street garden, was built during British rule. It was situated at the meeting point of three roads. Initially, it occupied only 2600 square metres. At the beginning of British rule, the colonial government planted trees and flowers here to form a garden. Because of its location close to the naval shipyard, it was named Wukou (meaning Shipyard) Garden. Also because of its triangular shape, it was later named the "Triangular

A village street, with characteristic stone flagging. (1933)

Garden". On 10th January 1916, the body of a large whale was discovered on the beach. Two huge jawbones from this whale were used to make an arch for the East Gate, and one bone was placed across each of the South and North Gates. That's why it was renamed yet again as the Whale Garden. During British rule, gardens became places in which to commemorate their achievements. In 1921, when Lockhart retired, two stone tablets were erected here by the Port Edward Chamber of Commerce and the village headmen to remember his just administration and his contributions to local business.

East Hill Park was situated in the same location as the present East Hill Hotel. It was completed on 6th June, 1928.4 A great variety of trees and rare flowers were planted inside the park for the public's enjoyment. Many of these were imported from foreign countries. The extension and re–construction of this park were begun in February 1934, and completed by 15th July of the same year. There was one assembly hall there, named "Lofty Room for Cloud–Watching" which was situated at the highest point of the park. At that time, it was the only large–sized hall which could accommodate more than 300 people. There was a terrace on the top of the building which offered fine views. Inside the park, there was a painted pavilion named the "Long Wind Pavilion", and a gymnasium equipped with all sorts of exercise equipment. In addition a small wood, orchard and gardens were planted there. For some time, East Hill was one of the great scenic spots in Weihaiwei for sightseeing, and a major tourist attraction. In 1945, it was set on fire by the Japanese soldiers when they left.

A father and son in the countryside. (1902)

A stone built house and its residents.

The village view, most buildings were made of rough stones. (1927)

During the British rule of Weihaiwei, the construction of facilities at Port Edward and the management of public health and the environment did achieve certain progress. However the changes within the countryside did not amount to much. Apart from the construction of a few roads everything else remained much the same as it had been in the old days.

The whole settlement was located in a hilly area. The hills were not very high, and the plain not very wide. The slopes of the hilly area were terraced for cultivation. The earth was rather poor due its high sand content. There were plenty of trees on the hills. Some areas were bare with huge rocks, some covered with green grasses and bushes. Hundreds of small streams spread themselves over the hills, but most of the time these were dry. Only when the rainy season came would there be a continuous flow of water and this would combine into turbulent rivers surging through the long dry river beds. Sometimes, it would also flood into the lower fields, destroying agri-cultural crops in its path.

Most of the villages were located on lower ground surrounded by hills, some also on the slopes. The local people favoured the practice of feng shui. Before building a house, they would always ask the feng shui master to choose the place and decide the direction it should face. Those locations with hills at the back and water in front and facing the sun were generally believed to possess good feng shui. Most of the village houses were built

Farmland outside the city walls. (1936)

Clothes–washing in the South River. The mountain spring river flows beneath the shade of the willows to make this one of the 'eight sights' of old Weihaiwei. (1927)

comparatively close together, with simple narrow streets in between. They were mostly of the traditional Chinese courtyard style. The streets were not very wide. Some of the surfaces of the streets were leveled with mud and sand; or covered with gravel. The houses were mostly built of stone, and only a few rich families could afford to use bricks. The roofs were usually covered with thatch of wheat, straw or seaweed. Only a few families could afford to use tiles. In the farming villages, none of the buildings were in very good shape. Apart from the large residences of some individual rich families, there were also temples and theatres. Within the villages, people mostly lived close together.

In each village, those families sharing the same surname would usually build a family temple in order to pay respect to their ancestors and for discussions about family affairs. Generally, these family temples were better built, with superior materials such as bricks and tiles, even red wooden pillars. Although the style was simple and uniform, they were wider, grander and more spacious than the houses. Apart from family temples, there were also 62 religious temples in the area. These temples were mostly built in a comparatively grand style. "In the larger villages may be seen theatrical pavilions in front of some local temples, and these pavilions are often the most elaborate buildings, as regards architectural structure and ornaments, in their respective neighbourhoods" "The stone–built pavilions usually faced north, opposite the front gate of the temple. The temple and the divine images inside the temple were all built facing south. Therefore, theoretically these spiritual

Huxian Temple outside of the city wall (now to the east of the White Swan Hotel), and Eight Tablets in memory of faithful and filial dead women. (1898)

beings could also watch the performance of the plays. As for the audience, they stood in between the temple and the stage." The quotations mentioned above describing the pavilions may be found in the book Lion and Dragon in North China, written by Reginald Johnston.

Fishing boats and cargo vessels in the bay of Weihaiwei.

The people of Weihaiwei during changing times

Traditionally, the inhabitants of present day Weihai were thought to have arrived from Yunnan hundreds of years ago. However according to discoveries by archaeologists, native people were to be found in that area as early as 6000 years ago, during the mid–Neolithic period. Following the various changes of dynasties and other historical events, the residents of this area moved away several times. Because of loss of land, or to escape the chaos and social upheaval brought about by war, other people continuously flooded into Weihai. These made up the early inhabitants of this region. They chose the location and settled down together to form primitive settlements. From the beginning of feudal society, there are various recorded facts concerning villages in the area to be found throughout classic history books. For example, during the West Han Dynasty, Weihai was known as Shiluo Village, and during the Yuan Dynasty, its name was changed to Qingquankuang.

During the Yuan and Ming Dynasties, frequent attacks by Japanese pirates became a major concern for Chinese national defence. After the establishment of the Ming Dynasty, the Chinese government began to set up systematic control of the coast, and chose significant areas in which to build up garrisons. Thus the military district of Weihaiwei came into being. The increase in its population reached a high point. Large numbers of emigrants flooded into Weihaiwei and the villages surrounding the central garrison quickly increased in size.

In the Qing Dynasty, after Weihaiwei became the base for the North–Ocean Navy, many merchants and transient residents flooded into Weihaiwei to seek their fortunes. The population of the area thus swelled still further. The British military supplier of the Beiyang Fleet, Armstrong, reported that all of this construction activity brought in many more people to Weihaiwei. Within five years the population of Liugong Island and the area around the harbour had grown considerably and a village of about five hundred families had sprung up outside the wall of the town on the mainland. Other villages emerged near each fort or camp. With this influx came various types of tradesmen and some beggars. During the herring season a large number of fishing vessels operated out of Weihaiwei and the Beiyang Fleet of the Qing imperial navy wintered there. This part of Shandong appeared to have a promising future.[5] However it was only a few years later that the Japanese shattered this hope and afterwards the British occupied it.

An old peasant. (1920s)

Initially, the people of Weihaiwei were not much concerned about the British. This was because intelligent men in Weihaiwei itself believed that "These British will stay here for only a short time. They intend to get the money for the buildings that are being pulled down, then they will up with their anchors and steam away never to return." No one guessed that this was the beginning of an occupation that was to last for thirty-two years.[6] However, when the local people realized that these foreign newcomers intended to settle down and lease their land, they did not yield but fought against them on several occasions during the early years of British rule. But after those initial difficulties, the local inhabitants came gradually to accept the British presence, and the British themselves soon became very satisfied with the behaviour of the people of Weihaiwei.

From the viewpoint of the British, "To speak as a whole, people here are not educated. But they, especially the farmers, are very friendly and courteous towards foreigners, obviously different from the rude and noisy Southerners. They are slow by nature, not offensive to other people. Generally speaking, their moral standards are completely the same as the Scots in most of the farming areas. They respect tradition, are respectful to the elderly, and affectionate to the young."[7] Lockhart felt very satisfied to discover that no more than 20 official staff could manage such a large population in Weihaiwei. He wrote in his Report to the Colonial Office, "The Chinaman in this part of the world at any rate is not as black as he is painted by those who have no real knowledge or experience of him. Regarded impartially from an administrative point of view, the Chinaman is a most desirable person to govern for being a great believer in home rule, his chief desire is to be left alone to govern himself and his family. He is as a rule sober, orderly, docile; kind to his parents and his children; thrifty, industrious and contented. When such qualities predominate, it is not surprising that the Chinese are in many respects much superior to those who affect to despise them or to superciliously criticize them."[8]

Commissioner Johnston analysed this phenomena: "One important reason why the people of Weihaiwei acquiesce with a good grace in British rule is their vague belief that we are in Weihaiwei at the request and with the thorough goodwill of the Chinese Government, and are in some way carrying out the august wishes of the Emperor. They still speak of us as the foreigners or "Ocean men", and of China as Da Guo, the Great Country. There is not the faintest vestige of a feeling of loyalty to the British sovereign, even among those who would be sorry to see us go away. Thus arises among the people the notion that their own Emperor has for some mysterious reason, best known to himself, temporarily entrusted the administration of Weihaiwei to some English officials, and will doubtless decide in his own good time when this arrangement is to be rescinded, but any attempt to persuade them

A street cobbler (1930s)

A village street in Mengjiazhuang. (1902)

Grandmother and grandchild at Port Edward. (1907)

that the Emperor could not, if he willed, cause the immediate departure of the foreigners would probably be a miserable failure. The long and short of the matter is that the Chinese of Weihaiwei acquiesce in British rule because their sovereign, as represented by the Governor of Shandong, shows them the example of acquiescence; but if diplomatic troubles were to arise between Great Britain and China, and the command, direct or indirect, were to go forth from the Governor that the British in Weihaiwei were no longer to be treated with respect, a few days or weeks would be sufficient to bring about a startling change in the direction of anti-foreign feeling among the inhabitants of the leased Territory."[9]

The British appreciated the industrious nature of the people of Weihaiwei. This was because the farmers made their own efforts to support the pressure of the dramatic increase of population. During the period of British rule, the

A mother and daughter washing clothes. (1920)

population of Weihaiwei increased rapidly. The results of the censuses of 1911 and 1921 were 146,840 and 154,416 respectively. The rates of increase in the population were both 5.3%. However if labourers whose home was within the territory, but who had left it to seek work outside, were counted, the rate would be 8%. Due to the fact that the territory consisted mainly of hills and the dry, sandy coastal land, agricultural land was quite scarce, and scattered throughout the valleys between hills. Therefore, the rapid increase in the population also increased the dramatic contrast between the increase in the population and the scarcity of land. Population density almost reached the

A Western style wedding on Liugong island. (1938)

limit that could be supported by the farming resources of that time. As a result, the struggle for survival in the area became very fierce. "Farmers had to increase food production by close cultivation and various kinds of plantation. During the winter season they went away to do other jobs or various kinds of other business to support their family. The better quality grains were usually sold out. Most of the common people ate coarse grains and root vegetables, or corns and maize." In the view of the British, "The only explanation for this was that people in the area were all extremely frugal.

A small businessman in the walled city of Weihaiwei. (1924)

A traditional wedding procession in the countryside. (1933)

Street stalls on market day. (1933)

A villager from Mengjiazhuang. (1905)

Local people gathered to celebrate the first Chinese Constitution. (1906)

Grandmother and grandson having a rest beside the road. (1902)

There was hardly any empty—handed leisure class. They were all most hard—working farmers."

As for the living conditions of the inhabitants of Weihaiwei, the British held a number of conflicting views. In the opinion of Swettenham, Weihaiwei was the poorest place in Shandong, "Every village contains large number of labourers who are without land or houses or cattle. These people spend their days in labouring for the landowners. When it comes to a bad year, there will be no money for their labour. It will be all right if they could earn some food to eat." On the other hand, in the views of Lockhart and Johnston, Weihaiwei was not poor. In 1903, Lockhart wrote: "I consider the people here neither rich nor poor. There are hardly any beggars, and people develop rather well physically. They must be counted as up to the level of well—to—do and secure." Whereas Johnston stated in his account: "If there were no lawsuits or family problems, their life would be very peaceful even blissful. They possess an excellent climatic environment. In the meantime, their fine physical and spiritual condition also proves that their daily life was not bad at all. During the harvest season, grown—ups and children are all busily engaged in the fields; while in the longish winter nights, they sat around the heated bed for warmth. In the daytime, they would go out to collect firewood, or stand on the field to watch the English horses racing on their ancestor's soil. Three times each week, they would use a donkey to carry goods on its back for sale in Weihaiwei market. Women would work on needlework at home and chat leisurely."[10]

Each period has its own way of life. During the period in which Weihaiwei was under British rule, Chinese society was undergoing a transition from a feudal society to a modern one. According to the popular saying, it was normal for the commercial coastal areas to be the first to be influenced by the Westerners. But in Weihaiwei, this was not so. During those one hundred and more years of social progress in China nothing seemed to happen to the people who dwelt on this ancient earth. These farmers, "wooden-headed, faced all wars and political storms almost without any response, as if nothing had changed."[11] Yet, this was not so strange. As a race, the Chinese were never very susceptible to any other culture. In any case, the colonial government established by the British was almost completely Chinese in style. To allow the Weihaiwei people to carry on living in the old-fashioned productive fashion was the ideal solution for the British. Both Johnston and Lockhart were successful in using this means of Chinese control to rule Weihaiwei. Under their protection, the thoughts and deeds of the Weihaiwei people differed little from the previous century right up to the early 1930s.

To take the family as an example, by the end of the Qing Dynasty, there was already a trend towards smaller numbers in the Chinese traditional large

Stalls outside Tianhou temple, these were not only places for business, but also where people would gather to socialise. (1902)

Rickshaw man having a rest on Liugong Island. (1937)

family. Yet, extended families containing four or five generations were not all that rare in Weihaiwei. According to the result of an investigation in 1911, there were two households whose family members exceeded 40 people; 15 households with between 30–40 people; more than 100 households with between 20–30. The largest household was the Meng–Yu family which had four generations living together. It contained 66 people plus one servant. Each meal needed to feed 67 mouths in total!

Again, let us take the hateful customs of growing pigtails and foot–binding as examples. By 1930, there were still 50 men with pigtails; and almost all the women still had bound feet. This did not mean that the opposition in Weihaiwei to these customs occurred later than in other places. In fact, Weihaiwei was one of the earliest places in Shandong Province to develop an anti–foot–binding movement. It was in 1907 that a number of people from Jiangsu and Anhui Provinces together with the commercial and educational sectors of Weihaiwei established the anti–foot–binding organization – the Natural Feet Association. Later on, local people in Weihaiwei also organized another natural feet association. In 1914, these two combined together to form the Weihaiwei Natural Feet Association. Propaganda materials were brought from Shanghai by members and distributed everywhere, in order to get rid of the old–fashioned practice of binding feet. In 1909, the Natural Feet Association also established the Shude Girls' School to encourage girls with unbound feet to learn the Chinese language, needlework and home economics, in order to promote the development of this movement. However, the colonial government took no interest in this, and all the efforts of the anti-binding feet organizations just vanished in the wind! It was only after the return of Weihaiwei to China that the movement began to get into full swing. The municipal government officially established the Female Persuasion Committee to mobilize people both in the City and villages. By 1933, the whole area had basically stopped foot-binding. The situation regarding pig-tails on the heads of Weihaiwei menfolk was similar to that of the bound feet of the women. Weihaiwei was the last place in China where they were abolished. The Revolution of 1911, which led to the overthrow of the Qing Dynasty, also brought with it the movement to cut off pigtails. After a few years' effort, this outdated custom was basically abolished nation-wide. However, even in 1930, there were still 50 men with pigtails in Weihaiwei. It was only after its return to Chinese control, thanks to the encouragement and efforts of the local officials, that men's pigtails finally totally disappeared by 1931.

Owing to its long periods of war and past upheavals and its militarily important location, there were a considerable number of emigrants, itinerant people and military personnel amongst the residents of Weihaiwei. This resulted in a tendency to strife within the population. For some time after the British arrived, this habit was became acute. No matter how important or

Women busy during the wheat harvest outside the city wall. (1898)

Children returning after collecting seafood from the beach. (1919)

After the Chinese Revolution of 1911, China went through a period of reform, getting rid of the remnants of the Qing empire. However, the people of Weihaiwei seem to have got left behind, some men are still wearing the 'pigtail' a remnant of the Qing empire. (1920s)

insignificant their dispute, ordinary people would take it to court without hesitation. It was said that: "The people of this Territory positively revel in going to Court & look upon it in very much the same light as going to the Theatre or other places of diversion. An injured husband will walk 20 miles to inform the Magistrate that he is quite unable to keep his wife in order, – An aggrieved rustic will plod wearily a distance of 10 miles to tell the Magistrate that his neighbour had stolen 6 handfuls of grass that belonged to him."[12]

Weihaiwei returns to the motherland

7

In the history of Weihai during the 20th century, the year 1930 is an especially important one because that was the year in which Weihaiwei was returned to China. Ever since the British had leased Weihaiwei, the gate to North China had been wide open, which was a threat to the military defence of the whole of China. From the day that Weihaiwei had been leased, all Chinese governments had made repeated efforts to get it back. But at that time, China was weakened by civil wars and political conflicts. The way for Weihaiwei to return to the motherland was to be long and difficult.

War between Russian and Japanese broke out in 1904. The victorious Japanese took over control of Port Arthur (L ü shun) from Russia. This change meant that the British had now lost their excuse for leasing Weihaiwei "to defeat Russians". According to the clause in the Convention for the Lease of Weihaiwei that "the lease term should be for as long as the Russians control Port Arthur" the British should have given Weihaiwei back to China at once. This was the first time there was any hope of Weihaiwei being returned. However the British War Office / Naval Office and the Colonial Office insisted that Weihaiwei was a valuable "Military enclave" which could be used to control Germany's influence in North China. As the ally of

Lockhart with some Japanese at a spa bath to celebrate the opening. (1905)

Britain, and in order to curb the German who occupied Jiaozhou Gulf, the Japanese were against handing Weihaiwei back too and insisted "The British should stay in Weihaiwei as long as Germany stays in the Jiaozhou Gulf". The British Government then decided on the strategy of not giving back Weihaiwei and the British Colonial Ministry tried to revise the treaty and place Weihaiwei under the control of Hong Kong in order to occupy Weihaiwei for a longer period of time. The Hong Kong Governor Sir Matthew Nathan was ready to take over Weihaiwei as soon as he got the order. As the British were busy with their preparations, the Chinese Qing Government requested that Weihaiwei should be returned according to the Treaty signed in 1906. The British Minister stated that although Port Arthur had changed its owner, it was still not under Chinese control and so Britain would not give up Weihaiwei, no matter what was stated in the treaty. The weak Qing Government withdrew. In order to avoid the intervention of other western countries, the British Government abandoned the idea of making Weihaiwei belong to Hong Kong. Since 1905, there had been suggestions inside the Hong Kong British Government that it should abandon its demands for Weihaiwei on the precondition of gaining the New Territories. For historical reasons, this suggestion failed.[1]

Lockhart inspecting Port Arthur recently a battleground. (1906)

Lockhart and Johnston with Clementi (on right of picture), a visiting senior British colonial official. (1905)

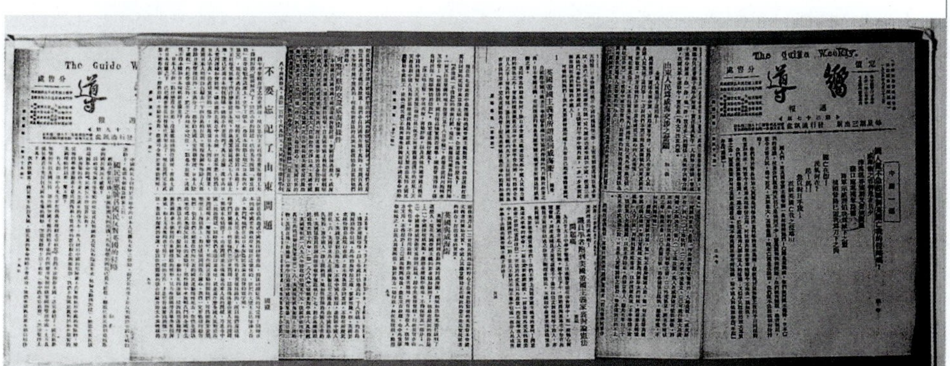

The Guide Weekly

嚮導

不要忘記了山東問題

Articles by Chen Duxiu and other early communist leaders in The Guide Weekly, demanding the unconditional return of Weihaiwei.

World War I ended in November 1918 with the Central Powers of Germany and Austria, etc. the losers. China had joined the Allied Forces during the war and thus belonged to the winning side. This brought new hope to China of recovering Weihaiwei. In January 1919, a Chinese delegation took part in the Paris Peace Conference. Before the meeting, the British Government modified its policies towards China, including Weihaiwei. Acting Administrator Reginald Johnston thought that Weihaiwei had not brought any prestige to Great Britain but only scorn from the Chinese because of the poor investment record of Britain compared with its other colonies. He proposed giving Weihaiwei back to China but retaining Liugong Island as a supply base for the Navy. Jordan, the British Minister in China, agreed and considered this an important element in the adjustment of British policies towards China. The British Navy Ministry insisted on retaining Weihaiwei as its supply base. Japan had expanded its influence in China and the Pacific Areas during World War I and threatened Britain's role in China, which led to severe conflicts between the two countries. The British Government finally decided that as long as Japan continued to advance in China, it would not give up its existing position there. During the Paris Peace Conference, all reasonable requests presented by the Chinese delegation to recover leased land and end the occupation were denied.

The Chinese delegation's failure at the Paris Peace Conference led to the

1st October 1930, Johnston welcomes the Chinese commissioner to receive the return of Weihaiwei at Edward Port.

May 4th Patriotic Movement throughout the whole of China, which forced the Chinese Beiyang Government to refuse to sign the Peace Treaty. The Paris Peace Conference strengthened Japanese influence and advantages in China and deepened its conflicts with USA and Great Britain. The USA organised the Washington Conference, held from 20th November, 1921 to 6th February, 1922, and attended by nine countries including China, the USA, Great Britain and Japan. Before the conference, the British Government tried to prevent any decision concerning the leased land. But as a prelude, E. Carpmael from the British Embassy in China prepared an internal report about Weihaiwei presenting Johnston's suggestion, which was to be used only within the British delegation. On 3rd December, 1921, the Chinese representative Gu Weijun put forward the proposal that leased lands in China be returned and demanded the "abolition of the leased land treaties". The British Government was reluctant to agree, but was forced by Chinese patriotic activities and conflicts inside Britain itself. The British representative and the head of the Privy Council, Arthur Balfour, was forced to announce that the Great Britain would return Weihaiwei to China once all other western countries had returned their leased lands to China.[2]

Weihaiwei was the first leased land to be returned through peaceful talks. Before the negotiations, Britain took a tough line. Balfour wrote to Shi Zhaoji demanding that negotiation groups from both sides should be formed,

1st October 1930, Vice Foreign Minister Wang Jiazheng(left second) and the first High Commissioner of Weihaiwei municipal government, Xu Zushan(left third), accompanied by Johnston, inspecting the British Guard of Honour, (1st October 1930)

taking the Settlement of Qingdao, formerly leased by Germany, as a model. The British proposed as preconditions to these negotiations that the British Navy should be free to use Weihaiwei during the summer with no limitation regarding the transportation and storing of military goods, free of tax charges and to retain all British properties; to conduct naval exercises in the sea around Weihaiwei; foreign people's rights to be represented in any decisions involving local affairs; China to build a railway at Weihaiwei, etc.. The British Minister in China passed Balfour's proposal to the Chinese Beiyang Government formally on 14th and 16th April, and suggested forming a Sino-British committee to investigate Weihai. After the Washington Conference, the Chinese Government formed the Pacific Conference Committee mainly through its Foreign Diplomatic Ministry to work for the implementation of the decisions of the Washington Conference. On 7th April, the Chinese Beiyang Government assigned Liang Ruhao to supervise the take-over of Weihaiwei. The British Government assigned Bertram Giles as the chairman and A. P. Blunt and G. F. B. Edward Collins as commissioners.[3]

Starting on 2nd October, 1922, the delegations from China and Great Britain held their fifth round of negotiations. The inflexibility of the British conditions and especially their refusal to withdraw from the continued lease of

The British Guard of Honour at the rendition ceremony. (1st October 1930)

Liugong Island, and the demand of the British side that foreigners' interests must be represented in local political decisions meant that no result could be achieved from the negotiations. The two sides restarted their negotiations in Beijing on 16th March, 1923 and after 34 rounds of negotiation, the <<Agreement on the Rendition of Weihaiwei >> was finally settled on 31st March. According to this agreement, the British Navy would lease Liugong Island for another ten years unconditionally and could continue to lease it for as long as it wished; the British Navy could hold military exercises and training on Liugong Island and in the seas around Weihaiwei, also the transportation and storage of military goods by the British Navy were all allowed; some of the official positions in Weihaiwei should be offered to foreign people, etc. This agreement infringed Chinese sovereignty and was actually just a repeat of Balfour's earlier proposal.[4]

The return of Weihaiwei to China caused dissatisfaction amongst those foreigners living there, and on 18th February, 1912, they sent to the British Government a demand guaranteeing the safety of foreigners' rights in Weihaiwei.[5] The Chinese people were even more dissatisfied with the conditions placed on the return of Weihaiwei. During the period of negotiation, demonstrations occurred in and outside Shandong Province. The Agreement brought about an angry reaction by the whole Chinese people. The Shandong Parliament announced to the other parliaments in China that there should be no conditions attached to the return of Weihaiwei after the termination of Britain's lease. Furthermore the Chinese representative on the Sino-British Committee, Liang Ruhao, had failed in his mission and should be punished because he had accepted the land-leasing and sovereignty infringing 24 treaties. Shandong Industries United Union announced to the Chinese Beiyang Government and the Diplomatic Ministry that the Agreement was an insult to the nation and would not be accepted by the Shandong People. Shao Ciming and other people, including representatives of the Shandong Beijing Residents Association, supported by the Shandong Students Association and the Wendeng County Independence Association etc., were sent to the State Council to present a petition,[6] which denounced the Chinese Beiyang Government as responsible for Britain's infringement of China's sovereignty and interference in Chinese domestic affairs, and demanded the punishment of Liang Ruhao for his betrayal. The early Chinese Communist Party Leaders, Chen Duxiu, Cai Hesen, and others published articles in the first public Party Newspaper The Guide Weekly to summon the Chinese people to resist the infringement of Chinese territory by the British. These displayed the Chinese Communist Party's principled stand against Imperialism and for safeguarding the nation's sovereignty through articles such as: <<The So-Called Return of Weihaiwei by the British Imperialists>>, <<The Shandong People Fight For the Return of Weihaiwei>>, <<Don't Forget the Shandong Affair>>, <<The Shocking

Conditions to the Return of Weihaiwei>> and <<Cannot the Chinese People defeat British Invasion Now?>>, etc.

These protest activities throughout China showed the people's determination to recover Weihaiwei without preconditions and forced the Chinese Beiyang Government to refuse to sign the treaty. On 20th September and 2nd October, 1923, the Beiyang Government demanded that the British Government should revise the agreement. The British Government refused and said if the Chinese Government did not sign the agreement, the British Government would not return Weihaiwei to China. On 28th May, 1924, Liang Ruhao was forced to resign in the face of whole nation's condemnation. The Diplomatic Ministry took over the work of recovering Weihaiwei. After further negotiations, Britain agreed to revise some words but made no substantive changes and stated that if the Chinese Government insisted on real changes, the British Government would postpone the return. On 12th June, 1924, the Foreign Minister Gu Weijun of the Beiyang Government restarted the negotiations with the British Minister. After ten rounds of negotiation, the Chinese side was forced to agree to only some minor changes in the wording, except for a slight modification of the terms of the British Navy's lease of Liugong Island. In October of the same year, both sides prepared the Rendition for the Lease of Weihaiwei (Draft) and signed this officially on 28th November. However on 24th November, 1924, Feng Yuxiang had taken over from the Cao Kun Government through a military coup d'etat. The British Government the postponed the return using the excuse of China's political instability.

The return of Weihaiwei came to a halt. The Beiyang Government was busy dealing with the civil war and made no further requests to the British Government for the return of Weihaiwei. In 1927, in order to gain more influence within Shandong, the Shandong Governor Zhang Zongchang suggested that the Beiyang Government should appoint Yang Du as the Special Commissioner of Weihaiwei and proposed taking the settlement of Qingdao as an example of how to make Weihaiwei a special area under the administration of Shandong. The Beiyang Government brought this suggestion to the British Government secretly but was refused. Meanwhile, as the Northern Expedition was in progress, patriotic uprisings were occurring throughout China, and the Chinese Guomindang Government announced the abolishment of the unequal treaties and independent diplomatic policies. The imperialist countries in China were facing even more severe challenges than ever before. The British Government became worried and kept close eyes on events in China and Weihaiwei. In March of 1927, the British Minister in China, Lampson, suggested that the British Government should immediately sign the Rendition (Draft) of 1924 with Zhang Zuolin to prevent the Guomindang Government's rejection of that treaty after the triumph of the Northern Expedition. At the

Johnston reading out the Rendition. From left to right: Wang Jiazheng, Archer – the first British Consul at Weihaiwei, Major J.M. Colchester Wemyss, Vice-Admiral Waitstell of the China Squadron of the British Fleet, Xu Zushan (1st October 1930)

end of the same year, the British House of Commons announced it would return Weihaiwei directly when any Chinese negotiators appeared. The Hong Kong Governor Cecil Clementi strongly opposed this attitude and he asked the British Government to be tough in its conditions for the return of Weihaiwei and suggested making the acquisition of the New Territories a precondition of Weihaiwei's return.[7] The British Weihaiwei Administrator Johnston had changed his attitude of returning Weihaiwei to one of continuing to lease Weihaiwei because many wealthy people had come to live in Weihaiwei as a result of the War, stimulating the local economy. In February 1928, Johnston suggested in his letter to Lampson that the British Government should intervene in the North and South dispute and choose Weihaiwei as the negotiating place, and that he wished to revise the Rendition (Draft) of 1924 to add more clauses to benefit the British Navy and to lease the land for further ten years. He even wished the British to take over the Administration of Weihaiwei.[8] His dream was not to be realised.

In June 1928, China was unified under the Nanjing Government which endowed that Government with greater authority in its diplomacy than any previous government. On 7th July of the same year, the Foreign Ministry announced that all treaties between China and foreign countries whose deadlines had expired were to be abolished, and new treaties to be negotiated accordingly. The return of Weihaiwei now became hopeful. In the face of this new situation, Johnston changed his opinion and suggested to the Colonial Office that the British Government should bring forward the return of Weihaiwei to China in order to prevent the Chinese rejection of the Rendition of 1924 and to avoid the embarrassment of being forced to withdraw from Hankou and Jiujiang. The British Government did not accept his suggestion. On 21st June, 1929, the Diplomatic Minister of the Nanjing Government, Mr Wang Zhengting, demanded the return of Weihaiwei through the British Minister in China, Lampson. The Chinese side would take back Weihaiwei unconditionally. But the British side wanted to abide by the Rendition for the Lease of Weihaiwei (Draft) without changing a single word. The British side insisted especially on the continued lease of Liugong Island and the protection of foreign people's interests and threatened to postpone the negotiations. Half a year passed without any progress. During this period of time, throughout China, people demanded the unconditional return of Weihaiwei. There were articles in various Chinese newspapers blaming Britain's shameful behaviour and urging the Nanjing Government to reclaim Weihaiwei unconditionally. Anti-British protests occurred in Weihaiwei. From February 1929, leaflets such as "An Independent Authority", "Chinese to govern Chinese", "Down

After 32 years, the Chinese flag flying once again over Weihaiwei. (1st October 1930)

1st October 1930, after the hand-over ceremony, Johnston on his way back to Britain at the end of his 32 years of political life in China.

with Imperialism" and "The Shame of Weihaiwei" appeared. When the negotiations restarted in 1930, the Zhongyuan War was about to break out as the conflicts between the warlords Chiang Kai-Shek, Feng Yuxiang and Yan Xishan deepened. The Nanjing Government did not want to spend time on the return of Weihaiwei and so compromised with the British. Finally the two sides agreed to include a section in the new treaty accepting Britain's continued presence on Liugong Island for a limited period of time. On 13th February, the drafts of the Rendition for the Lease of Weihaiwei and the Agreement were completed. According to these, Weihaiwei and Liugong Island and the Islands around Weihai Harbour should be returned to China. On 1st October Liugong Island could be leased to Britain for another ten years and at the end of this period any possible extension of that lease would be discussed again. The property of foreign people in Weihaiwei could be leased forever. On 18th April, Wang Zhengting and Lampson signed their names on behalf of their respective governments. The negotiations over Weihaiwei's return had ended after eight years. However the end of the negotiations did not mean that Weihaiwei could be returned smoothly to China on 1st October. According to a secret agreement, only when the Nanjing Government was in control of the whole of Shandong, could Weihaiwei be returned. As the Zhongyuan War broke out, it became less likely that Weihaiwei would be returned. In order to avoid the postponement of that return, the Guomindang Government planned to assist the administration of Weihaiwei using Zhang Xueliang's North-east Navy to take responsibility for the coastal defence of Weihaiwei. But not until 12th September, after Han Fuqu had been ap-

pointed as Governor of Shandong, was the problem solved. On 15th September, the British Colonial Office requested Johnston to return Weihaiwei to China according to the agreed plan.[9]

On 14th June, 1930, the Guomindang Government's Foreign Ministry set up an office to handle the rendition of Weihaiwei, and appointed Xu Zushan as the High Commissioner. On 23rd September, the Guomindang Government appointed the vice Foreign Minister Wang Jiazhen as special commissioner for Weihaiwei. On 1st October, a reception delegation formed of Wang Jiazhen, Xu Zushan and others headed a 300 strong group of marines which arrived in Weihaiwei in two cruisers: the Haichen and the Zhenhai. At 10:45 am, the Returning Ceremony was held in the British Weihaiwei Administrative Office. At 11:45 am, the British Weihaiwei Commissioner Johnston left Weihaiwei by boat, thus ending the 32 years of British colonial control over Weihaiwei.

1st October 1931, a memorial marking the return of Weihaiwei to China was built in the Triangle Garden (old name Whale Garden) by the Weihaiwei municipal government. The memorial is 32–feet tall in remembrance of the 32–year lease period. (1937)

Notes

Notes to Poem

1 Weihaiwei is a port overlooking the Yellow Sea

2 Confucius is buried within Shandong Province

3 Liugong Island is situated at the entrance to Weihai Bay

4 Refers to the anticipated return of Weihai to China (this poem was written in 1925)

5 Confucius and Mencius

6 The seven territories: Hong Kong, Macau, Taiwan, Kowloon, Guangzhouwan, Weihaiwei, Port Arthur.

Notes to Chapter 1

1 Qiao Ming-shun(乔明顺): World Modern History, Beijing, Beijing University Press, 1990, pp.224-5.

2 Young, L.K: British Policy in China, 1895-1902. Oxford, Oxford University Press, 1970, p.19.

3 Telegraph, MacDonald to Salisbury, Dec. 22nd, 1897, quoted in Weihai Municipal Political Consultative Conference Scientific, Educational, Cultural and Historical Commission: The 32 years of Britain's leasing of Weihaiwei (restricted version), Weihai, 1998, p.203.

4 McCordock, R.S: British Far Eastern Policy, 1894-1900. New York, Octagon Books, 1976, P.241.

5 Liu Cun Kuan(刘存宽): Hong Kong Lishi Wenti Ziliao Xuanping,Zujie Xinjie.《香港历史问题资料选评，租借新界》 Hong Kong, Sanlian Publishing Co. Ltd. 1995, p8.

6 Jin Wei(金炜): Zhonghua Minzu Chiru Shi. 《中华民族耻辱史》, Beijing, China Broadcasting and TV Press, 1995, P.553.

7 Weng Tong-he (翁同和): Weng Wen Gong Gong' Diary《翁文恭公日记》, Shanghai, Commercial Press, 1925, Vol.37, p.19.

8 Jin Wei(金炜): Zhonghua Minzu Chiru Shi. 《中华民族耻辱史》, P.554.

9 Daiyi(戴逸): Zhonguo Jindaishi Tongjian 《中国近代史通鉴》, 1840-1949, Beijing, Red Flag Press, 1997, Vol.4, P.78.

10 McCordock, R.S.: British Far Eastern Policy, 1894-1900. P.174.

11 FO17/1340, Secret Cable from MacDonald to Salisbury, 25th February, 1898.

12 Salisbury to MacDonald, 25th February, 1898. Weihai Municipal Political Consultative Conference Scientific, Educational, Cultural and Historical Commission: The 32 years of Britain's leasing of Weihaiwei (restricted version), p.227.

13 Jin Wei(金炜): Zhonghua Minzu Chiru Shi. 《中华民族耻辱史》, P.553.

14 Atwell, P: British Mandarins and Chinese Reformers, The British Administration of Weihaiwei(1898–1930) and the Territory's Return to Chinese Rule. Hong Kong, Oxford University Press, 1985, pp.6–7.

15 Atwell, P: British Mandarins and Chinese Reformers, pp.7–8,11

16 Salisbury to MacDonald, 25 March 1898. The 32 years of Britain's leasing of Weihaiwei (restricted version), p.228.

17 The 32 years of Britain's leasing of Weihaiwei (restricted version), Weihai, p.2.

18 Sheng Xuan–huai (盛宣怀): Yuzhai Cungao 《愚斋存稿》, Vol. 29, pp31,33; Vol. 31, p23.

19 Sheng Xuan–huai (盛宣怀): Yuzhai Cungao 《愚斋存稿》, Vol. 31, p23.

20 Dai Yi(戴逸): Zhongguo Jindaishi Tongjian 《中国近代史通鉴》 1840–1949, p298.

21 Dai Yi(戴逸): Zhongguo Jindaishi Tongjian 《中国近代史通鉴》 1840–1949, p297.

22 Jin Wei(金炜): Zhonghua Minzu Chiru Shi. 《中华民族耻辱史》, 1995, P.556.

23 Donald to Salisbury, 16th April, 1898. The 32 years of Britain's leasing of Weihaiwei (restricted version), pp.279–283.

24 Donald to Salisbury, 16th April, 1898. The 32 years of Britain's leasing of Weihaiwei (restricted version), pp.284–285.

25 Salisbury to Russel, 26th March, 1898. The 32 years of Britain's leasing of Weihaiwei (restricted version), p.228.

26 Russel to Salisbury, 21th April, 1898. The 32 years of Britain's leasing of Weihaiwei (restricted version), p.253.

27 Salisbury to Satow, 31th March, 1898. The 32 years of Britain's leasing of Weihaiwei (restricted version), p.228.

28 Jin Wei(金炜): Zhonghua Minzu Chiru Shi. 《中华民族耻辱史》, P.556.

29 Jin Wei(金炜): Zhonghua Minzu Chiru Shi. 《中华民族耻辱史》, P.556–7.

30 MacDonald to Salisbury, 29 April 1898. The 32 years of Britain's leasing of Weihaiwei (restricted version), p.228.

31 Royal Naval Office to Seymour, two letters, 9 May; 13 May 1898. The 32 years of Britain's leasing of Weihaiwei (restricted version), p.267–270.

32 Dai Yi(戴逸): Zhongguo Jindai Shitongjian 《中国近代史通鉴》 1840–1949, Vol.4, p300.

33 CO770/3, the letter from Seymour to Royal Naval Commission about the takeover of Weihaiwei. 2 June 1898.

34 Dai Yi(戴逸): Zhongguo Jindai Shitongjian 《中国近代史通鉴》 1840–1949, Vol.4, p28.

35 CO521/1, Barton to Dorward, May 1900.

36 Zhao Ban–xin (赵泮馨): Yingzu Weihai Huajie Can'an Jilue 《英租威海划界惨案纪略》. Shandong provincial collection commission on local historical material: Shandong Sheng Zhi Zi Liao 《山东省志资料》. Jinan, Shandong People Press, 1958, p8.

37 FO233/44, Minutes of talks between MacDonald and Tsungli Yamen, 29 May 1899.

38 CO873/4, A letter from Dorward to Macdonald, 23 May 1900.
39 Barnes, A.A.S: On Active Service with the Chinese Regiment, Grant Richards, Leicester Square London, 1902, p1.
40 CO52 1/1, letter from Dorward to the War Office, 6 April 1900.
41 CO873/4, letter from Dorward to MacDonald, 23 May 1900.
42 CO521/1, letter from Dorward to the War office, 6 April 1900.
43 Barnes, A.A.S: On Active Service with the Chinese Regiment. 1902, p5.
44 CO873/4, letter fromDorward to MacDonald, 19 May 1900.
45 CO873/4, letter from Dorward to MacDonald, 19 May 1900.
46 Barnes, A.A.S: On Active Service with the Chinese Regiment. 1902, p5-11.
47 Barnes, A.A.S: On Active Service with the Chinese Regiment. 1902, p11-13.
48 CO873/4, letter from Dorward to MacDonald, 12 June, 1900.

Notes to Chapter 2

1 CO521/1, Swettenham to Colonial Office, 26th July 1900.
2 CO521/41, Annual Report, 1927.
3 Airlie, S: Thistle and Bamboo, The Life and Times of Sir James Stewart Lockhart, Hong Kong, Oxford University Press, 1989, Chap 1 to Chap 6.
4 Airlie, S: Thistle and Bamboo, The Life and Times of Sir James Stewart Lockhart, Hong Kong, Oxford University Press, 1989, p112.
5 Airlie, S: Thistle and Bamboo, The Life and Times of Sir James Stewart Lockhart, Hong Kong, Oxford University Press, 1989, p113.
6 CO873/97, Annual Report of Secretary to Government, 1902.
7 CO873/239, Annual Report of Secretary to Government, 1906.
8 CO521/18, Annual Report, 1916.
9 ACC4138/7, Farewell Address to the Chamber of Commerce by Lockhart during his Retirement Ceremony, 19th April, 1921.
10 Airlie, S: Thistle and Bamboo, The Life and Times of Sir James Stewart Lockhart, Hong Kong, Oxford University Press, 1989, p113.
11 Johnston R.F.: Lion and Dragon in Northern China, Hong Kong, Oxford University Press, 1986, p2.
12 Tong Daoming (童道明): Hua Wuseshi Bu Nantianlie (化五色石补南天裂), Beijing Youth Daily, 21st May 1949.
13 ACC4138/7, Farewell Address to the Chamber of Commerce by Lockhart during his Retirement Ceremony, 19th April, 1921.
14 Airlie, S: Thistle and Bamboo, The Life and Times of Sir James Stewart Lockhart, Hong Kong, Oxford University Press, 1989, p42.
15 Airlie, S: Thistle and Bamboo, The Life and Times of Sir James Stewart Lockhart, Hong Kong, Oxford University Press, 1989, Chap12.
16 CO521/12, Lockhart to the Colonial Secretary, 14th April 1911.
17 Airlie, S: Reginald Johnston, Edinburgh, NMS Publishing Limited, 2001, p20.
18 Johnston R.F.: Lion and Dragon in Northern China, Hong Kong, Oxford University

Press, 1986, p449.

19 CO873/175, Annual Report of the Secretary to Government, 1905.

20 Johnston to Lockhart, 13th Oct. 1905.

21 Carol G. S. Tan: Going to Court in Weihaiwei, Some Support for Civil Litigation in the Qing. Beijing, Global Law Review, Autumn 2002.

22 FO371/15448, Archer to Foreign Office, 31st Oct. 1930.

23 Airlie, S: Thistle and Bamboo, The Life and Times of Sir James Stewart Lockhart, Hong Kong, Oxford University Press, 1989, p171.

24 Zhao Yiheng (赵毅衡): The Second Half of Johnston's Life, Writer's Digest, Issue 85, 2001.

25 Airlie, S: Reginald Johnston, Edinburgh, NMS Publishing Limited, 2001, p48.

26 CO744/1, Government Gazette 1918, No.8.

27 CO521/20, Johnston's Report, 25th Jan. 1919.

28 CO521/42, Johnston to Beckett, 28th Feb. 1928.

29 ACC4138/64, Commissioner's Speech at the Government Offices, Weihaiwei, 29th Sep. 1930.

30 Xiangsi. Hanbu(向斯.寒布): Xieyangxia De Gongdian – Minguo Shiqi Gugong Wangshi (斜阳下的宫殿 – 民国时期故宫往事). Beijing, Changhong Publishing Press, p45.

31 Airlie, S: Reginald Johnston, Edinburgh, NMS Publishing Limited, 2001, p97.

32 Ibid.

33 Xiangsi. Hanbu: Xieyangxia De Gongdian – Minguo Shiqi Gugong Wangshi. Beijing, Changhong Publishing Press, p45.

34 Xiao Li(肖黎), Ma Baozhu(马宝珠) and Lü Yanqing(吕延清) edited: 100 Westerners Influential in the History of China, Guangzhou, Guangdong People's Publishing Press, 2001, pp293–7.

35 The Weihaiwei Order-in-Council of 1901, Article 9.

36 Johnston R.F.: Lion and Dragon in Northern China, Hong Kong, Oxford University Press, 1986, pp80–1

37 Johnston R.F.: Lion and Dragon in Northern China, Hong Kong, Oxford University Press, 1986, p81.

38 Airlie, S: Thistle and Bamboo, The Life and Times of Sir James Stewart Lockhart, Hong Kong, Oxford University Press, 1989, p172.

39 Johnston R.F.: Lion and Dragon in Northern China, Hong Kong, Oxford University Press, 1986, p80.

40 CO841/1, Weihaiwei Acts,

41 Johnston R.F.: Lion and Dragon in Northern China, Hong Kong, Oxford University Press, 1986, p81.

42 CO841/1, The Protection of Women and Girls' Ordinance, 1905, Section 17.

43 CO841/1, The Peace Preservation Ordinance, 1921, Section 7.

44 CO744/2, Regulations for the Control of Motor Traffic, 1928, Section 44.

45 Punishment for not Returning the Lost Property to the Owner, The Midday Post of Weihaiwei, 25th May 1928

46 CO744/2, Regulations for the Control of Motor Traffic, 1928, Section 44.
47 CO841/1, The Protection of Woman and Girl's Ordinance, 1905, Section 7; CO841/1, The Offences against the Person Ordinance, 1905, Section 53.
48 CO841/1, The Offences against the Person Ordinance, 1905, Section 25, 26.
49 CO841/1, The Offences against the Person Ordinance, 1905, Section 38.
50 ACC4138/67, Annual Report, 1928.
51 CO841/1, The Public Health and Buildings Ordinance, 1903, Section29, 30.
52 ACC4138/43, Weihaiwei Police Rules, Section 31.
53 CO841/1, The Public Health and Buildings Ordinance, 1903, Section2(13), 11(7).
54 CO521/15, Annual Report, 1913.
55 CO841/1, The Government Waste Lands Ordinance, 1919.
56 CO841/1, The Chinese Marriage Preservation Ordinance, 1913, Section 2.
57 Weihaiwei Order-in-Council of 1901, Section 12.
58 Johnston R.F.: Lion and Dragon in Northern China, Hong Kong, Oxford University Press, 1986, p99.
59 Order-in-Council, Article16, 18.
60 Johnston R.F.: Lion and Dragon in Northern China, Hong Kong, Oxford University Press, 1986, p100-1.
61 CO841/1, The Rehearings Ordinance, 1913.
62 Order-in-Council, Article18.
63 Order-in-Council, Article18(2).
64 Order-in-Council, Article21(2).
65 Order-in-Council, Article34(1).
66 Order-in-Council, Article21(3).
67 CO770/3, Seymour to the Naval Secretary, 2nd June 1898.
68 Dorward to the War Office, 7th Jan. 1900.
69 CO873/97, Annual Report of Secretary to Government.
70 CO873/239, Annual Report of Secretary to Government, 1906.
71 CO521/18, Annual Report, 1916.
72 Johnston R.F.: Lion and Dragon in Northern China, Hong Kong, Oxford University Press, 1986, p99.
73 CO521/10, Annual Report, 1907.
74 Ibid.
75 Order-in-Council, Article 9, 19.
76 Order-in-Council, Article 20.
77 CO841/1, The Jury Ordinance, 1905.
78 CO873/175,Annual Report of Secretary to Government, 1905.
79 CO873/97, Annual Report of Secretary to Government, 1902.
80 Johnston R.F.: Lion and Dragon in Northern China, Hong Kong, Oxford University Press, 1986, p7.
81 Johnston R.F.: Lion and Dragon in Northern China, Hong Kong, Oxford University Press, 1986, p104.

82 Johnston R.F.: Lion and Dragon in Northern China, Hong Kong, Oxford University Press, 1986, p123.
83 Johnston R.F.: Lion and Dragon in Northern China, Hong Kong, Oxford University Press, 1986, p104.
84 CO873/97, Annual Report of Secretary to Government, 1902.
85 CO873/150, The Settlement of the Dispute over Land, 25th November 1905.
86 CO873/163, Annual Report of Secretary to Government, 1904.
87 CO873/97, Annual Report of Secretary to Government, 1902.
88 Johnston R.F.: Lion and Dragon in Northern China, Hong Kong, Oxford University Press, 1986, p95.
89 CO873/265, Annual Report of Secretary to Government, 1907.
90 Johnston R.F.: Lion and Dragon in Northern China, Hong Kong, Oxford University Press, 1986, p114.
91 CO744/1, Government Gazette, 1910, No.21, 15th June 1910.
92 CO873/543, Notice on Petition-fee, September 1913.
93 CO873/543, Notice on Petition-fee, 28th July and 14th December 1916.
94 CO521/1, Swettenham to Colonial Office, 26th July 1900, AppendixA.
95 CO521/2, Bruce to Dorward, 30th May 1901.
96 CO521/2, Dorward to Deputy-Secretary of the War Office, 3rd June 1901.
97 CO873/97, Annual Report of Secretary to Government, 1902.
98 Annual Report, 1903.
99 CO521/9, Lockhart to the Colonial Secretary, 13th February 1906.
100 CO521/9, Lockhart to the Colonial Secretary, 14th February 1906.
101 CO873/239, Annual Report 1906.
102 CO841/1, The Police Force Ordinance, 1903, Section2; ACC4138/43, Weihaiwei Police Rules, Section1; CO873/673, Annual Report, 1921.
103 CO873/277, Rules and Regulations for the Police Force of Weihaiwei, Section2.
104 Zhu Shiquan (朱世全): The Weihaiwei Question, Shanghai, The Commercial Press Ltd, September 1931, p139.
105 ACC4138/43, Weihaiwei Police Rules, Sectuion52.
106 CO873/239, Annual Report of Secretary to Government, 1906.
107 Weihai Municipal Archives 229-1-29, Annual Report, 1925.
108 CO841/1, The Offences against the Person Ordinance, 1905, Section34.
109 CO873/239, Annual Report of Secretary to Government, 1906.
110 CO873/238, Petition to Lockhart Presented by District and Village Headmen, 1907.
111 CO873/239, Annual Report of Secretary to Government, 1906.
112 CO873/692, Annual Report of Senior District Officer, 1924.
113 CO873/673, Annual Report, 1921.
114 CO873/692, Annual Report of Senior District Officer, 1924.
115 ACC4138/67, Annual Report, 1928.
116 CO873/99, Annual Report of Secretary to Government, 1903.
117 CO873/239, Annual Report of Secretary to Government, 1906.

118 CO521/13, Lockhart to the Colonial Secretary, 13th December 1912.

119 CO873/634, Memorandum on the Police Work by Senior District officer, 2nd May 1921.

120 CO521/15, Annual Report, 1913.

121 Zhu Shiquan (朱世全): The Weihaiwei Question, Shanghai, The Commercial Press Ltd, September 1931, p133.

122 CO873/692, Annual Report of Senior District Officer, 1924.

123 CO873/634, Memorandum on the Police Work by Senior District officer, 2nd May 1921.

124 Zhu Shiquan (朱世全): The Weihaiwei Question, Shanghai, The Commercial Press Ltd, September 1931, p141.

125 CO873/97, Annual Report of Secretary to Government, 1902.

126 CO873/97, Annual Report of Secretary to Government, 1902.

127 Zhu Shiquan (朱世全): The Weihaiwei Question, Shanghai, The Commercial Press Ltd, September 1931, p141.

128 Zhu Shiquan (朱世全): The Weihaiwei Question, Shanghai, The Commercial Press Ltd, September 1931, p141.

129 ACC4138/67, Annual Report,1909.

130 CO744/1, Government Gazette, 1917, No.17, 19th March 1917.

131 Zhu Shiquan (朱世全): The Weihaiwei Question, Shanghai, The Commercial Press Ltd, September 1931, p141.

132 CO841/1, The Prisons Ordinance, 1903, section18.

133 Zhu Shiquan (朱世全): The Weihaiwei Question, Shanghai, The Commercial Press Ltd, September 1931, p141.

134 Zhang Zhichao(张志超):The Prison System during the British Lease Period of Weihaiwei, Beijing, Global Law Review, Issue5, 2005, pp555-6.

135 CO873/277, Rules and Regulations for the Police Force of Weihaiwei, Section2.

136 CO873/612, Regulations for Sergeants or Other Police Officers in Charge of Police Posts in the Territory, 1920.

137 CO873/634, Memorandum on the Police Work by Senior District officer, 2nd May 1921.

138 Zhu Shiquan (朱世全): The Weihaiwei Question, Shanghai, The Commercial Press Ltd, September 1931, p133.

139 CO873/97, Annual Report of Secretary to Government, 1902.

140 CO841/1, The Police Force Ordinance, 1903, Section15.

141 CO521/8, Lockhart to Colonial Secretary, 10th July 1905.

142 CO521/10, Annual Report, 1907.

143 ACC4138/67, Annual Report, 1909.

144 CO873/673, Annual Report, 1921.

145 CO873/571, Regulations on Organizing Peace Preservation Union, 16th October 1918.

146 Annual Report, 1911.

147 CO873/377, Annual Report of Secretary to Government, 1913.

148 CO841/1, The Peace Preservation Ordinance, 1921, Section2.

149 CO841/1, The Peace Preservation Ordinance, 1921, Section3.

150 CO521/1, Swettenham to Colonial Office, 26th July 1900.

151 Lockhart's Instructions to Village Headmen, 8th May 1902.
152 CO873/239, Annual Report of Secretary to Government, 1906.
153 Johnston R.F.: Lion and Dragon in Northern China, Hong Kong, Oxford University Press, 1986, p95.
154 CO873/384, Rules on Village Headmen Election and Appointment, 8th May 1902.
155 Johnston R.F.: Lion and Dragon in Northern China, Hong Kong, Oxford University Press, 1986, p95.
156 CO873/163, Annual Report, 1904.
157 CO873/184, The Exemplary Conduct of Haixitou Village Headman.
158 CO872/7, McDonald to Zongli Yamen, 13th December 1899.
159 Evolution of Shandong Provincial Government Series' Compilation Committee: Administration of All the Previous Governments of Shandong Province, Jinan, Xinhua Publishing Press, 1993, p44.
160 CO521/70, Johnston to Miles W. Lampson, Confidential, 2nd January 1930.
161 Atwell, P: British Mandarins and Chinese Reformers, The British Administration of Weihaiwei (1898–1930) and The Territory's Return to Chinese Rule. Hong Kong, Oxford university Press, 1985, p16.
162 Evolution of Shandong Provincial Government Series' Compilation Committee: Chronicle of Events of Shandong Provincial Government, Jinan, Xinhua Publishing Press, 1993, p60.
163 CO873/4, Letter on Weihaiwei Boundary Demarcation, 1900.
164 Zhao Panxin (赵泮鑫), Yingzu Weihai Huajie Canan Jilue (英租威海划界惨案纪略), Collection Committee on Local Chronicle of Shandong Province: Chronicle of Shandong Province. Jinan, Shandong People's Publishing Press, 1958, p8.
165 Johnston R.F.: Lion and Dragon in Northern China, Hong Kong, Oxford University Press, 1986, p89.
166 ACC4138/66, A Confidential Report of a Journey in the Province of Shandong including a Visit to Jiaozhou, printed by Noronha & Co, 1903.
167 Atwell, P: British Mandarins and Chinese Reformers, Hong Kong, Oxford University Press, 1985, p60.
168 Airlie, S: Thistle and Bamboo, The Life and Times of Sir James Stewart Lockhart, Hong Kong, Oxford University Press, 1989, p123.
169 Johnston R.F.: Lion and Dragon in Northern China, Hong Kong, Oxford University Press, 1986, pp87–8.
170 CO521/12, Lockhart to Colonial Secretary, 24th November, 1911.
171 Atwell, P: British Mandarins and Chinese Reformers, Hong Kong, Oxford university Press, 1985, p82.
172 CO521/13, Lockhart to Colonial Secretary, 1912.
173 Atwell, P: British Mandarins and Chinese Reformers, Hong Kong, Oxford university Press, 1985, p90.
174 CO521/70, Johnston to Miles W. Lampson, Confidential, 2nd January 1930.

Notes to Chapter 3

1 Weihai Municipal Political Consultative Conference for Science, Education, Literature and History Committee: The 32 Years of Britain's Leasing Weihaiwei (restricted version), "The British Fleet on Liugong Island for 42 years." 1998, Weihaiwei, pp129–137.
2 Ibid.
3 Harfield, A: British and Indian Armies on the China Coast, 1785–1985, A & J. Partnership, 1990, p281.
4 Harfield, A: British and Indian Armies on the China Coast, 1785–1985, A & J. Partnership, 1990, p283.
5 Harfield, A: British and Indian Armies on the China Coast, 1785–1985, A & J. Partnership, 1990, p281.
6 Ibid.
7 Weihai Municipal Archives229–1–1453, Uniform of the Chinese Regiment at Weihaiwei.
8 229–1–15, Telegrams on British Recruitment at Weihaiwei from Zongli Yanmen and Shandong Governor's Yamen, 1899, p4.
9 229–1–15, Telegrams on British Recruitment at Weihaiwei from Zongli Yanmen and Shandong Governor's Yamen, 1899, p6.
10 Wright, A & H. A. Cartwright: Twentieth Century Impressions of Hong Kong Shanghai and other Treaty Ports of China, Their History People Commerce Industries and Resources. Lloyd's Greater Britain Publishing Company Ltd, 1908, p773.
11 Harfield, A: British and Indian Armies on the China Coast, 1785–1985, A & J. Partnership, 1990, p283.
12 Shandong Shibao《山东时报》, pp174–5.
13 ACC4138/66, Military Report and General Information Concerning the Dependency of Weihaiwei, 1904.
14 Shandong Shiba《山东时报》, p175.
15 Harfield, A: British and Indian Armies on the China Coast, 1785–1985, A & J. Partnership, 1990, p284.
16 229–1–1453, Uniform of the Chinese Regiment at Weihaiwei.
17 Robert Coventry Forsyth: Shandong, The Sacred Province of China, In Some of Its Aspects, Shanghai, Christian Literature Society, 1912, p111.
18 Harfield, A: British and Indian Armies on the China Coast, 1785–1985, A & J. Partnership, 1990, p283.
19 ACC4138/66, Military Report and General Information Concerning the Dependency of Weihaiwei, 1904.
20 229–1–1453, Uniform of the Chinese Regiment at Weihaiwei.
21 Barnes, A.A.S.: On Active Service with the Chinese Regiment. Grant Richards, Leicester Square, London, 1902, Preface.
22 Harfield, A: British and Indian Armies on the China Coast, 1785–1985, A & J. Partnership, 1990, p302.
23 Barnes, A.A.S.: On Active Service with the Chinese Regiment. Grant Richards, Leicester Square, London, 1902, p3.
24 Barnes, A.A.S.: On Active Service with the Chinese Regiment. Grant Richards,

Leicester Square, London, 1902, p4.

25 Barnes, A.A.S.: On Active Service with the Chinese Regiment. Grant Richards, Leicester Square, London, 1902, p6.

26 Barnes, A.A.S.: On Active Service with the Chinese Regiment. Grant Richards, Leicester Square, London, 1902, p16.

27 Barnes, A.A.S.: On Active Service with the Chinese Regiment. Grant Richards, Leicester Square, London, 1902, p12.

28 Barnes, A.A.S.: On Active Service with the Chinese Regiment. Grant Richards, Leicester Square, London, 1902, p18.

29 Barnes, A.A.S.: On Active Service with the Chinese Regiment. Grant Richards, Leicester Square, London, 1902, p19.

30 Barnes, A.A.S.: On Active Service with the Chinese Regiment. Grant Richards, Leicester Square, London, 1902, p203.

31 Barnes, A.A.S.: On Active Service with the Chinese Regiment. Grant Richards, Leicester Square, London, 1902, p19.

32 Barnes, A.A.S.: On Active Service with the Chinese Regiment. Grant Richards, Leicester Square, London, 1902, p11.

33 Barnes, A.A.S.: On Active Service with the Chinese Regiment. Grant Richards, Leicester Square, London, 1902, p205.

34 Barnes, A.A.S.: On Active Service with the Chinese Regiment. Grant Richards, Leicester Square, London, 1902, p21.

35 Barnes, A.A.S.: On Active Service with the Chinese Regiment. Grant Richards, Leicester Square, London, 1902, preface.

36 Barnes, A.A.S.: On Active Service with the Chinese Regiment. Grant Richards, Leicester Square, London, 1902, p78.

37 Barnes, A.A.S.: On Active Service with the Chinese Regiment. Grant Richards, Leicester Square, London, 1902, p37.

38 Barnes, A.A.S.: On Active Service with the Chinese Regiment. Grant Richards, Leicester Square, London, 1902, p37.

39 Barnes, A.A.S.: On Active Service with the Chinese Regiment. Grant Richards, Leicester Square, London, 1902, pp36-7.

40 Barnes, A.A.S.: On Active Service with the Chinese Regiment. Grant Richards, Leicester Square, London, 1902, p50.

41 Dai Yi(戴逸)edited: Zhongguo Jindashi Tongjian《中国近代史通鉴》, 1840-1949. Beijing, Hongqi Publishing Press, 1997, Vol.4, p134.

42 Barnes, A.A.S.: On Active Service with the Chinese Regiment. Grant Richards, Leicester Square, London, 1902, p216.

43 Dai Yi(戴逸)edited: Zhongguo Jindashi Tongjian《中国近代史通鉴》, 1840-1949. Beijing, Hongqi Publishing Press, 1997, Vol.4, pp141-2.

44 Barnes, A.A.S.: On Active Service with the Chinese Regiment. Grant Richards, Leicester Square, London, 1902, pp75-6.

45 Barnes, A.A.S.: On Active Service with the Chinese Regiment. Grant Richards,

Leicester Square, London, 1902, p208.
46 Lightness and Darkness of the Chinese People's Life, wrote by Mai Gaowen, translated by Zhu Tao(朱涛)and Nijing(倪静), from China in Westerners' View, edited by Huang Xingtao(黄兴涛), Beijing, Shishi Publishing Press, 1998, p46.
47 Barnes, A.A.S.: On Active Service with the Chinese Regiment. Grant Richards, Leicester Square, London, 1902, p220
48 Harfield, A: British and Indian Armies on the China Coast, 1785-1985, A & J. Partnership, 1990, p299.
49 Barnes, A.A.S.: On Active Service with the Chinese Regiment. Grant Richards, Leicester Square, London, 1902, p226.
50 Harfield, A: British and Indian Armies on the China Coast, 1785-1985, A & J. Partnership, 1990, p306.
51 Barnes, A.A.S.: On Active Service with the Chinese Regiment. Grant Richards, Leicester Square, London, 1902, p80.
52 Lightness and Darkness of the Chinese People's Life, from China in Westerners' View, edited by Huang Xingtao(黄兴涛), Beijing, Shishi Publishing Press, 1998, p46.
53 Barnes, A.A.S.: On Active Service with the Chinese Regiment. Grant Richards, Leicester Square, London, 1902, p206.
54 Barnes, A.A.S.: On Active Service with the Chinese Regiment. Grant Richards, Leicester Square, London, 1902, p88.
55 C. E. Bruce-Mitford: The Territory of Wei Hai Wei, Shanghai, Kelly & Walsh Limited, 1902, p24.
56 Harfield, A: British and Indian Armies on the China Coast, 1785-1985, A & J. Partnership, 1990, p290.
57 Barnes, A.A.S.: On Active Service with the Chinese Regiment. Grant Richards, Leicester Square, London, 1902, p225.
58 C. E. Bruce-Mitford: The Territory of Wei Hai Wei, Shanghai, Kelly & Walsh Limited, 1902, p24.
59 Wright, A & H. A. Cartwright: Twentieth Century Impressions of Hong Kong Shanghai and other Treaty Ports of China, Their History People Commerce Industries and Resources. Lloyd's Greater Britain Publishing Company Ltd, 1908, p774.
60 Barnes, A.A.S.: On Active Service with the Chinese Regiment. Grant Richards, Leicester Square, London, 1902, p120.
61 Wright, A & H. A. Cartwright: Twentieth Century Impressions of Hong Kong Shanghai and other Treaty Ports of China, Their History People Commerce Industries and Resources. Lloyd's Greater Britain Publishing Company Ltd, 1908, p774.
62 Barnes, A.A.S.: On Active Service with the Chinese Regiment. Grant Richards, Leicester Square, London, 1902, p225.
63 Dai Yi(戴逸)edited: Zhongguo Jindaishi Tongjian《中国近代史通鉴》, 1840-1949. Beijing, Hongqi Publishing Press, 1997, Vol.4, p151.
64 Dai Yi(戴逸)edited: Zhongguo Jindaishi Tongjian《中国近代史通鉴》, 1840-1949. Beijing, Hongqi Publishing Press, 1997, Vol.4, p155.

65 Barnes, A.A.S.: On Active Service with the Chinese Regiment. Grant Richards, Leicester Square, London, 1902, pp147-8.

66 Barnes, A.A.S.: On Active Service with the Chinese Regiment. Grant Richards, Leicester Square, London, 1902, p198.

67 Harfield, A: British and Indian Armies on the China Coast, 1785-1985, A & J. Partnership, 1990, p302.

68 Lockhart, J. H. S.: A Confidential Report of A Journey in the Province of Shandong include A Visit to Jiaozhou, Hong Kong, Printed by Noronha & Co, 1903.

69 Johnston, R.F.: Lion and Dragon in Northern China, Hong Kong, Oxford University Press, 1986, p84.

70 Harfield, A: British and Indian Armies on the China Coast, 1785-1985, A & J. Partnership, 1990, p302.

71 Robert Coventry Forsyth: Shandong, The Sacred Province of China, In Some of Its Aspects, Shanghai, Christian Literature Society, 1912, p112.

72 Robert Coventry Forsyth: Shandong, The Sacred Province of China, In Some of Its Aspects, Shanghai, Christian Literature Society, 1912, p111.

73 McDonald to Salisbury, 27 May 1898. Weihai Municipal Political Consultative Conference for Science, Education, Literature and History Committee: The 32 Years of Britain's Leasing Weihaiwei (restricted version), 1998, Weihai, pp278-9.

74 Carol, G. S. Tan: Going to Court in Weihaiwei, Some Support for Civil Litigation in the Qing. Beijing, Global Law Review, Autumn, 2002.

75 Airlie, S: Thistle and Bamboo, The Life and Times of Sir James Stewart Lockhart, Hong Kong, Oxford University Press, 1989, p113.

76 CO521/9, Lockhart to the Colonial Office, 14th February, 1906.

77 CO521/17, Annual Report, 1915.

78 ACC4138/67, Annual Report, 1918.

79 ACC4138/67, Annual Report, 1927.

80 CO521/2, Dorward to the Colonial Office, 1st January 1901.

81 The statement on extradition, please refer to CO873/778, Correspondences on Extradition between Johnston and the Authorities Concerned, from 1928 to 1930.

82 The statement on political refugees at Weihaiwei, please refer to CO521/42, Correspondences on Political Refugees between Johnston and the Authorities Concerned in 1928.

83 Dai Yi(戴逸)edited: Zhongguo Jindashi Tongjian《中国近代史通鉴》, 1840-1949. Beijing, Hongqi Publishing Press, 1997, Vol.6, p91.

84 Xu Guoqi(徐国琦),The Study on the Scheme to Send Labourers rather than Soldiers to Europe During World War 1, Hong Kong, The 21st Century, December 2000, pp55-62.

85 Dai Yi(戴逸)edited: Zhongguo Jindashi Tongjian《中国近代史通鉴》, 1840-1949. Beijing, Hongqi Publishing Press, 1997, Vol.6, p836.

86 Editor in Chief - Li Xin(李新); Editors - Han Xinfu(韩信夫) and Jiang Kefu(姜克夫): Chronicles of the Republic of China, Beijing, China Literature and History Publishing Press, 1996, Book1, p349.

87 Chronicles of the Republic of China, Beijing, China Literature and History Publishing

Press, 1996, Book1, p358.

88 Ibid.

89 Xu Guoqi(徐国琦),The Study on the Scheme to Send Labourers rather than Soldiers to Europe During World War 1, Hong Kong, The 21st Century, December 2000, pp55-62.

90 Editor in Chief – Li Xin(李新); Editors – Han Xinfu(韩信夫) and Jiang Kefu(姜克夫): Chronicles of the Republic of China, Beijing, China Literature and History Publishing Press, 1996, Book1, p429.

91 Chronicles of the Republic of China, Beijing, China Literature and History Publishing Press, 1996, Book1, p430.

92 Dai Yi(戴逸)edited: Zhongguo Jindashi Tongjian《中国近代史通鉴》, 1840-1949. Beijing, Hongqi Publishing Press, 1997, Vol.6, p137.

93 Xu Guoqi(徐国琦),The Study on the Scheme to Send Labourers rather than Soldiers to Europe During World War 1, Hong Kong, The 21st Century, December 2000, pp55-62.

94 Ibid.

95 Summerskill, M; China on the Western Front, Britain's Chinese Work Force in the First World War, p49.

96 Summerskill, M; China on the Western Front, Britain's Chinese Work Force in the First World War, p74.

97 Summerskill, M; China on the Western Front, Britain's Chinese Work Force in the First World War, p62.

98 Summerskill, M; China on the Western Front, Britain's Chinese Work Force in the First World War, p64.

99 Summerskill, M; China on the Western Front, Britain's Chinese Work Force in the First World War, pp52-3.

100 Summerskill, M; China on the Western Front, Britain's Chinese Work Force in the First World War, p39.

101 Summerskill, M; China on the Western Front, Britain's Chinese Work Force in the First World War, p50.

102 Summerskill, M; China on the Western Front, Britain's Chinese Work Force in the First World War, p39.

103 Summerskill, M; China on the Western Front, Britain's Chinese Work Force in the First World War, p39

104 Summerskill, M; China on the Western Front, Britain's Chinese Work Force in the First World War, p39.

105 Summerskill, M; China on the Western Front, Britain's Chinese Work Force in the First World War, p47.

106 Summerskill, M; China on the Western Front, Britain's Chinese Work Force in the First World War, p51.

107 Summerskill, M; China on the Western Front, Britain's Chinese Work Force in the First World War, pp52-3.

108 Summerskill, M; China on the Western Front, Britain's Chinese Work Force in the First World War, p48.

109 Summerskill, M; China on the Western Front, Britain's Chinese Work Force in the First World War, p66.

110 Dai Yi(戴逸)edited: Zhongguo Jindashi Tongjian《中国近代史通鉴》, 1840-1949. Beijing, Hongqi Publishing Press, 1997, Vol.6, p1216.

111 Dai Yi(戴逸)edited: Zhongguo Jindashi Tongjian《中国近代史通鉴》, 1840-1949. Beijing, Hongqi Publishing Press, 1997, Vol.6, p1217.

112 229-1-611, Notice on British Honest Recruitment of Chinese Labourers; Wage Levels for Chinese Labourers by British Recruitment Office at Weihaiwei, 1916.

113 Dai Yi(戴逸)edited: Zhongguo Jindashi Tongjian《中国近代史通鉴》, 1840-1949. Beijing, Hongqi Publishing Press, 1997, Vol.6, p1217.

114 Summerskill, M; China on the Western Front, Britain's Chinese Work Force in the First World War, p55.

115 Summerskill, M; China on the Western Front, Britain's Chinese Work Force in the First World War, pp73-4

116 Summerskill, M; China on the Western Front, Britain's Chinese Work Force in the First World War, p2.

117 Summerskill, M; China on the Western Front, Britain's Chinese Work Force in the First World War, p77.

118 ACC4138/67, Annual Report, 1918.

119 Editor in Chief - Li Xin(李新); Editors - Han Xinfu(韩信夫) and Jiang Kefu(姜克夫): Chronicles of the Republic of China, Beijing, China Literature and History Publishing Press, 1996, Book1, p464.

120 Summerskill, M; China on the Western Front, Britain's Chinese Work Force in the First World War, p54.

121 Chronicles of the Republic of China, Beijing, China Literature and History Publishing Press, 1996, Book1, pp464-469.

122, Chronicles of the Republic of China, p471, p497.

123 Xu Guoqi(徐国琦),The Study on the Scheme to Send Labourers rather than Soldiers to Europe During World War 1, Hong Kong, The 21st Century, December 2000, pp55-62.

124 Luo Luo(罗罗): The Truth of Chinese Labourers to Europe, from Oriental Magazine《东方杂志》, 1918, Vol.15, No.6, p37.

125 Summerskill, M; China on the Western Front, Britain's Chinese Work Force in the First World War, p3.

126 Summerskill, M; China on the Western Front, Britain's Chinese Work Force in the First World War, p70.

127 Dai Yi(戴逸)edited: Zhongguo Jindashi Tongjian《中国近代史通鉴》,1840-1949. Beijing, Hongqi Publishing Press, 1997, Vol.6, pp1220-1221.

128 Wu Huiyi(吴蕙仪),Approaching the Cemetery Asleep. Http://dzrb.dzwww.com/dazk/dzfs/tz0050408_1023971.htm/2006-5-24.

129 E. Manico Gull, The Story of the Chinese Labor Corps. Far Eastern Review, 1918.

130 Summerskill, M; China on the Western Front, Britain's Chinese Work Force in the First World War, p2.

131 Xu Guoqi(徐国琦),The Study on the Scheme to Send Labourers rather than Soldiers to Europe During World War 1, Hong Kong, The 21st Century, December 2000, pp55-62.

132 Dai Yi(戴逸)edited: Zhongguo Jindashi Tongjian《中国近代史通鉴》, 1840-1949. Beijing, Hongqi Publishing Press, 1997, Vol.6, p1221.

133 Xu Guoqi(徐国琦),The Study on the Scheme to Send Labourers rather than Soldiers to Europe During World War 1, Hong Kong, The 21st Century, December 2000, pp55-62.

134 Wu Huiyi(吴蕙仪), Approaching the Cemetery Asleep. Http://dzrb.dzwww.com/dazk/dzfs/tz0050408_1023971.htm/2006-5-24.

135 Xu Guoqi(徐国琦),The Study on the Scheme to Send Labourers rather than Soldiers to Europe During World War 1, Hong Kong, The 21st Century, December 2000, pp55-62.

136 Dai Yi(戴逸)edited: Zhongguo Jindashi Tongjian《中国近代史通鉴》, 1840-1949. Beijing, Hongqi Publishing Press, 1997, Vol.6, p1221, p1223.

137 Wu Huiyi(吴蕙仪),Approaching the Cemetery Asleep. Http://dzrb.dzwww.com/dazk/dzfs/tz0050408_1023971.htm/2006-5-24.

138 Chen Xiaoqing(陈晓卿)edited: Century China C1899-1949), Jinan, Shandong Pictorial Publishing Press, 2000, p105.

139 Xu Guoqi(徐国琦), The Study on the Scheme to Send Labourers rather than Soldiers to Europe During World War 1, Hong Kong, The 21st Century, December 2000, pp55-62.

140 CO744/1, Government Gazette, 1918, No.34, 20 November 1918.

141 Xu Guoqi(徐国琦), The Study on the Scheme to Send Labourers rather than Soldiers to Europe During World War 1, Hong Kong, The 21st Century, December 2000, pp55-62.

142 Kanwairen(槛外人): My 1919. Http://dubook.blogchina.com/3615266.html.

143 Xu Guoqi(徐国琦), The Study on the Scheme to Send Labourers rather than Soldiers to Europe During World War Hong Kong, The 21st Century, December 2000, pp55-62.

144 Huaren Fengbei Houren Wei Linghun(华人丰碑 后人慰灵魂), Http://hangzhou.com.cn/20020127/ca95630.htm.

Notes to Chapter 4

1 C.E.Bruce-Midford: The Territory of Wei Hai Wei. Shanghai, Kelly and Walsh, Limited, 1902.

2 Airlie Shiona: Thistle and Bamboo, the Life and Times of Sir James Stewart Lockhart, Hong Kong, Oxford University Press, 1989.

3 CO873/163, Annual Report 1904.

4 Weihai Municipal Political Consultative Conference for Science, Education, Literature and History Committee: 32 Years of Britain's Lease of Weihaiwei (restricted publication), "The Survey of Weihaiwei", 1998, Weihai, pp116-125.

5 Ibid.

6 32 Years of Britain's Lease of Weihaiwei (restricted publication), 1998, Weihai.

7 Ibid

8 Ibid

9 Ibid

10 Ibid

11 Ibid
12 C.E.Bruce-Midford: The Territory of Wei Hai Wei. Shanghai, Kelly and Walsh, Limited, 1902.

Notes to Chapter 5

1 The Weihaiwei Lyre (published daily), Weihai Municipal Archives Repository, Vol:229-1-306.
2 The Midday Post of Weihaiwei, Weihai Municipal Archives Repository, Vol:229-1-312.
3 The Origin of Weihaiwei Daily, Weihai Municipal Archives Repository, Vol:229-1-305.
4 1925 Annual Report, Weihai Municipal Archives Repository, Vol:229-1-29
5 CO873/9, Henry J Brown to Lockhart, 5th June 1902.
6 CO873/163, 1904 Annual Report.
7 CO873/585, 1919 Department Annual Report.
8 CO873/263, The Advice on the Foundation of Girl School, 12th December 1907.
9 CO873/722, The Management of Qidong Middle School.
10 CO873/649, Weihaiwei Census Report of 1921
11 CO521/70, Johnston to Lampson, 1929.
12 CO521/1, Report on Weihaiwei and Its Future Administration, 26th July, 1900.
13 1929 Annual Report.
14 CO873/292, 1909 Annual Report.
15 CO873/649, Weihaiwei Census Report of 1921.
16 The Weihaiwei Lyre (published daily), Weihai Municipal Archives Repository, Vol: 229-1-306.
17 CO873/253, Ask for Instructions about the establishment of the Sports Organization, 4th September, 1907.
18 The Weihaiwei Lyre (published daily), Weihai Municipal Archives Repository, Vol: 229-1-306.
19 Shandong, The Sacred Province of China: Shanghai Christian Literature Society, 1912.
20 Weihai Municipal Political Consultative Conference for Science, Education, Literature, and History Committee: The 32 years of Britain's leasing of Weihaiwei (restricted version), 1998, Weihai, pp312-324.
21 CO873/694, Weihaiwei Census Report of 1921.

Notes to Chapter 6

1 CO521/1, Report on Weihaiwei and Its Future Administration, 26th July 1900.
2 CO873/97, 1902 Annual Report.
3 Ibid.
4 The Midday Post of Weihawei, Weihai Municipal Archives Repository, Vol: 229-1-316, 6th June, 1928.
5 Atwell P., British Mandarins and Chinese Reformers, The British Administration of Weihaiwei (1898-1930) and the Territory's Return to Chinese Rule. Hong Kong Oxford University Press, 1985, p4.

6 Atwell P., British Mandarins and Chinese Reformers, Hong Kong Oxford University Press, 1985, p17.

7 CO873/649, Weihaiwei Census Report of 1921.

8 CO873/163, 1904 Annual Report.

9 Johnston R.F.: Lion and Dragon in Northern China, Hong Kong Oxford University Press, 1986, pp88-9.

10 CO873/163, 1904 Annual Report.

11 Johnston R.F.: Lion and Dragon in Northern China, Hong Kong Oxford University Press, 1986, p3.

12 CO873/97, 1902 Annual Report.

Notes to Chapter 7

1 Atwell P: British Mandarins and Chinese Reformers. Foreword by N.J.Miners.

2 Chu S.C.: The Weihaiwei Question. The Commercial Press, Ltd, Shanghai, 1931.

3 Ibid.

4 Ibid.

5 CO873/661, British Businessmen at Weihaiwei to Commissioner A.P.Blunt.

6 Han Xinfu(韩信夫): Chronicle of Events in the Republic of China (Book 2), Beijing, China Literature and History Press, 1996, p64.

7 CO521/43, Clementi to the Colonial Office, 25th November, 1928.

8 CO521/42, Johnston to Lampson, 16th February 1928.

9 Chu S.C.: The Weihaiwei Question. The Commercial Press, Ltd, Shanghai, 1931.

Index

Text Original	Alternative (pinyin/Wade Giles)	Chinese characters
Andong		安东
Anhui		安徽
Anleyuan		安乐园
Balitai		八里台
Baolong		宝隆(木匠商号)
Baoquantang		宝泉汤
Bao Tu Quan		趵突泉
Baoxin	P'ao Tu Ch'uan	报信(村)
BeiCang		北仓
Beikou		碑口(庙)
Beiyang		北洋
Beizhudao		北竹岛
Boshan		博山
Buliucun		埠柳村
Cai Hesen	Puliuts'un	蔡和森
Cai Tinggan		蔡廷干
Cao Kun	Tsao Tingkau	曹锟
Caomiaozi	Ts'ao K'un	草庙子
Changchun	Tsao-miao-tze	长春
Changxing		昌兴（火柴厂）
Chefoo		烟台
Chen Jingxing	Yantai	陈景星
Chen Duxiu		陈独秀
Cheng Jen Yu Wei		“拯人于威”
Cheng Peiqing	hen Ren Yu Wei	程培清
Che Shuoxue		车硕学
Chiang Kai-Shek	Ch' ē Shuohs ǘ eh	蒋介石
Ch'ing Court	Jiang Jieshi	清朝
Cisheng Temple	Qing Court	慈圣寺

Cong Shuhan		丛淑汉
Cui Shoushan		崔寿山
Cundong	Tsun Tung	村董
Da Guo		大国
Dagu	Daku	大沽
Dalantou		大岚头
Dalian	Dairen	大连
Dalian Ribao	Dalian Shimbun	《大连日报》
Da Ming Lake	Ta Ming Lake	大明湖
Daqiangmen		大前门
Datong		大同
Dao	Tao	道
Daotai	tao-t'ai	道台
Denglaiqing	Tenglaich'ing	登莱青
Dengzhou	Deng Chow	登州
Dewei		德威（火柴厂）
Dihua		迪化（街）
Dong Baiyang		董百阳
Dongcang		东仓(村)
Dongdaotou		东道头(村)
Donghua		东华(医院)
Dong Shaohui		董绍辉
Dongya		东亚(木匠商号)
Duliu	Tu Liu	独流
Duoding mountain		垛顶山
Fanjiabu		范家埠(村)
Fangzi		坊子（煤矿）
feng shui		风水
Feng Yuxiang	Feng Yuhsiang	冯玉祥
Fuchi	Fuji	"复济"号
Fujian		福建
Fu Tingyu		傅廷遇
Fuzhou		福州
Gaoxi		高熙
Gaoyuan		高苑
Gong Huiqing		宫惠卿
Gu Hongming		辜鸿铭
Gu huiting		谷辉庭
Gu Mingxun		谷铭训
Gu Shanyi		谷善益
Gu Weijun	Ku Weijun	顾维钧
Guangdong		广东

Guang Ming		光明（电气公司）
Guangzhouwan	Kwangchowwan	广州湾
Guomindang		国民党
Haichen		“海琛”舰
Haixitou	Haihsit'ou	海西头
Haixing		海星(小学)
Haizhou		海州
Han Fuqu		韩复渠
Hankou	Hankou	汉口
Hongwu		洪武
Hsien	Xian	县
Huancui		环翠(楼)
Huangtaiqiao		黄台桥
Huangtianqiao	Wang Tien Ch'iao	黄天桥
Huangren		皇仁（学校）
Huimin		惠民(公司)
Jishengchang		吉升昌(书坊)
Jianggezhuang		姜格庄
Jiangnanzhuang		姜南庄
Jiangsu		江苏
Jinan	Tsinan	济南
Jining		济宁
Jiaodong		胶东(半岛)
Jiaozhou	Kiaochou	胶州
Jiaoji railway		胶济线
Jinghai	Ching Hai	“靖海”号
Jinxianding		金线顶
Jinzhen		津镇(铁路)
Jiujiang		九江
Kangji		"康济"号
Kang Youwei		康有为
Kong Lingyi		孔令贻
Kowloon	Jiulong	九龙
Kuomintang	Guomindang	国民党
Kwantung	Guandong	关东
Laihai		莱海(村)
Lang Binghua		朗炳华
Laolongtou		老龙头
Laoshan Bay		崂山湾
Lao Xikai		老西开
Li Hongzhang		李鸿章
Li Huae		李华鄂

Li Jianshan		李兼善
Li Jingmai		李经迈
Li Xijie	Li Hischieh	李希杰
Li Yizhi		李翼之
Li Zunian		李祖年
Liang Rucheng		梁汝成
Liang Ruhao		梁如浩
Liang Shiyi		梁士诒
Liaodong		辽东
Liao Shouheng		廖寿恒
Linquan		林泉(河)
Lin Yingqi		林颖启
Lin Siting		林泗亭
Liugongdao	Liukungtao	刘公岛
Liu Kunyi	Liu K'uni	刘坤一(两江总督)
Liu Zhennian	Liu Chennien	刘珍年
Liu Zhonghai		刘中海
L ü shun		旅顺
Ludaokou		鹿道口
Luo Bi		骆壁
Luo Fenglu	Lo Fenglu	罗丰禄
Luo Hanguang		罗汉光
Luo Kou	Lo K'ou	洛口
Luo Renting		骆仁廷
Luo Xi		骆檄
Luo Zhongming	Lo Chung Ming	罗忠铭
Majingzi		麻井子
Mashanzui		马山嘴
Mei Dongyi		梅东益
Meng Guangxun	Meng Kuanghs ù n	孟广训
Mengjiazhuang		孟家庄
MengYu		孟于(氏)
Meng Zhaoqian		孟昭乾
Miao Woming		苗我明
Ming Dynasty		明朝
Mingxing		明星
Mou	Mou	亩
Mouping		牟平
Nanjing	Nanking	南京
Nie Shicheng		聂士成
Peking	Beijing	北京
Penglai		蓬莱

Pien	Bian	匾
Ping Chengli		品称黎
Prince Gong (Puwei)	Prince Kung	恭亲王（溥伟）
Prince Yi Kuang		庆亲王弈匡
Pukou		埔口
Puyi		溥仪
Qi Diankui	Chi-dien-kwei	戚殿魁
Qidong		齐东(中学)
Qi Qingsu		戚庆素
Qi Xiaotian		戚筱田
Qi Yutan		戚玉潭
Qingdao	Tsingtao	青岛
Qinghe Lou		庆和楼
Qingming Festival		清明节
Qingquan School		清泉学校
Qingquankuang		清泉夼
Qingzhou		青州
Rongcheng	Jungch'eng	荣成
Sa Zhenbing		萨镇冰
Shandong:	Shantung	山东
Shang Qiheng		尚其亨（按察使）
Shao Ciming		邵次明
Sheng Xuanhuai		盛宣怀
Shidao		石岛
Shiluo		石落(村)
Shi Zhaoji		施肇基
Shi Zhi Yu Dao		士志于道
Shude		淑德(女校)
Shuangsikuang		双寺夼
Song Guangfu	Sung Kuangfu	宋广富
Sun Baoqi	Sun Paoch'I	孙宝琦
Sun Fushan		孙福山
Sun Hanchuan		孙汉川
Sun Qichang	Sun ChiCh'ang	孙启昌
Sun Qinxuan		孙琴轩
Sun Xintian		孙心田
Taian		泰安
Taibo		太薄（山）
Taidong Ribao	Taitung Jihpao	《泰东日报》
Taigu		太古
Taihua		泰华(木匠商号)
Taiji		太极

Taishan		泰山
Tiananmen		天安门
Tiancun		田村
Tianhou		天后(宫)
Tianjin	Tientsin	天津
Tongle		同乐（剧院）
Tongzhou	Tungchow	通州
Tun Ho Wan	Dun He Wan	敦贺丸
Wang Jiazhen		王家桢
Wang Wenshao (Governor of Zhili)		王文韶（直隶总督）
Wang Yingzhi		王营之
Wang Zhengting		王正廷
Wang Zuogang		王佐刚
Weihaiwei		威海卫
Weixian		潍县
Wenhua		文华(木匠商号)
Wenquantang	Wen Ch' ü an T'ang	温泉汤
Wendeng	Wenteng	文登
Wuhan		武汉
Wu Jianmin		吴建民
Wukou		坞口
Xishawo		西沙窝
Xianlu		仙鹿
Xiao Qing River	Hsiao Ch'ing Ho	小清河
Xie Zuantai		谢缵泰
Xinheju		新和居
Xinzhuang		新庄
Xu Beihong		徐悲鸿
Xu Guoqi		徐国琦
Xu Shichang	Ts ŭ Shichang	徐世昌
Xu Zhenjiang	Hs ŭ ChenChiang	徐振江
Xu Zushan	Hs ŭ Tsu-shan	徐祖善
Xuantong		宣统
Yamen		衙门
Yan Daohong		严道洪(候补道)
Yanhui		颜回(庙)
Yan Yangchu		晏阳初
Yan Xishan		阎锡山
Yang Du		杨度
Yangjiaogou	Yang Chiao Kou	羊角沟
Yang Shixiang		杨士骧
Yangtzi		长江

Yangjiatan		杨家滩
Yantai	Chefoo	烟台
Yanzhou		兖州
Ye Gongchuo		叶恭绰
Yifang		怡芳
Yifeng		义丰（绣花厂）
Yihetuan		义和团
Yimin		益民(磨面厂)
Yixing		峄兴（煤矿）
Yongle		永乐
Yongzeng		永增（织布厂）
Yu Chunxuan		于春暄
"Yuta"		“玉塔”号
Yu Xian		毓贤
Yuan Shikai	Y ǚ an Shihk'ai	袁世凯
Yuan Keding	Y ǔ an K'oting	袁克定
Yuanxingdong		源兴东(酱园)
Yue Baoshu		岳宝树
Yunnan		云南
Zhaizi		寨子
Zhang Bangyong		张邦永
Zhangcun		张村
Zhang Fulai		张福来
Zhang Lianfen		张莲芬
Zhang Mingqi	Cheung MingCh'I	张鸣歧
Zhang Rumei		张汝梅
Zhang Suian		张遂安
Zhang Xueliang		张学良
Zhang Yuanji		张元济
Zhang Zhidong	Chang Chihtung	张之洞（湖广总督）
Zhang Zongchang	Chang Tsungch'ang	张宗昌
Zhang Zuolin	Chang Tsolin	张作霖
Zhao Dingyu		赵定宇
Zhaofang		兆芳（相馆）
Zhenhai		“镇海”舰
Zhi Dao		志道
Zhili		直隶
Zhongwei		中威（橡皮厂）
Zhongyuan War		中原大战
Zhou Fu	Chou Fu	周馥
Zhougong		周公(庙)
Zhou Tianquan		周田泉

Zhudao		竹岛
Zhu Xiru		朱喜儒
Zhu Xin		祝鑫
Zhuang Shidun		庄士敦
Zichuan		淄川
Zizhulin		紫竹林
Zongdong	tsungtung	总董
Zongli yamen	Tsungli Yamen	总理衙门

Epilogue

During the 13th International Archive Conference which was held in Beijing in 1996 we met Mrs Sarah Tyacke the Chief Executive of the British National Archives and we asked her to inquire into the possibility of acquiring a copy of the archives of the history of Weihaiwei during the period of its lease to Britain. In July 1997, Mrs Tyacke sent us the relevant archive catalogue and an invitation to come to Britain. In March 1998, the first archive acquisition group travelled to the UK, headed by Mr Yu Lanmo, a Party Committee deputy member of the Weihai Municipal Government and Secretary Chief of the Municipal Party Committee.

When we opened this old archive on the other side of the ocean, we discovered many historical events which were previously unknown to us and many high quality historical photographs. As the first Chinese to view that precious archive, we were surprised and excited, and it is hard to express our feelings and thoughts in words. We made another two journeys to the UK in 1999 and 2002, and visited several British historical experts on the history of Weihaiwei's lease to Britain and cleared up some questions and then we started to write this book.

During the process of editing, we were guided by the principle of respecting that history and the first-hand materials, and to offer a greater opportunity for the readers to learn from that history. We simply presented the information from our acquired archive, with exception of some analyses and statements concerning one or two specific events. As to the photographs, we included some taken in the decade up to 1940, because even after Weihaiwei had been returned to China in 1930, Britain continued to lease Liugong Island for another 10 years. During this period of time, the British still played an important role in Weihaiwei although Weihaiwei had now come under the control of the Nanjing Government.

We will not forget all those foreign experts, scholars and friends who helped us with this book.

Mrs Sarah Tyacke, the Chief Executive of the UK National Archives, has played a very important role in its creation. It is thanks to her support that we were able to acquire this archive and thus to produce this book.

Lieutenant Commander Ronald E. H. Childs, Royal Navy, who has researched into the history of British Navy in Weihaiwei. He is a warm-hearted friend and has provided many important historical materials and photographs and answered many of our questions concerning that period.

We twice visited George Watson's College and were welcomed there by the Chancellor, Mr Gareth Edwards. Mr Michael Gill, the keeper of the Stewart Lockhart Archive, offered us a collection of copies of many historical photos and kindly invited us into his home. His wife, Shiona Airlie, had carried out research into the history of Weihaiwei while it was leased by Great Britain and her books <<Thistle and Bamboo: Life and Times of Sir James Stewart Lockhart>> and <<Reginald Johnston: Chinese Mandarin (Scots' Lives Series) >> proved very informative.

Mr I. F. Maciver, head of the manuscript division of the National Library of Scotland, helped us a great deal and provided us with facilities to duplicate the archive photographs which guaranteed the quality of those photographs.

Dr Pamela Atwell of the Hobart and William Smith College in America is an expert in the history of the leasing of Weihaiwei by the British. Her book <<British Mandarins and Chinese Reformers: British Administration of Weihaiwei, 1898-1930, and the Territory's Return to Chinese Rule (East Asian Historical Monographs)>> provided much important historical material. Dr Atwell visited Weihai in 2002, together with her husband Professor William S. Atwell, Dean of the History Department of the Hobart and William Smith College and an expert on the Chinese Ming Dynasty. Their visit cleared up a lot of questions.

Mr Duncan Clark, who was born in Weihaiwei, is the grandson of the first foreign businessman in Weihaiwei---the owner of the company D. Clark & Co. The Clark family had a business in Weihaiwei for more than 40 years. Besides providing the materials of the D. Clark & Co, Mr Clark provided us with many precious historical photographs free of charge and also presented us with the flag of the territory of Weihaiwei when under its lease by Britain, which belonged to a time almost one century ago.

Mr Wang Guangqi, an overseas' Chinese who lives in London, helped us a lot with the acquisition of the Archives. He assisted us with our communications and helped transfer most of the archives back to Weihai.

Alderman J. H. Pennington, who is an honorary freeman both of Weihai, and of Cheltenham, the twin-city of Weihai in the UK, has worked tirelessly for friendship and cooperation between our two cities and assisted us a great deal.

Mr Ian Johnson, another friend from Cheltenham, has undertaken a great amount of research work to discover the places to find the lost archives and has provided us with many precious historical photographs and a copy of the archive catalogue even before the catalogue from the UK National Archives was sent to us.

Dr Sonia Lightfoot, a fellow of St Hilda's College, Oxford University, is very knowledgeable about Chinese art and Lockhart's collection in particular. She hosted us in her home when we visited Oxford and helped us with the acquisition of the archive.

Ms Carol G. S. Tan, an expert in Chinese Law at the University of Newcastle in the UK, has made a study of the legal system in Weihaiwei when it was leased to Britain and in May 2001 sent us her publication <<Going to Court in Weihaiwei: Some support for Civil Litigation in the Qing>> added a lot to our book.

Prof Paul Bailey from Edinburgh University, who is a lecturer who has specialized in the history of Chinese Labourers during World War I visited Weihai in April 2000 and provided us with many archive materials about those Chinese labourers which contributed greatly to our book.

We would like to thank the many people from the British National Archives, the National Library of Scotland, the School of Oriental and African Studies of London University, the University of London Library, the Royal Navy Museum, the Rhodes House Library of Oxford University, and Daintree Lodge, Fareham, who have all helped us in our work. We want to thank the keepers of The Custodians of the Stewart Lockhart Collection, The Merchant Company Education Board, Edinburgh and The School Governing Council of George Watson College for providing us the use of their photographs.

We have obtained help from many units and persons in China during the compiling of this book. First of all, we want to thank Mr Liu Deyi, an expert on Weihai history and a retiree from the Party History Office of Huancui District, who contributed greatly to the checking of historical events, providing historical materials and the revising of the book. Thanks to Mr Cong Weidong, vice director of the Weihai Municipal Government Foreign Affairs Office for his work in providing clues in our search for the archive and checking the original British archive. Thanks also to Mr Zhang Hong, director of the Yantai International Book Communication Centre. Thanks to Mr Liu Deqiang, Vice General Editor of the Weihai Daily, who offered us many useful suggestions. Thank to Ms Cong Juan, Ms Ma Xianghong, Ms Li Yanyan, Ms Hu Xiujie and to several teachers and students from Shandong University's English Department for their translation work. Thanks to Li Chunze, former gardener to Reginald Johnston, and Lin Juren from Linjiayuan Village, Che Fangkai and Che Fangxia from Haixitou Village, Liu Jusheng from Wolong Village, Liu Yide Deng Xizen and Liang Fangjing from Majingbo Village, Liu Yulun from Baoxin Village, Ji Liansheng from Beikou Village,

Yu Hongren and Deng Yulian from Dongshenge Village, Fu Deyi from Menjiazhuang Village, Lin Zhichen from Caomiaozi Village, etc., who all provided valuable information for our work. We want to especially to thank Mr Ding Xiangyang and Mr Cong Yangzi, who are director and vice director of the Liugong Island Administrative Committee for their support. Thanks finally to the Museum of the First Sino-Japanese War (1894-1895) on Liugong Island, and also to the Qingdao Municipal Archive Bureau for their help.

Zhang Jianguo
October 2002, Weihai